U/S

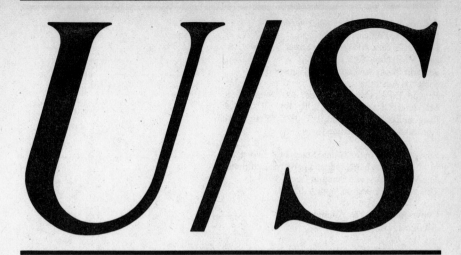

U/S

A STATISTICAL PORTRAIT OF THE AMERICAN PEOPLE

EDITED BY
ANDREW HACKER

WITH THE ASSISTANCE OF
LORRIE MILLMAN

THE VIKING PRESS / NEW YORK
PENGUIN BOOKS

Penguin Books Ltd, Harmondsworth,
Middlesex, England
Penguin Books, 40 West 23rd Street,
New York, New York 10010, U.S.A.
Penguin Books Australia Ltd, Ringwood,
Victoria, Australia
Penguin Books Canada Limited, 2801 John Street,
Markham, Ontario, Canada L3R 1B4
Penguin Books (N.Z.) Ltd, 182–190 Wairau Road,
Auckland 10, New Zealand

First published in the United States of America
in simultaneous hardcover and paperback editions by
The Viking Press and Penguin Books 1983
This paperback edition reprinted 1983

Copyright © 1983 by Andrew Hacker
All rights reserved

LIBRARY OF CONGRESS CATALOGING IN PUBLICATION DATA
Main entry under title:
U/S: a statistical portrait of the American people.
  Bibliography: p.
  Includes index.
  1. United States—Statistics. I. Hacker, Andrew.
  II. Millman, Lorrie. III. Title: US.
HA214.U15 1983   317.3   82-70120
ISBN 0 14 00.6579 2

Printed in the United States of America by
R.R. Donnelley & Sons Company, Harrisonburg, Virginia
Set in Times Roman

Except in the United States of America,
this book is sold subject to the condition
that it shall not, by way of trade or otherwise,
be lent, re-sold, hired out, or otherwise circulated
without the publisher's prior consent in any form of
binding or cover other than that in which it is
published and without a similar condition
including this condition being imposed on
the subsequent purchaser

PREFACE

U/S may be used as a reference book. It has been organized and indexed for that specific purpose. It is also a book to be read as a source of information, or simply for enjoyment.

U/S presents a comprehensive picture of the people of America. It explains what kinds of individuals we are and the ways we lead our lives, the similarities we share and how we differ from one another. All this is depicted with precision, for *U/S* sets forth the facts of American life in a unique way: the information in this book takes the form of statistics. More than that, they are all official figures, compiled by various government agencies.

Of course not everything about a nation can be reduced to statistics. Still, *U/S* shows just how much we can discover by translating facts into figures. Far from compressing human beings into chilly columns of numbers, statistics highlight the qualities that make individuals interesting and varied. Indeed, anyone leafing through this book will find some facets of his or her own self on virtually every page.

U/S is a book for Americans who want to understand their country—and themselves—in these unsettled times. Even now, the decade of the 1980s has yet to show its shape. Old labels no longer apply, and the future seems uncertain. Yet much of the knowledge we need is within our reach. The United States leads the world in collecting information, but most of it is dispersed in documents few citizens ever see. Each year federal agencies publish several thousand studies charting trends and conditions in American society. These reports are public property; indeed, they have been produced for the public's benefit. It is our right as citizens not only to know what they say, but to use their findings to enlarge our understanding. *U/S* draws on these official figures to open new perspectives on the present and the future.

At this point it should be emphasized that the material in *U/S* has not simply been reproduced from government reports. On the contrary, in virtually all cases, figures have been recomputed and categories recast so that their significance is readily apparent. In other instances, findings from several sources have been brought together to draw relevant conclusions. By the same token, almost all the rankings that appear here were not in the original studies but required further calculations. Keys to source materials are given with each set of figures, and the documents from which they came are listed at the end of the book. These references contain the basic statistics from which all the figures in *U/S* have been derived.

An introductory chapter explains why we collect statistics and how they play a role in the governmental process. Particular attention is given to the Bureau of the Census, the major source of our official figures. There is also a brief discussion of the 1980 Census, describing how it was conducted and what can be expected from its results. The chapter concludes with some ground rules for the use of statistics, including how they come into being and the validity of their claim to represent reality.

Readers of *U/S* need no special background in mathematics or statistics. The figures presented here are all ordinary numbers: the most complicated are percentages carried to a decimal place. Most of the material may be read as in any other book. When tables seem appropriate, every effort has been made to keep them clear and concise.

I owe a great debt of gratitude to the many individuals who helped me obtain the reports and documents necessary for *U/S*. In particular, I would like to thank Lois Afflerbach of the Queens College Library; Irene Itina and Frances Breidenbach at the New York Public Library; and Margaret Padin-Bialo, Marie Morales, and Beverly Wright of the New York office of the Bureau of the Census. Linda Weinberger and Patricia Richards also provided invaluable assistance in preparing the manuscript.

Robin Straus, my literary agent, offered every possible encouragement and helped in shaping the initial conception of *U/S*. William Strachan of The Viking Press showed me how to transform an unwieldy stack of pages into a finished book. And Lorrie Millman, as much as any single person, made this entire project possible. As my editorial assistant she not only triple-checked thousands of statistics, but played a vital role in the basic organization of *U/S*.

—ANDREW HACKER

CONTENTS

U/S

CHAPTER ONE

FACTS INTO FIGURES

William James, the psychologist and philosopher, once described the universe as "a booming, buzzing confusion." One way to introduce some order is by keeping count of what is going on. Thus societies make an effort to find out how many marriages have been performed and how many cars are on their roads, the frequency of homicides and the incidence of diphtheria. Collecting information of this kind is a sign that a nation takes itself seriously.

Generally speaking, statistics are collected for very practical reasons. If policies are to be effective, they must be geared to actual conditions. Businesses keep careful track of how their products are doing and draw up figures to estimate future needs. Governments do much the same, but on a more extensive scale. The finding that unemployment has risen by a full percentage point signals a serious change in the state of the economy. Indeed, all the economic "indicators" we use are statistical, ranging from bankruptcy rates and inventories to the level of inflation and the balance of payments. The following examples illustrate some of the ways official figures can affect our lives.

- Each month the Bureau of Labor Statistics computes its Consumer Price Index, an account of what we have to pay for products and services. That figure is then used to adjust Social Security pensions, as well as wage rates in many private industries.

- More than 100 federal programs distribute money to the states on the basis of figures from the Census Bureau and several other agencies. For example, the Department of Education apportions grants for "reading improvement" according to each state's population of children from ages 5 through 12. Funding from the Department of Health and Human Services to assist "the nutrition of the elderly" depends on how many residents of a state are 60 or over. Drug abuse prevention grants are distributed in part according to how many cases of hepatitis have been reported in the state. And Civil Defense is supported in proportion to how many people in a state reside in "critical target areas."

- While Congress makes laws and agencies administer them, we need statistics to discover their actual effect. For example, the income tax statutes contain tables with the rates for every bracket, but incomes come from varied sources and are eligible for deductions. Therefore, the Internal Revenue Service turns out annual reports showing what people actually pay. Its most recent study revealed that among returns in the $100,000 to $200,000 range, federal taxes averaged 33.4 percent of declared adjusted gross income. And a report by the Social Security Administration showed that as of June 1981, while pensions for retired workers could go as high as $9,035, the average retiree was only receiving $4,735. Studies of this kind provide a perspective on how legislation works in practice, and what other legislation may be necessary.

- Statistics can give us a glimpse of the coming shape of our society. Between 1970 and 1980, a total of 33,499,000 births were registered in this country, 14.2 percent fewer than in the previous decade. It is important to have this information if we want to know how many children will be starting school during the 1980s and how many jobs should be available in the 1990s. This is not to say that we will set plans in motion to meet these future needs, but it is imperative to have these statistical forewarnings.

- Statistics can be used to call attention to a problem. In recent years the Bureau of the Census has been issuing studies on child support and alimony. Its most recent report shows that more than half—51.1 percent—of the women who were supposed to get child support payments did not receive the agreed-upon amounts. Simply releasing this figure suggests that child support agreements may require more rigorous enforcement.

- Gathering statistics goes back to the birth of the Republic. The Census was mandated by the Constitution, which called for an "enumeration" every decade to determine how many seats each state would have in the House of Representatives. The 1790 count found 3,929,214 persons, and from that figure apportioned the first 106 Congressional seats. With the Census of 1910, the House of Representatives decided to stop growing and limited itself to 435 members. That year New York led the states with 43 seats and California was well down on the list with only eleven. By 1980, due to population changes charted by the Census, New York's delegation had declined to 34 while California's had grown to 45.

These are just a few illustrations of the purposes statistics serve, though not every set of figures will have an immediate application, and some are published simply because they are available. Thus a National Center for Health Statistics report contains a table revealing that Saturday is the most popular day for weddings (914,220 at last count), with Friday (339,596) in second place, and Tuesday (74,235) and Wednesday (71,762) bringing up the rear.

THE CENSUS AND *U/S*

The figures in *U/S* come from many different departments, but the central source of statistics is the Bureau of the Census. Indeed, much of the Bureau's effort goes into collecting figures for other governmental agencies. For example, it ascertains the monthly unemployment rate for the Department of Labor and carries out an annual survey of "criminal victimization" for the Justice Department. But its best-known responsibility is the decennial Census, the only full-scale survey of the American people.

The decennial Census is a huge operation, and for many years it has been managed in a highly professional manner. The Bureau is located in Suitland, Maryland, about a half-hour drive from downtown Washington. You pass a Gino's drive-in, a Goodyear tire store, and a row of Chinese restaurants, all suburban-style, but across the road, in a complex of barrackslike buildings, are some of the country's finest geographers, cartographers, demographers, and statisticians. They constitute a national resource of inestimable value; cutbacks in the Bureau's budget should not be suggested lightly. So while the 1980 count has had its share of problems, it should be stressed at the outset that the benefits from having Census figures far outweigh the limitations.

During the first week of April 1980, the Census mailed its forms to every family and household in the country, as well as persons living by themselves. It made the best attempt it could to reach every household. If families did not send back the forms, Census personnel called on people's homes to retrieve the questionnaires and assist in filling them out. Even lodging houses were visited, so individuals with no settled address could be added to the count.

The Census was intended to reach everyone living in the United States in April 1980, with the count to include all men, women, and infants, but not foreign visitors here for only a short stay. This meant that the total would contain both citizens and resident aliens, whether the latter were here legally or not. The Census said it did its best to obtain filled-in forms from illegal aliens, assuring them that their whereabouts would not be reported to other official agencies.

By the end of the summer, a total of 58,882,153 families plus 21,507,520 persons living alone had submitted information for the Census' files, and on December 31, 1980, the Bureau reported its final count. There were, it announced, a total of 226,504,825 persons residing in the United States.

But the Census is more than a head count. Its basic form, which went to every household, contained 18 questions: 6 on age, race, sex, and marital status, and another 12 on residential conditions. In addition, a much longer form was given to every sixth household or, in some areas, to every second one. This so-called "long form" included the 18 basic questions, plus 81 more on personal attributes and housing characteristics, which covered a remarkably wide range. Individuals were asked, for example, whether they "speak a language other than English at home" and to estimate "how long it usually takes to get from home to work." If a woman was filling in the form, she was asked to reveal "how many babies she has ever had," and homeowners were requested to report their "annual premium for fire and hazard insurance." When a residence got its water from a well, the Census wanted to know if it was "drilled" or "dug." The "long form" also questioned whether the respondent was a citizen; but those who said they were not were not asked about their legal status. So while the 1980 Census will eventually publish a total figure for the number of aliens in the population, it will not be able to tell us how many are here legally and how many are not.

How Complete is the Census? No one has ever claimed that the decennial Census succeeds in reaching everyone. Even so, we cannot know for sure how many people it has missed. Its own estimate is that in 1970 its "undercount" came to 2.5 percent. (To compensate for this, Census statisticians created 4.9 million fictional "individuals," based on the results they received, whom they then inserted in the tables. They even gave these paper persons occupations and other attributes.)

In 1980 the problem took a somewhat different turn. Early that year, before the count was taken, the Census Bureau had estimated that there were approximately 221,719,000 people in the country. As has been indicated, the Census ultimately got forms listing 226,504,825 individuals, or 2.2 percent *more* than the estimate. Does this mean that the 1980 count is probably complete? At first the Census insisted that it was, especially in response to lawsuits from various cities which claimed that many of their residents had been overlooked.

But by 1982 Census officials were willing to give some ground. They went so far as to admit that their official figure for the black population—26,488,218—was short by 4.8 percent, which put the true total of blacks in the vicinity of 27.8 million. However, the Census was not willing to estimate how many white persons or those of other races may also have been missed. The Bureau also acknowledged the presence of uncounted aliens, but refused to speculate on their possible numbers. So at best the Census was willing to raise its national figure from the original 226,504,825 to something like 227,800,000 to accommodate 1.3 million black Americans who were never reached. But despite this adjustment the Census does not intend to revise the reports it has already issued or the figures it has ready for future publication.*

In consequence, we have a situation in which the full-count statistics are impressively precise, even though they are not completely accurate. The Census tells us that as of April 1980, there were exactly 806,027 Americans of Chinese descent; that the country had a total of 2,945,482 women aged 75 to 79; and at the time the Census was taken the population of Catoosa County, Georgia, came to 36,991. Obviously, precision of this sort can be misleading if we take the figures too literally. In a sense, every Census statistic is an estimate, even when it is explicit to the final digit.

Still, the decennial Census is the only overall count we have. While far from perfect, it tells us more about ourselves than we could ever know without it. It is a useful source of information, and U/S draws on its findings because they are often the best we have, offering warnings when they seem in order.

Releasing the Results. The amount of information elicited by the Census is nothing short of staggering, with a potential for producing billions of statistics. The 1970 count eventually yielded over 200,000 pages of tables plus many miles of computer tape; some publications were still coming out in 1975. It will certainly take the Census Bureau several years to compute and publish its 1980 findings, and, moreover, because of budgetary cutbacks, the Bureau has said it may not be able to publish in

*However, after the first edition of U/S went to press, the Census discovered 40,980 additional questionnaires, raising the 1980 population to 226,545,805, an increase of two one-hundredths of one percent (0.02%). Altogether, 39 states had their totals raised, ranging from 24 more people for Oklahoma to 7,337 more in North Carolina. Subsequent editions of U/S will include these and other adjustments, and will amend the title of Chapter Two.

printed form as many reports as it did in previous years. In addition, staff reductions mean we will have to wait longer for those publications that do appear. In some cases Census statistics will be released only on magnetic tape, and while this presents no problems for organizations with computer facilities, it means the general reader will not have access to many statistics that were previously available.

For this reason *U/S* also uses figures from an alternative Census source. Every month the Census Bureau conducts what it calls its Current Population Survey, which is based on interviews with persons in some 65,000 households all across the country, and whose basic purpose is to ascertain the nation's monthly unemployment rate. However, each month some further questions are added, and the results are published in a Census series called the Current Population Reports. The households that make up the sample are carefully selected and constantly updated as conditions change. (A "household" can be a family, a single individual, or two or more nonrelated people sharing living quarters.) People in the survey field agree that a sample of 65,000 households provides a reliable cross-section of the total population, and findings from it can be used with confidence.

There is also an appearance of precision in the Survey's publications. For example, its recent study on "Geographical Mobility" reported that during the 5-year period from 1975 to 1980, a total of 94,959,000 Americans changed their residence. In fact, that figure was determined by extrapolating from the responses of persons in the 65,000-household sample. That is, the number of movers in the sample were multiplied so that their total appeared as a proportion of the national population. The Current Population Survey signifies that its figures are approximations by ending them with three zeroes.

The value of the Current Population Reports is that their results are rapidly available. With the one on geographic mobility, the interviews were carried out in March 1980, and the findings were released in October 1981. On the other hand, information on mobility from the full 1980 Census is not scheduled for publication until late in 1983. The chief limitation of the Current Population Survey is that while its statistics are reliable on a nationwide basis, it cannot provide detailed information on state and local conditions. In cases where figures from the full Census are not available, *U/S* draws on statistics from the Current Population Survey.

SETTING STANDARDS FOR STATISTICS

An allusion was made earlier to "collecting" statistics. Strictly speaking, this is not what really happens. Numbers are not scattered on the ground, merely waiting to be found. Figures must be created, and bringing them into being is the work of human beings.

Statistics emerge when someone decides to count something, an activity in which all of us engage several times a day. We intuitively understand that figures are a very efficient way of representing reality. However, if they are to serve that purpose, the numbers we create must have four basic characteristics: precision, compression, consistency, and reliability.

Precision. In everyday discussions we use words like "more" and "most" and "some" to denote degrees of quantity. For example, ordinary observation suggests that "most" people who drive to work apparently do so alone. However, statistics allow us to be precise. The 1980 Census reported that 81,350,994 Americans travel to their jobs by "car, truck, or van" and of these, 62,275,065, or 76.6 percent, have the vehicle to themselves. In a similar vein, someone may remark that the various armed services seem to differ in their acceptance of women. With statistics we can say that of the 118,469 members of the Marine Corps, only 6,219, or 3.3 percent, are women. By way of contrast, in the Air Force, 60,394 out of 553,558, or 10.9 percent, of personnel are women. Of course these figures are only valid for a specific date; in this case the count was made on September 30, 1980. We might also want to know how many women have actually applied to the various services and how each branch defines its duties. Still, precise figures are a beginning; we can refine them later on.*

It should also be noted that some figures are truly precise, while others only give an appearance of reality. We can be fairly sure that the Marine Corps made an accurate count of its women members. However, the figure of 62,275,065 people said to drive to work alone is actually a semi-fictitious statistic derived from a Census "long form" sample.

Compression. Everyone is aware that men earn more than women—but statistics can tell us exactly what that differential is. In 1980 the typical income of men who worked throughout the year came to $20,521; for women the comparable sum was $12,083, or 58.9 percent of the men's amount. These figures were arrived at by computing the average earnings of all the men and women who held full-time jobs during 1980. In all, there were 41,923,000 men and 23,025,000 women in that category. Quite obviously, compressing the incomes of so many people into a pair of averaged figures conceals a range of variations. If we want more specific information, we can turn to more detailed tables, which show,

*Throughout *U/S* the totals for columns of percentages have all been rounded to 100.0 percent, although the actual figures occasionally add up to 99.9 percent or 100.1 percent.

for instance, in what kinds of occupations women's incomes come closer to rivaling men's. The wages of women security guards turn out to be 90.7 percent of those received by men, and the salaries of women who are postal clerks stand at 93.9 percent of the figure for men. In other cases the effects of compression are readily apparent. The Reno, Nevada, metropolitan area was reported in 1979 to have a per capita income of $12,317, amounting to a supposed $49,268 income for a typical family of four. It would be reasonable to suspect that a few extremely wealthy families helped to lift Reno's average to that lofty level.

Consistency. If statistics begin with counting, the next step consists of distributing whatever has been counted into groups or categories. Some groupings are fairly standard: men and women, individuals' ages, or states and cities. However, in other cases it is necessary to draw up special definitions, so numbers can be distributed with a measure of consistency. Thus the Census defines a "family" as any two or more related persons who share a residence. This means that a daughter who has an apartment of her own is no longer regarded by the Census as a member of a family. The Bureau of Labor Statistics lists a person as having been "employed" if he or she "did a minimum of an hour's work for pay or profit" during a given week. The Federal Bureau of Investigation explains in some detail how a "burglary" differs from a "robbery," or an "attempted rape" from an "aggravated assault."

Definitions like these are necessary if we are to draw meaningful comparisons. In examining the "robbery" rate across the states, we would like to feel that Kansas and Kentucky define that crime in a consistent way. In some cases the choice of category is left to the individual. Thus the 1980 Census asked each American to select an ethnic category. In 1970 a total of 792,730 persons described themselves as American Indians; whereas 10 years later 1,361,869—not too far from twice as many—chose to do so. The category of "Indian" is still consistent; however, we should be aware that it expresses an identity people choose for themselves. In the chapters that follow, an effort will be made to show the standards of consistency for series of statistics.

Reliability. Figures don't lie, the adage goes, but liars can figure. On the whole, United States government statistics are produced by professional civil servants who have no axes to grind. A President running for reelection may not like the unemployment rate, but the Bureau of Labor Statistics will not change its method of computation to make the White House look better. Rather, the issue of reliability takes other forms.

There is first of all the fact that people are not always truthful when responding to interviews or questionnaires. For example, in a recent Census survey, 59.2 percent of those questioned said they had voted in the 1980 election. However, the actual turnout in 1980 came to only 52.3 percent of the eligible population, which suggests that not everyone who answered was absolutely honest. In another survey 619,000 persons said they had been victims of robberies and reported the offense to the police. But police departments across the country pointed out they had received a total of only 467,000 robbery reports. Our best recourse is to cite such discrepancies when we find that they occur and use common sense to see how far the statistics still serve a useful purpose.

On other occasions we may be presented with statistics that seem remarkably precise but may not tell the entire story. The Immigration and Naturalization Service reported that in 1980 exactly 5,381,107 aliens in this country turned in registration forms. But the INS offers no guesses on how many did not; its statistics are "reliable" in that they are accurate counts of cases available for counting. While they are clearly not complete, we can still use them as a starting point for further investigations.

SAMPLE SURVEYS OR COMPLETE COUNTS?

In some areas complete counts are possible, and we can assume they are on the whole reliable. The provisional 1981 figures of 3,633,826 births and 2,311,496 marriages come from counting certificates made out at those events. Other full-scale counts are not nearly so complete. In 1981 the Centers for Disease Control reported that exactly 984,330 cases of gonorrhea were known to physicians and officially recorded. Obviously there were more, but it isn't easy to obtain information from people who do not want to be counted. In addition, full surveys are tremendously expensive. In consequence, many of our statistics are derived from samples.

In some cases, an agency will choose not to use all the information it has on hand. Thus the Internal Revenue Service works with a 25 percent sample—every fourth tax return—for its statistical studies, but draws up its reports as if they came from a full count. So while its findings concerning incomes between $200,000 and $500,000 are derived from examining 24,308 forms, the results are multiplied out so they appear to cover the 97,232 returns that actually fell in that range.

The real doubts about reliability arise from samples that claim to be a cross-section of an entire population. Mention was made earlier of the Current Population Survey, which conducts interviews with only 65,000 households. The average earnings figures of those "41,923,000 men" and "23,025,000 women," or the "94,959,000 individuals" who changed their residence, were all extrapolated from that 65,000-household sample. It should be noted that the people who collect and create government statistics want them to be as accurate as possible, and those who select the samples employ professional methods that can be tested and verified, one of which is to measure the makeup of the sample against the general population.

We can see what happens when such a comparison is made. The March 1980 Current Population Survey conducted interviews with its 65,000-household sample to discover general family characteristics. One month later the Census distributed its forms to every household in the country, with similar questions on family characteristics. The officials who made the computations for the March sample survey could not know what figures would result from the April count; in fact, the latter were not fully processed until almost two years later. Here is how the sample stacked up against the complete count:

	MARCH 1980 CENSUS SURVEY	APRIL 1980 COMPLETE COUNT
Number of households	65,000	80,389,673
All family households	*73.9%*	*73.2%*
Those headed by married couples	60.9%	60.2%
Those with single female heads	10.8%	10.5%
Those with single male heads	2.2%	2.6%
All nonfamily households	*26.1%*	*26.8%*
Persons living alone	22.5%	22.7%
Persons living together	3.6%	4.1%

This is not a bad approximation, suggesting that the March sample was a pretty good parallel of the April total. The most serious difference is in the figures for nonrelated persons living together, which means future samples will have to pay more attention to locating such households.

The figures in *U/S* are the most recent that were available as the book went to press in the fall of 1982. Still, by the time any statistics have been published they are already out-of-date. It takes time to collect and process figures and get them into print. In addition, agencies vary greatly in how long they take to prepare this information. Some departments had figures on 1980 ready early in 1981; in other cases reports were still unavailable by 1982. Sometimes the lag is even longer: full statistics on births, marriages, and deaths for 1977 did not appear in finished form until late in 1981. Similar figures for 1982 are scheduled to be published in 1986.

Despite occasional criticism, United States statistics—whether from samples or full counts—have proved remarkably reliable. They are the best we have. While there are times when it is proper to challenge official figures, a more productive approach is to view them as a basic source of information and an aid in understanding. The purpose of *U/S* is to show how this can be done.

CHAPTER TWO

226,504,825 AMERICANS

According to the most recent Census count, there were 226,504,825 persons residing in the United States. However, the Census is more than a head count: its forms have always asked for additional information, particularly on sex and age and race, plus place of residence. This chapter draws chiefly on the 1980 Census to portray the basic characteristics of our current population. These figures are ranked and interwoven in a variety of ways, and in addition, population trends are charted over time, with special attention to changes that have taken place during the past decade.

THE FIRST CENSUS

A good way to set these statistics in perspective is to look at the findings of the first United States Census, which was conducted in 1790. By contemporary standards it was a very modest survey, asking for responses to only 6 questions. However, it set a precedent by reporting its results with remarkable precision. This is what that initial Census found:

- The population totaled 3,929,214 persons, of whom 3,172,006 were white and 757,208 were black or other races. (The latter figure did not include Indians, who were not given full Census status until 1860.)

- The white population contained 1,615,434 males and 1,556,572 females. (The genders of other races were not recorded until 1820.)

- As far as age was concerned, only white males were questioned, and they were simply asked if they were older or younger than 15. It emerged that 800,492 were 15 or younger, while the other 814,942 were 16 or older. (White women were asked their age in the 1800 Census, and nonwhites were asked in 1820 and thereafter.)

- The 1790 Census revealed that Virginia was by far the largest state, with 747,610 residents, followed by North Carolina with 393,751 and Massachusetts with 378,787. Delaware was the least populous state, with 59,096 people, after which came Rhode Island with 68,825.

- Of the 3,929,214 total population, only 201,655 Americans—a mere 5.1 percent—lived in "urban places," defined as localities with at least 2,500 persons. There were 24 such places, of which New York was the largest (49,401), followed by Philadelphia (28,522) and Boston (18,320). Other important urban centers were Baltimore (13,503); Providence (6,380); and Richmond (3,761); along with Albany (3,498) and the whaling town of New Bedford (3,313).

- Finally, of the 757,208 nonwhite Americans, 697,681 were slaves and 59,527 were free. With the 1870 Census this item no longer appeared on the official questionnaires.

POPULATION GROWTH: IN NUMBERS AND PERCENTAGES

Between 1970 and 1980, the nation's population rose from 203,211,926 to 226,504,825, an increase of 23,292,899, or 11.5 percent, the second-lowest rate of growth in the country's history.

From 1960 to 1970, the population went from 179,310,655 to 203,211,926, an increase of 23,901,271, or 13.3 percent. In the 1950–1960 decade—the height of the "baby boom" years—the growth was 19.0 percent. And between 1940 and 1950, half of that period being wartime, the increase was 14.5 percent.

The lowest growth was during the 1930–1940 Depression decade, or only 7.2 percent. The fastest was in the nation's first 70 years, which averaged a rate of 34.6 percent for each of its decades, when immigration caused substantial additions to the existing population.

[11, 14]

These are the official totals from the nation's twenty Censuses, with each count's percentage increase over the one that came before it.

YEAR	POPULATION	PERCENT INCREASE
1980	226,504,825	11.5%
1970	203,211,926	13.3%
1960	179,323,175	19.0%
1950	150,697,361	14.5%
1940	131,669,275	7.2%
1930	122,775,040	16.1%
1920	105,710,620	14.9%
1910	91,972,266	21.0%
1900	75,994,575	20.7%
1890	62,947,714	25.5%
1880	50,155,783	26.0%
1870	39,818,449	26.6%
1860	31,443,321	35.6%
1850	23,191,876	35.9%
1840	17,069,453	32.7%
1830	12,866,020	33.5%
1820	9,638,453	33.1%
1810	7,239,881	36.4%
1800	5,308,483	35.1%
1790	3,929,214	– **[11, 14]**

REASONS FOR THE RISE

Three factors contributed to the 1970–1980 population rise of 23,292,899. The first came from "natural" growth: there were 34,499,000 births and 19,322,000 deaths between the two Censuses, yielding a net natural increase of 15,177,000. The second was the return of 567,000 members of the armed services who had been serving overseas, mainly in Vietnam. The third was the arrival of persons from abroad—8,549,000 more than had departed—over the 10-year period.

The surplus of births over deaths accounted for 60.9 percent of the population growth, with net immigration providing 36.7 percent and returning service personnel the remaining 2.4 percent.

Stated another way, "natural" growth contributed 7.0 percent within the 11.5 percent 1970–1980 population rise; new arrivals comprised 4.2 percent; and military personnel the other 0.3 percent.

[40]

STATES, CITIES, COUNTIES

The next several pages contain tables showing:

- The States Ranked by Population, 1980
- Changes in the States' Populations, 1970–1980
- The Ten Most Populous States in 1980 and Their Populations in 1880, 1900, 1920, 1940, 1960, and 1980
- The Ten Most Populous States in 1800, 1820, 1840, 1860, 1880, 1900, 1920, 1940, 1960, and 1980
- The Fifty Largest Cities in 1980
- The Ten Largest Cities in 1980 and Their Populations in 1880, 1900, 1920, 1940, 1960, and 1980
- The Ten Largest Cities in 1800, 1820, 1840, 1860, 1880, 1900, 1920, 1940, 1960, and 1980
- The Sixty Largest Counties in 1980

THE STATES RANKED BY POPULATION

1. California	23,668,562	26. Oklahoma	3,025,266
2. New York	17,557,288	27. Iowa	2,913,387
3. Texas	14,228,383	28. Colorado	2,888,834
4. Pennsylvania	11,866,728	29. Arizona	2,717,866
5. Illinois	11,418,461	30. Oregon	2,632,663
6. Ohio	10,797,419	31. Mississippi	2,520,638
7. Florida	9,739,992	32. Kansas	2,363,208
8. Michigan	9,258,344	33. Arkansas	2,285,513
9. New Jersey	7,364,158	34. West Virginia	1,949,644
10. North Carolina	5,874,429	35. Nebraska	1,570,006
11. Massachusetts	5,737,037	36. Utah	1,461,037
12. Indiana	5,490,179	37. New Mexico	1,299,968
13. Georgia	5,464,265	38. Maine	1,124,660
14. Virginia	5,346,279	39. Hawaii	965,000
15. Missouri	4,917,444	40. Rhode Island	947,154
16. Wisconsin	4,705,335	41. Idaho	943,935
17. Tennessee	4,590,750	42. New Hampshire	920,610
18. Maryland	4,216,446	43. Nevada	799,184
19. Louisiana	4,203,972	44. Montana	786,690
20. Washington	4,130,163	45. South Dakota	690,178
21. Minnesota	4,077,148	46. North Dakota	652,695
22. Alabama	3,890,061	47. Delaware	595,255
23. Kentucky	3,661,433	48. Vermont	511,456
24. South Carolina	3,119,208	49. Wyoming	470,816
25. Connecticut	3,107,576	50. Alaska	400,481

[3]

STATE INCREASES OR DECREASES IN POPULATION IN ABSOLUTE NUMBERS AND BY PERCENTAGE CHANGE FROM 1970 to 1980

	STATE	NUMBER	STATE	PERCENTAGE CHANGE
1.	California	3,697,493	Nevada	63.5%
2.	Texas	3,029,728	Arizona	53.1%
3.	Florida	2,948,574	Florida	43.4%
4.	Arizona	942,467	Wyoming	41.6%
5.	Georgia	876,335	Utah	37.9%
6.	North Carolina	790,018	Alaska	32.4%
7.	Washington	716,919	Idaho	32.4%
8.	Virginia	694,831	Colorado	30.7%
9.	Colorado	679,238	New Mexico	27.8%
10.	Tennessee	664,732	Texas	27.1%
11.	Louisiana	559,335	Oregon	25.9%
12.	Oregon	541,130	Hawaii	25.3%
13.	South Carolina	528,495	New Hampshire	24.8%
14.	Oklahoma	465,803	Washington	21.0%
15.	Alabama	445,707	South Carolina	20.4%
16.	Kentucky	440,722	Georgia	19.1%
17.	Utah	401,764	Arkansas	18.8%
18.	Michigan	376,518	California	18.5%
19.	Arkansas	362,191	Oklahoma	18.2%
20.	Nevada	310,446	Tennessee	16.9%
21.	Illinois	308,176	North Carolina	15.5%
22.	Mississippi	303,644	Louisiana	15.3%
23.	Indiana	294,787	Vermont	15.0%
24.	Maryland	292,549	Virginia	14.9%
25.	Wisconsin	287,514	Mississippi	13.7%
26.	New Mexico	282,913	Kentucky	13.7%
27.	Minnesota	291,045	Montana	13.3%
28.	Missouri	239,821	Maine	13.2%
29.	Idaho	230,920	Alabama	12.9%
30.	West Virginia	205,407	West Virginia	11.8%
31.	Hawaii	195,087	Delaware	8.6%
32.	New Jersey	193,046	Maryland	7.5%
33.	New Hampshire	182,929	Minnesota	7.1%
34.	Ohio	139,996	Wisconsin	6.5%
35.	Wyoming	138,400	Nebraska	5.7%
36.	Maine	130,938	Indiana	5.7%
37.	Kansas	114,137	North Dakota	5.6%
38.	Alaska	97,898	Kansas	5.1%
39.	Montana	92,281	Missouri	5.1%
40.	Iowa	88,019	Michigan	4.2%

(continued)

(continued)

	STATE	NUMBER	STATE	PERCENTAGE CHANGE
41.	Nebraska	84,673	South Dakota	3.6%
42.	Connecticut	75,359	Iowa	3.1%
43.	Vermont	66,724	Illinois	2.8%
44.	Pennsylvania	65,962	New Jersey	2.7%
45.	Massachusetts	47,867	Connecticut	2.5%
46.	Delaware	47,121	Ohio	1.3%
47.	North Dakota	34,903	Massachusetts	0.8%
48.	South Dakota	23,921	Pennsylvania	0.6%
49.	Rhode Island	−2,569	Rhode Island	−0.3%
50.	New York	−684,103	New York	−3.8%

[3]

THE TEN MOST POPULOUS STATES IN 1980 AND THEIR POPULATIONS: 1880 THROUGH 1980

	CALIFORNIA	NEW YORK	TEXAS	PENNSYLVANIA	ILLINOIS
1980	23,668,562	17,557,288	14,228,383	11,866,728	11,418,461
1960	15,717,204	16,782,304	9,579,667	11,319,366	10,081,158
1940	6,907,387	13,479,142	6,414,824	9,900,180	7,897,241
1920	3,426,861	10,385,227	4,663,228	8,720,017	6,485,280
1900	1,485,053	7,268,894	3,048,710	6,302,115	4,821,550
1880	864,694	5,082,871	1,591,749	4,282,891	3,077,871

	OHIO	FLORIDA	MICHIGAN	NEW JERSEY	NORTH CAROLINA
1980	10,797,419	9,739,992	9,258,344	7,364,158	5,872,429
1960	9,706,397	4,951,560	7,823,194	6,066,782	4,556,155
1940	6,907,612	1,897,414	5,256,106	4,160,165	3,571,623
1920	5,759,394	968,470	3,668,412	3,155,900	2,559,123
1900	4,157,545	528,542	2,420,982	1,883,669	1,893,810
1880	3,198,062	269,493	1,636,937	1,131,116	1,399,750

[11,14]

THE NATION'S TEN MOST POPULOUS STATES: 1800–1980

1980	1960	1940	1920	1900
1. California	New York	New York	New York	New York
2. New York	California	Pennsylvania	Pennsylvania	Pennsylvania
3. Texas	Pennsylvania	Illinois	Illinois	Illinois
4. Pennsylvania	Illinois	Ohio	Ohio	Ohio
5. Illinois	Ohio	California	Texas	Missouri
6. Ohio	Texas	Texas	Massachusetts	Texas
7. Florida	Michigan	Michigan	Michigan	Massachusetts
8. Michigan	New Jersey	Massachusetts	California	Indiana
9. New Jersey	Massachusetts	New Jersey	Missouri	Michigan
10. North Carolina	Florida	Missouri	New Jersey	Iowa

1880	1860	1840	1820	1800
1. New York	New York	New York	New York	Virginia
2. Pennsylvania	Pennsylvania	Pennsylvania	Virginia	Pennsylvania
3. Ohio	Ohio	Ohio	Pennsylvania	New York
4. Illinois	Illinois	Virginia	North Carolina	North Carolina
5. Missouri	Virginia	Tennessee	Ohio	Massachusetts
6. Indiana	Indiana	Kentucky	Kentucky	South Carolina
7. Massachusetts	Massachusetts	North Carolina	Massachusetts	Maryland
8. Kentucky	Missouri	Massachusetts	South Carolina	Connecticut
9. Michigan	Kentucky	Georgia	Tennessee	New Jersey
10. Iowa	Tennessee	Indiana	Maryland	New Hampshire

[11, 14]

THE NATION'S LARGEST CITIES

1980 RANK	1980 POPULATION	POPULATION CHANGE SINCE 1970
1. New York	7,071,639	−10.4%
2. Chicago	3,005,072	−10.7%
3. Los Angeles	2,966,850	+ 5.4%
4. Philadelphia	1,688,210	−13.4%
5. Houston	1,595,138	+29.4%
6. Detroit	1,203,339	−20.4%
7. Dallas	904,078	+ 7.1%
8. San Diego	875,538	+25.7%
9. Phoenix	789,704	+35.9%
10. Baltimore	786,775	−13.1%
11. San Antonio	785,880	+20.1%
12. Indianapolis	700,807	− 5.9%
13. San Francisco	678,974	− 5.1%

(continued)

(continued)

1980 RANK	1980 POPULATION	POPULATION CHANGE SINCE 1970
14. Memphis	646,356	+ 3.7%
15. Washington, D.C.	638,333	−15.6%
16. Milwaukee	636,212	−11.3%
17. San Jose	629,442	+41.2%
18. Cleveland	573,822	−23.6%
19. Columbus, Ohio	564,826	+ 4.7%
20. Boston	562,994	−12.2%
21. New Orleans	557,515	− 6.1%
22. Jacksonville	540,920	+ 2.3%
23. Denver	493,846	− 4.4%
24. Seattle	492,365	− 7.2%
25. Nashville-Davidson	455,651	+ 1.7%
26. St. Louis	453,085	−27.2%
27. Kansas City, Missouri	448,159	−11.6%
28. El Paso	425,259	+32.0%
29. Atlanta	425,022	−14.5%
30. Pittsburgh	423,938	−18.5%
31. Oklahoma City	403,213	+10.0%
32. Cincinnati	385,457	−14.8%
33. Fort Worth	385,164	− 2.1%
34. Minneapolis	370,951	−14.6%
35. Portland, Oregon	366,383	− 4.2%
36. Honolulu	365,048	+12.4%
37. Long Beach	361,334	+ 0.8%
38. Tulsa	360,919	+ 8.8%
39. Buffalo	357,870	−22.7%
40. Toledo	354,635	− 7.6%
41. Miami	346,865	+ 3.6%
42. Austin	345,496	+37.2%
43. Oakland	339,337	− 6.1%
44. Albuquerque	331,767	+36.1%
45. Tucson	330,537	+25.7%
46. Newark, New Jersey	329,248	−13.9%
47. Charlotte	314,447	+30.4%
48. Omaha	314,255	− 9.5%
49. Louisville	298,451	−17.4%
50. Birmingham	282,413	− 5.5%

[5]

THE TEN LARGEST CITIES IN 1980 AND THEIR POPULATIONS IN EARLIER YEARS

	NEW YORK	CHICAGO	LOS ANGELES	PHILADELPHIA	HOUSTON
1980	7,071,639	3,005,072	2,966,850	1,688,210	1,595,138
1960	7,781,984	3,550,404	2,479,015	2,002,512	938,219
1940	7,459,995	3,396,808	1,504,277	1,913,334	384,514
1920	5,620,048	2,701,705	576,673	1,823,779	138,276
1900	3,427,202	1,698,575	102,479	1,293,697	44,633
1880	1,911,698	503,185	38,991	847,170	16,513

	DETROIT	DALLAS	SAN DIEGO	PHOENIX	BALTIMORE
1980	1,203,339	904,078	875,538	789,704	786,775
1960	1,670,144	679,684	573,224	439,170	939,024
1940	1,623,452	294,734	203,341	65,414	859,100
1920	993,678	158,976	74,361	29,053	733,826
1900	285,704	42,638	17,700	5,544	508,957
1880	116,340	10,358	2,637	—	332,313

[5,14]

THE NATION'S TEN LARGEST CITIES: 1800–1980

	1980	1960	1940	1920	1900
1.	New York	New York	New York	New York	New York
2.	Chicago	Chicago	Chicago	Chicago	Chicago
3.	Los Angeles	Los Angeles	Philadelphia	Philadelphia	Philadelphia
4.	Philadelphia	Philadelphia	Detroit	Detroit	St. Louis
5.	Houston	Detroit	Los Angeles	Cleveland	Boston
6.	Detroit	Baltimore	Cleveland	St. Louis	Baltimore
7.	Dallas	Houston	Baltimore	Boston	Cleveland
8.	San Diego	Cleveland	St. Louis	Baltimore	Buffalo
9.	Phoenix	Washington, D.C.	Boston	Pittsburgh	San Francisco
10.	Baltimore	Milwaukee	Pittsburgh	Buffalo	Cincinnati

	1880	1860	1840	1820	1800
1.	New York	New York	New York	New York	New York
2.	Philadelphia	Philadelphia	Baltimore	Philadelphia	Philadelphia
3.	Chicago	Baltimore	New Orleans	Baltimore	Baltimore
4.	Boston	Boston	Philadelphia	Boston	Boston
5.	St. Louis	New Orleans	Boston	New Orleans	Providence
6.	Baltimore	Cincinnati	Cincinnati	Albany	Norfolk
7.	Cincinnati	Chicago	Albany	Richmond	Richmond
8.	San Francisco	Buffalo	Washington, D.C.	Providence	Albany
9.	New Orleans	Newark	Providence	Cincinnati	Savannah
10.	Cleveland	Louisville	Richmond	Norfolk	Alexandria

[5, 14]

THE NATION'S LARGEST COUNTIES

1.	Los Angeles	California (Los Angeles)	7,477,657
2.	Cook	Illinois (Chicago)	5,253,190
3.	Harris	Texas (Houston)	2,409,544
4.	Wayne	Michigan (Detroit)	2,337,240
5.	Kings	New York (Brooklyn)	2,230,936
6.	Orange	California (Los Angeles)	1,931,570
7.	Queens	New York (New York)	1,891,325
8.	San Diego	California (San Diego)	1,861,846
9.	Philadelphia	Pennsylvania (Philadelphia)	1,688,210
10.	Dade	Florida (Miami)	1,625,979
11.	Dallas	Texas (Dallas)	1,556,549
12.	Maricopa	Arizona (Phoenix)	1,508,030
13.	Cuyahoga	Ohio (Cleveland)	1,498,295
14.	Allegheny	Pennsylvania (Pittsburgh)	1,450,085
15.	New York	New York (Manhattan)	1,427,533
16.	Middlesex	Massachusetts (Boston)	1,367,034
17.	Nassau	New York (Long Island)	1,321,582
18.	Santa Clara	California (San Jose)	1,295,071
19.	Suffolk	New York (Long Island)	1,284,231
20.	King	Washington (Seattle)	1,269,749
21.	Bronx	New York (New York)	1,169,115
22.	Alameda	California (San Francisco)	1,105,379
23.	Broward	Florida (Miami)	1,029,979
24.	Erie	New York (Buffalo)	1,015,472
25.	Oakland	Michigan (Detroit)	1,011,793
26.	Bexar	Texas (San Antonio)	988,800
27.	St. Louis	Missouri (St. Louis)	974,815
28.	Milwaukee	Wisconsin (Milwaukee)	964,988
29.	Hennepin	Minnesota (Minneapolis)	941,461
30.	San Bernardino	California (Los Angeles)	893,157
31.	Hamilton	Ohio (Cincinnati)	873,136
32.	Franklin	Ohio (Columbus)	869,109
33.	Westchester	New York (New York)	866,599
34.	Tarrant	Texas (Fort Worth)	860,800
35.	Essex	New Jersey (Newark)	850,451
36.	Bergen	New Jersey (Northern New Jersey)	845,385
37.	Hartford	Connecticut (Hartford)	807,946
38.	Fairfield	Connecticut (Western Connecticut)	807,143
39.	Baltimore City	Maryland (Baltimore)	786,775
40.	Sacramento	California (Northern California)	783,381
41.	Shelby	Tennessee (Memphis)	777,113
42.	Marion	Indiana (Indianapolis)	765,233
43.	Honolulu	Hawaii (Honolulu)	762,874
44.	New Haven	Connecticut (New Haven)	758,337
45.	Pinellas	Florida (St. Petersburg)	728,409

(continued)

(continued)

46.	Monroe	New York (Rochester)	702,238
47.	Macomb	Michigan (Detroit)	694,600
48.	Jefferson	Alabama (Birmingham)	684,793
49.	San Francisco	California (San Francisco)	678,974
50.	Jefferson	Kentucky (Louisville)	671,197
51.	Prince George's	Maryland (District of Columbia)	665,071
52.	Riverside	California (Southern California)	663,923
53.	Du Page	Illinois (Chicago)	658,177
54.	Contra Costa	California (San Francisco)	657,252
55.	Baltimore	Maryland (Baltimore)	655,615
56.	Suffolk	Massachusetts (Boston)	650,142
57.	Hillsborough	Florida (Tampa)	646,960
58.	Worcester	Massachusetts (Worcester)	646,352
59.	Montgomery	Pennsylvania (Philadelphia)	643,621
60.	Essex	Massachusetts (Boston)	633,632

[5]

CHANGES IN CONGRESSIONAL REPRESENTATION

Due to shifts in population, states gain or lose members in the House of Representatives. The following 14 states had delegations of at least 10 members in 1960 and 1980:

1960		1980	
New York	41	California	45
California	38	New York	34
Pennsylvania	27	Texas	27
Illinois	24	Pennsylvania	23
Ohio	24	Illinois	22
Texas	23	Ohio	21
Michigan	19	Florida	19
New Jersey	15	Michigan	18
Florida	12	New Jersey	14
Massachusetts	12	Massachusetts	11
Indiana	11	North Carolina	11
North Carolina	11	Indiana	10
Georgia	10	Georgia	10
Virginia	10	Virginia	10
	277		275

Of these states, 8 of them (New York, Pennsylvania, Illinois, Ohio, Michigan, New Jersey, Massachusetts, and Indiana) lost a total of 20 seats; while 3 (California, Texas, and Florida) gained 18 seats in the Congress.

The membership of the House of Representatives remains constant, at 435 seats, so districts grow in size as the population increases. In 1960 an "average" district would have had 412,237 persons. By 1980 the comparable figure had grown to 520,701.

[10]

WHERE AMERICANS LIVE

The Census has two systems for classifying the kinds of areas in which Americans live. The first is a straight division along "urban" and "rural" lines. The second identifies certain sections as "metropolitan areas," which allows for a different division on "metropolitan" and "nonmetropolitan" lines. And, as will be seen, each metropolitan area contains a "central city" (sometimes more than one) plus a surrounding area (sometimes referred to as suburbs).

URBAN VS. RURAL

The Census defines as "urban" any city or town or village having at least 2,500 residents. The United States has more than 7,000 such localities. Using this generous definition, the 1980 Census found that 166,965,380 persons—73.7 percent of the population—live in urban settings. These ranged from New York City (7,015,608) and Chicago (2,969,570) to Centreville, Alabama (2,504) and Ellinwood, Kansas (2,508).

The remaining 59,539,445 Americans—26.3 percent of the population—live either in smaller places or out in open country beyond the village line. There are more than 13,000 communities with fewer than 2,500 people, like Alicia, Arkansas (246) and Frannie, Wyoming (138).

The nation has become progressively more urban, but the rate of change has varied over the decades. The following are the urban proportions of the population in each of the last ten Censuses, plus the percentage increase from the preceding Census:

	PERCENTAGE URBAN POPULATION	PERCENTAGE INCREASE
1890	35.1%	24.5%
1900	39.6%	12.8%
1910	45.6%	15.2%
1920	51.2%	12.3%
1930	56.1%	9.6%
1940	56.5%	0.7%
1950	64.0%	13.3%
1960	69.9%	9.2%
1970	73.6%	5.3%
1980	73.7%	0.1%

Since 1950 the urban rate of growth has been winding down, and the 1970–1980 decade saw almost no increase at all. However, during the 1970s no fewer than 19 states actually had an increase in the rural part of their populations. The greatest shifts were in Michigan (where the rural share rose by 12.7 percent); New Hampshire (up 9.6 percent); New York and Pennsylvania (both up 7.7 percent); Maine (6.7 percent); Delaware (5.4 percent); and Wisconsin (5.0 percent).

PROPORTION OF THE POPULATION LIVING IN URBAN AND METROPOLITAN AREAS

IN URBAN AREAS	PERCENTAGE PER STATE	IN METROPOLITAN AREAS	PERCENTAGE PER STATE
U.S.A.	73.7%	U.S.A.	74.8%
1. California	91.3%	California	94.9%
2. New Jersey	89.0%	Rhode Island	92.2%
3. Rhode Island	87.0%	New Jersey	91.4%
4. Hawaii	86.5%	New York	90.1%
5. Nevada	85.3%	Maryland	88.8%
6. New York	84.6%	Connecticut	88.3%
7. Utah	84.4%	Florida	87.9%
8. Florida	84.3%	Massachusetts	85.3%
9. Massachusetts	83.8%	Michigan	82.7%
10. Arizona	83.8%	Nevada	82.0%
11. Illinois	83.0%	Pennsylvania	81.9%

(continued)

(continued)

IN URBAN AREAS	PERCENTAGE PER STATE	IN METROPOLITAN AREAS	PERCENTAGE PER STATE
12. Colorado	80.6%	Illinois	81.0%
13. Maryland	80.3%	Colorado	80.9%
14. Texas	79.6%	Washington	80.4%
15. Connecticut	78.8%	Ohio	80.3%
16. Washington	73.6%	Texas	80.0%
17. Ohio	73.3%	Hawaii	79.1%
18. New Mexico	72.2%	Utah	79.0%
19. Michigan	70.7%	Arizona	75.0%
20. Delaware	70.7%	Indiana	69.8%
21. Pennsylvania	69.3%	Virginia	69.6%
22. Louisiana	68.6%	Delaware	67.0%
23. Missouri	68.1%	Wisconsin	66.8%
24. Oregon	67.9%	Missouri	65.3%
25. Oklahoma	67.3%	Oregon	64.9%
26. Minnesota	66.8%	Minnesota	64.6%
27. Kansas	66.7%	Louisiana	63.4%
28. Virginia	66.0%	Tennessee	62.8%
29. Alaska	64.5%	Alabama	62.0%
30. Wisconsin	64.2%	Georgia	60.0%
31. Indiana	64.2%	South Carolina	59.7%
32. Wyoming	62.8%	Oklahoma	58.5%
33. Nebraska	62.7%	North Carolina	52.7%
34. Georgia	62.3%	New Hampshire	50.7%
35. Tennessee	60.4%	Kansas	46.8%
36. Alabama	60.0%	Kentucky	44.5%
37. Iowa	58.6%	Nebraska	44.2%
38. South Carolina	54.1%	Alaska	43.2%
39. Idaho	54.0%	New Mexico	42.4%
40. Montana	52.9%	Iowa	40.1%
41. New Hampshire	52.2%	Arkansas	39.1%
42. Arkansas	51.6%	West Virginia	37.1%
43. Kentucky	50.8%	North Dakota	35.9%
44. North Dakota	48.8%	Maine	33.0%
45. North Carolina	48.0%	Mississippi	27.1%
46. Maine	47.5%	Montana	24.0%
47. Mississippi	47.3%	Vermont	22.3%
48. South Dakota	46.4%	Idaho	18.3%
49. West Virginia	36.2%	South Dakota	15.9%
50. Vermont	33.8%	Wyoming	15.3%

[6,8]

Back in 1950 the Census Bureau created a classification it called the "Standard Metropolitan Statistical Area." These metropolitan areas—as they will be called here—usually consist of a "central city" having a population of at least 50,000, plus the counties adjacent to it.

There can be variations to this pattern. Some metropolitan areas contain more than one city. Minneapolis–St. Paul is an obvious example. Dallas and Fort Worth are in the same area even though they are 30 miles apart. So far as the surrounding counties are concerned, there can be as many as 8 (as in St. Louis's case) or even 14 (as with Atlanta). At the other extreme, the Great Falls, Montana, area contains simply the city of Great Falls plus the rest of Cascade County, in which Great Falls is situated.

THE 25 LARGEST METROPOLITAN AREAS: 1980 CENSUS

		TOTAL POPULATION	CENTRAL CITIES	PERCENTAGE	SURROUNDING AREAS	PERCENTAGE
1.	New York	9,119,737	7,071,030	77.5%	2,048,707	22.5%
2.	Los Angeles	7,477,657	3,328,097	44.5%	4,149,560	55.5%
3.	Chicago	7,102,328	3,005,072	42.3%	4,097,256	57.7%
4.	Philadelphia	4,716,818	1,688,210	35.8%	3,028,608	64.2%
5.	Detroit	4,352,762	1,203,339	27.6%	3,149,423	72.4%
6.	San Francisco–Oakland	3,252,721	1,018,262	31.3%	2,234,459	68.7%
7.	Washington, D.C.	3,060,240	637,651	20.8%	2,422,589	79.2%
8.	Dallas–Fort Worth	2,974,878	1,289,219	43.3%	1,685,659	56.7%
9.	Houston	2,905,350	1,594,086	54.9%	1,311,264	45.1%
10.	Boston	2,763,357	562,994	20.4%	2,200,363	79.6%
11.	Long Island, N.Y.	2,605,813	-	-	2,605,813	100.0%
12.	St. Louis	2,355,276	453,085	19.2%	1,902,191	80.8%
13.	Pittsburgh	2,263,894	423,938	18.7%	1,839,956	81.3%
14.	Baltimore	2,174,023	786,775	36.2%	1,387,258	63.8%
15.	Minneapolis–St. Paul	2,114,256	641,181	30.3%	1,473,075	69.7%
16.	Atlanta	2,029,618	425,022	20.9%	1,604,596	79.1%
17.	Newark	1,965,304	329,248	16.8%	1,636,056	83.2%
18.	Anaheim	1,931,570	548,911	28.4%	1,382,659	71.6%
19.	Cleveland	1,898,720	573,822	30.2%	1,324,898	69.8%
20.	San Diego	1,861,846	875,504	47.0%	986,342	53.0%
21.	Miami	1,625,979	346,931	21.3%	1,279,048	78.7%
22.	Denver	1,619,921	568,081	35.1%	1,051,840	64.9%
23.	Seattle	1,606,765	548,259	34.1%	1,058,506	65.9%
24.	Tampa–St. Petersburg	1,569,492	508,416	32.4%	1,061,076	67.6%
25.	Riverside–San Bernardino	1,557,080	377,753	24.3%	1,179,327	75.7%

[6]

METROPOLITAN AREAS: 1950–1980

	1950	1960	1970	1980
Number of metropolitan areas at each census	168	209	243	284
Percentage of population in:				
Metropolitan areas	56.1%	63.0%	68.6%	74.8%
Central cities	32.8%	32.3%	31.4%	30.0%
Adjacent territory	23.3%	30.6%	37.2%	44.8%
Nonmetropolitan areas	43.9%	37.0%	31.4%	25.2%
	100.0%	100.0%	100.0%	100.0%
	1950	1960	1970	1980
Within metropolitan areas:				
Central cities	58.5%	51.4%	45.8%	40.1%
Adjacent territory	41.5%	48.6%	54.2%	59.9%
	100.0%	100.0%	100.0%	100.0%
Number of counties (or comparable subdivisions) included in metropolitan areas at each census	473	600	760	1,126

[6]

The largest metropolitan area in 1980 was New York's, with 9,119,737. As it happens, it might have been even larger, but the Census decided to make Long Island (2,605,813) an area in its own right. The same holds for the Los Angeles area (7,477,657), since nearby cities like Anaheim and Oxnard have areas of their own. The smallest metropolitan area is for Meriden, Connecticut (57,118), after which comes Enid, Oklahoma (62,820) and Lawrence, Kansas (67,640).

Metropolitan Population. The 1980 Census calculated there were 284 metropolitan areas in the country. Altogether they contained 169,405,018 persons, or 74.8 percent of the nation's population. The remaining 57,099,807 people, or 25.2 percent, lived in the rest of the country not included in metropolitan areas.

Over the years, the number of Americans living in metropolitan areas has been increasing, partly because the Census Bureau has been adding more cities to the metropolitan area list. At the same time, the proportion of persons within the areas who reside in their central cities has been declining. But that, too, is partly due to the fact that the Census has added more adjacent counties to the areas' surrounding territory.

Moreover, a metropolitan area includes the *entire* adjacent county or counties, regardless of its size. Thus the Tucson, Arizona, area takes in all of Pima County, which runs 150 miles across the state and exceeds New Hampshire in size. Reno, Nevada's area includes the whole of Washoe County, which is 195 miles long and meets the Oregon line. As a result, many metropolitan areas contain people and places the Census also classes as "rural." By the same token, it is stretching things a bit to designate all of an area's *noncity* territory as "surburban."

Indeed, the noncity parts of metropolitan areas are now so elongated that in most cases the majority of people who live in them no longer commute to the central city. For example, a recent Census survey showed that in the counties around Cincinnati, only 32.2 percent of the residents traveled to work in the city. For Chicago, the figure was 24.0 percent, and in Miami it was 23.8 percent. In Philadelphia's case, only 16.9 percent of those residing in its so-called suburbs were employed within the city.

A MORE "METROPOLITAN" AMERICA?

Common sense alone would tell us that more people now reside in "metropolitan areas" than was the case in the past. However, Census statistics are not very helpful in computing this movement. According to the Bureau's figures, the "metropolitan" portion of the population rose from 56.1 percent to 74.8 percent between 1950 and 1980.

But a considerable part of this growth comes from the fact that the Census itself created 116 new metropolitan areas during this period, raising the total from 168 to 284. Not only that, but in many cases extra counties were added as adjacent territory to already existing areas. In 1950, for example, the Atlanta area consisted of three counties (one of which contained Atlanta) encompassing 1,138 square miles. By 1980 "metropolitan" Atlanta included no less than 15 counties covering 4,326 square miles. Indeed, one of these "metropolitan" counties contained only 3,987 households and was largely "rural" in composition. Thus it was statistical sleight-of-hand that made more Georgians into "metropolitan" citizens.

How Much Urban Decline? The same problem arises with the status of the central cities. The Census tells us that the city component within metropolitan areas dropped from 58.5 percent in 1950 to 40.1 percent in 1980. While we know that most central cities have lost population, the figures are misleading insofar as they inflate "surburban" growth by adding new counties to the urban fringe. In 1950, for example, the Minneapolis–St. Paul metropolitan area contained only 4 counties, 2 of which included the Twin Cities, and they in turn accounted for 74.6 percent of the area's population. Between 1950 and 1980, Minneapolis and St. Paul together lost a total of 191,886 people, which would obviously decrease the cities' share of the area. According to the Census, by 1980 that share was down at 30.3 percent.

However, during that period the Census added 6 new counties to the area, and their very presence would make St. Paul and Minneapolis look even smaller. In 1980 those 6 new counties had 322,952 people, in itself providing the noncity part of the area with 28.1 percent more persons than it would have had with its 1950 boundaries.

All in all, then, it is best to exercise caution when reading Census statistics for so-called "metropolitan areas." Each such area should be scrutinized to ascertain the territory actually contained. As for how much of America is "rural" or "urban," or "metropolitan" or "suburban," at this stage about all we can say is that no one knows for sure.

AGE

AN AGING POPULATION

In the two decades from 1960 to 1980, the part of the population composed of children under the age of 5 declined from 20,321,901 to 16,344,407, or by 19.6 percent. During the same period, the number of persons aged 65 or over increased from 16,559,580 to 25,544,133, or by 54.3 percent.

Stated another way, in 1960, for every 100 children under 5 there were only 81 persons aged 65 or over. By 1980, for every 100 children there were 156 senior citizens.

This shift had two principal causes: fewer children are being born, and older people are living longer. Back in 1955–1959, the fertility rate was 3.7, representing the number of children an average woman would have at the rate then prevailing. By 1980 the fertility rate was 1.9, down to almost half the previous figure.

And in 1955 average life expectancy was 69.6 years of age. By 1980 it had climbed to 73.6 years. More than that, an individual who reached the age of 65 could expect to live another 16.7 years, to 81.7. (Further figures on life expectancy appear in the next chapter.)

[2]

Between 1970 and 1980 the nation grew older, with the median age rising from 28.0 to 30.0. Altogether, the number of children 14 years and younger fell by 6,653,495, whereas the number of persons 55 and older rose by 8,669,893.

	POPULATION IN 1980	CHANGE 1970–1980	1980 DISTRIBUTION PERCENTAGE	1970 DISTRIBUTION PERCENTAGE
Under 5	16,344,407	− 818,429	7.2%	8.4%
5–9	16,697,134	− 3,271,922	7.4%	9.8%
10–14	18,240,919	− 2,563,144	8.1%	10.2%
15–19	21,161,667	+ 2,077,696	9.3%	9.4%
20–24	21,312,557	+ 4,929,644	9.4%	8.1%
25–34	37,075,629	+12,153,118	16.4%	12.3%
35–44	25,631,247	+ 2,530,074	11.3%	11.4%
45–54	22,797,367	− 437,423	10.1%	11.4%
55–64	21,699,765	+ 3,098,096	9.6%	9.2%
65–74	15,577,586	+ 3,135,013	6.9%	6.1%
75–84	7,726,826	+ 1,605,199	3.4%	3.0%
85 and up	2,239,721	+ 831,585	1.0%	0.7%
	226,504,825	+23,292,899	100.0%	100.0%

[2]

AGE AND SEX

The 1980 Census found the following age distributions divided according to sexes:

sex ratio

	MALES	FEMALES	MALES PER 1000 FEMALES
Under 5	8,360,135	7,984,272	1047
5–9	8,537,903	8,159,231	1046
10–14	9,315,055	8,925,864	1044
15–19	10,751,544	10,410,123	1033
20–24	10,660,063	10,652,494	1001
25–29	9,703,259	9,814,413	989
30–34	8,675,505	8,882,452	977
35–39	6,860,236	7,102,772	966
40–44	5,707,550	5,960,689	958
45–49	5,387,511	5,700,872	945
50–54	5,620,474	6,088,510	923
55–59	5,481,152	6,132,902	894

(continued)

(continued)

sex ratio

	MALES	FEMALES	MALES PER 1000 FEMALES
60–64	4,669,307	5,416,404	862
65–69	3,902,083	4,878,761	800
70–74	2,853,116	3,943,626	723
75–79	1,847,115	2,945,482	627
80–84	1,018,859	1,915,370	532
85 and over	681,428	1,558,293	437
TOTAL	110,032,295	116,472,530	945
Median Age	28.8	31.3	

[2]

AGE AND RACE

The following were the numbers of white and black Americans in each age range in the 1980 Census:

	WHITE	BLACK	BLACKS PER 1000 WHITES
Under 5	12,631,197	2,435,915	193
5–9	13,031,017	2,489,947	191
10–14	14,460,283	2,672,908	185
15–19	16,957,541	2,983,440	176
20–24	17,283,385	2,724,355	158
25–34	30,625,328	4,208,892	137
35–44	21,584,367	2,708,418	125
45–54	19,612,854	2,271,182	116
55–64	19,210,785	1,907,335	99
64–74	13,905,249	1,339,974	96
75–84	6,994,079	586,991	84
85 and up	2,044,705	158,861	78
TOTAL	188,340,790	26,488,218	141
Median age	31.3	24.9	

Black and white Americans currently comprise 94.8 percent of the total population. Detailed figures on age distributions of individuals in the other 5.2 percent will not be available until late in 1983 or early 1984.

[2]

THE STATES: RELATIVE AGE-RANGES

The states can be ranked by their "youth" in three different ways. The first column shows the percentage of their inhabitants who are 10 years old or younger. The second column gives the median age of each state's population. And the third column ranks the states by the percentage of their inhabitants who are 65 or older.

	PERCENTAGE OF POPULATION 10 YEARS OLD OR YOUNGER		MEDIAN AGE OF POPULATION		PERCENTAGE OF POPULATION 65 YEARS OLD OR OLDER	
1.	Utah	23.0%	Utah	24.2	Alaska	2.9%
2.	Idaho	18.7%	Alaska	26.1	Utah	7.5%
3.	Alaska	18.4%	Wyoming	27.1	Wyoming	7.9%
4.	Wyoming	17.9%	Louisiana	27.4	Hawaii	7.9%
5.	Mississippi	17.2%	New Mexico	27.4	Nevada	8.2%
6.	New Mexico	17.2%	Mississippi	27.4	Colorado	8.6%
7.	Louisiana	16.8%	Idaho	27.6	New Mexico	8.9%
8.	Texas	16.4%	Texas	28.2	South Carolina	9.2%
9.	South Dakota	16.1%	South Carolina	28.2	Maryland	9.4%
10.	North Dakota	15.9%	North Dakota	28.3	Virginia	9.4%
11.	Montana	15.8%	Hawaii	28.4	Georgia	9.5%
12.	Georgia	15.8%	Colorado	28.6	Louisiana	9.6%
13.	South Carolina	15.8%	Georgia	28.7	Texas	9.6%
14.	Alabama	15.7%	South Dakota	28.9	Michigan	9.8%
15.	Arizona	15.6%	Michigan	28.9	Idaho	9.9%
16.	Hawaii	15.6%	Montana	29.0	Delaware	10.0%
17.	Kentucky	15.6%	Kentucky	29.1	California	10.2%
18.	Arkansas	15.6%	Arizona	29.2	North Carolina	10.2%
19.	Indiana	15.5%	Minnesota	29.2	Washington	10.4%
20.	Nebraska	15.3%	Indiana	29.2	Indiana	10.7%
21.	West Virginia	15.3%	Alabama	29.3	Montana	10.7%
22.	Oklahoma	15.3%	Vermont	29.4	Ohio	10.8%
23.	Michigan	15.2%	Wisconsin	29.4	Illinois	11.0%
24.	Ohio	14.9%	North Carolina	29.6	New Hampshire	11.2%
25.	Colorado	14.9%	Nebraska	29.7	Kentucky	11.2%
26.	Iowa	14.8%	Delaware	29.7	Tennessee	11.3%
27.	Illinois	14.8%	Washington	29.8	Arizona	11.3%
28.	Minnesota	14.8%	Virginia	29.8	Alabama	11.3%
29.	Kansas	14.8%	Ohio	29.9	Vermont	11.4%
30.	Tennessee	14.7%	Illinois	29.9	Mississippi	11.5%
31.	Oregon	14.7%	California	29.9	Oregon	11.5%
32.	Wisconsin	14.7%	Iowa	30.0	New Jersey	11.7%

(continued)

PERCENTAGE OF POPULATION 10 YEARS OLD OR YOUNGER		MEDIAN AGE OF POPULATION		PERCENTAGE OF POPULATION 65 YEARS OLD OR OLDER	
33. Washington	14.6%	Oklahoma	30.1	Connecticut	11.7%
34. North Carolina	14.5%	Tennessee	30.1	Minnesota	11.8%
35. Maine	14.5%	New Hampshire	30.1	Wisconsin	12.0%
36. Vermont	14.4%	Kansas	30.1	West Virginia	12.2%
37. Missouri	14.4%	Oregon	30.2	New York	12.3%
38. California	14.2%	Nevada	30.3	North Dakota	12.3%
39. New Hampshire	14.2%	Maryland	30.3	Oklahoma	12.4%
40. Delaware	14.0%	Maine	30.4	Maine	12.5%
41. Virginia	14.0%	West Virginia	30.4	Massachusetts	12.7%
42. Nevada	13.9%	Arkansas	30.6	Pennsylvania	12.9%
43. Maryland	13.4%	Missouri	30.9	Kansas	13.0%
44. New York	13.2%	Massachusetts	31.2	Nebraska	13.1%
45. New Jersey	13.2%	Rhode Island	31.8	Missouri	13.2%
46. Pennsylvania	13.1%	New York	31.9	South Dakota	13.2%
47. Connecticut	12.6%	Connecticut	32.0	Iowa	13.3%
48. Rhode Island	12.5%	Pennsylvania	32.1	Rhode Island	13.4%
49. Massachusetts	12.4%	New Jersey	32.2	Arkansas	13.7%
50. Florida	12.2%	Florida	34.7	Florida	17.3%
U.S.A.	14.6%	U.S.A.	30.0	U.S.A.	11.3%

[2]

RACIAL AND NATIONAL ORIGINS

The way the Census deals with race and nationality needs explanation. Its method is to draw up a list of choices and let respondents pick the one that best describes their origins. So first the Census must decide which groups will go on its lists. As it happens, the lists have included races (white, black), nationalities (Japanese, Chinese), and even several islands (Guam, Samoa). What emerges is an eclectic collection, containing various expressions of ethnicity.

In 1970, for example, the question on the form was headed "Color or Race," followed by 9 choices from which respondents could choose. In

1980 the question simply began with a query: "Is this person . . . ?" and the list had lengthened to include *15* choices. The 1970 and 1980 lists ran as follows:

1970	1980
( ) WHITE	( ) WHITE
( ) NEGRO or BLACK	( ) BLACK or NEGRO
( ) INDIAN (AMERICAN)	( ) INDIAN (AMERICAN)
( ) JAPANESE	( ) JAPANESE
( ) CHINESE	( ) CHINESE
( ) FILIPINO	( ) FILIPINO
( ) HAWAIIAN	( ) HAWAIIAN
( ) KOREAN	( ) KOREAN
( ) OTHER	( ) INDIAN (ASIAN)
	( ) VIETNAMESE
	( ) GUAMANIAN
	( ) SAMOAN
	( ) ESKIMO
	( ) ALEUT
	( ) OTHER

The responses were as follows:

RACIAL AND NATIONAL ORIGINS 1970 AND 1980

	1970 Number	1970 Percentage	1980 Number	1980 Percentage	PERCENTAGE CHANGE
White	177,748,975	87.475%	188,340,790	83.153%	+ 6.0%
Black	22,580,289	11.112%	26,488,218	11.695%	+ 17.3%
American Indian	792,730	0.390%	1,361,869	0.601%	+ 71.8%
Chinese	435,062	0.214%	806,027	0.356%	+ 85.3%
Filipino	343,060	0.169%	774,640	0.342%	+ 125.8%
Japanese	591,290	0.291%	700,747	0.309%	+ 18.5%
Asian Indian	—	—	361,544	0.160%	—
Korean	69,130	0.034%	354,529	0.157%	+ 412.8%
Vietnamese	—	—	261,714	0.116%	—
Hawaiian	100,179	0.049%	167,253	0.074%	+ 67.0%
Eskimo	28,186*	0.014%	42,149	0.019%	+ 49.5%
Samoan	—	—	42,050	0.019%	—
Guamanian	—	—	32,132	0.014%	—
Aleut	6,352*	0.003%	14,177	0.006%	+ 123.2%
Other	516,673	0.254%	6,756,989	2.983%	+1,207.8%
TOTAL	203,211,926	100.000%	226,504,825	100.000%	+ 11.5%

[4, 20]

*The 1970 figures include only Aleuts and Eskimos living in Alaska. Those for 1980 are for the entire country.

Whites. The number of people who identified themselves as "white" rose by only 6.0 percent from 1970 to 1980, a rate just slightly over half of the 11.5 percent increase for the country as a whole. As a result, the "white" component of the population fell from 87.5 percent to 83.2 percent during the decade.

Blacks. The 17.3 percent increase among black Americans was almost three times that registered by white Americans. Between 1960 and 1970, the black population rose by 19.6 percent; and from 1950 to 1960 it went up by 25.4 percent.

American Indians and Hawaiians. Both these groups are noteworthy because they grew by impressive rates, without having been augmented by arrivals from abroad. New births can only account for a small proportion of the 71.8 percent American Indian increase and the 67.0 percent rate for persons of Hawaiian origin. It seems that many people who chose some other designation in 1970 decided to identify as American Indians or Hawaiians in 1980. We have no way of ascertaining what their 1970 choices may have been, although it would seem likely that many if not most had selected "white."

Chinese, Filipinos, and Japanese. Among these three groups, persons of Japanese origin led the list in the 1970 Census. By 1980, the Chinese came first, having grown by 85.3 percent; followed by the Filipinos, whose numbers more than doubled, rising by 125.8 percent. These shifts reflect large-scale emigrations from Hong Kong and Taiwan and the Philippines. There was much less emigration from Japan, resulting in only an 18.5 percent rise for that group. (Japanese citizens who were here temporarily on business assignments were not counted in the Census.)

Koreans and Asian Indians. The number of Koreans underwent a five-fold expansion from 1970 to 1980, for an increase of 412.8 percent. As the Census did not include Asian Indians on its "color or race" list in 1970, it is not possible to calculate their rate of increase. However, on another part of the 1970 Census form, which dealt with the "national origins," 75,533 persons said that they or their parents had been born in India. If that is taken as the 1970 figure, the Asian Indian group increased by 378.7 percent. On the whole this seems a fair estimate.

Eskimos and Aleuts. Unfortunately, the 1970 Census counted only Eskimos and Aleuts who were living in the state of Alaska. Those figures came to 28,186 and 6,352. If we compare them with Alaska's 1980 Eskimo and Aleutian totals, which were 34,135 and 8,063, it emerges that those groups had respective increases of 21.1 percent and 26.9 percent. In addition to growths due to new births, these relatively high rates also include people who had chosen some other identification in 1970 and switched in 1980 to Eskimo or Aleut. The 1980 Census also shows that 19.0 percent of America's Eskimos and 43.1 percent of the Aleuts were residing in states other than Alaska.

Vietnamese, Samoans, and Guamanians. The 1970 Census made no specific count of persons from these places, so no growth percentages can be computed. In 1970 persons of these origins would have checked the "other" category.

"Other": The Group with the Largest Growth. The thirteenfold increase in persons choosing "other"—1,307.8 percent—was the biggest surprise of the 1980 Census. In earlier Censuses, relatively few people picked that residual option; in 1970 only slightly more than half a million did so. Typically they were persons of Middle Eastern or Asian Indian origins, along with some individuals of mixed parentage. What we do know is that in the past most persons of Spanish origin identified themselves as "white." Indeed, in 1970 no fewer than 93.3 percent did so.

By 1980 that had changed. No fewer than 40.0 percent of persons of Spanish origin chose *not* to check any of the 14 choices of a race or nationality. These individuals picked "other," which was their way of saying that their Spanish origin was their full identity. That is, they did not desire a further designation (such as "white") for their personal description. Moreover, it seems clear that Americans of Spanish origin accounted for most of the growth in the "other" category.

SPANISH ORIGIN

"Spanish" was not among the racial and national choices on the 1970 and 1980 Census lists. However, both Censuses had a completely separate question, which allowed individuals to specify if they were of Spanish (or Hispanic) origin or descent.

In 1970 a total of 9,072,602 persons said they were of Spanish origin. In 1980 the figure was 14,605,883, a rise of 61.0 percent, higher than that for either white or black Americans.

Individuals of Spanish origin, along with everyone else, were asked to locate themselves on the race and nationality list. These were their choices in 1970 and 1980:

| | 1970 | | 1980 | |
	Number	Percentage	Number	Percentage
White	8,466,126	93.3%	8,113,648	55.6%
Black	454,934	5.0%	390,733	2.7%
Other Specific Choices	63,342	0.7%	260,850	1.7%
General "Other"	87,930	1.0%	5,840,648	40.0%
TOTAL	9,072,602	100.0%	14,605,883	100.0%

The number of persons of Spanish origin who chose to identify as "white" declined by 4.2 percent, while those identifying as "black" dropped by 14.1 percent. The sharp rise of 311.8 percent among those choosing other specific categories is due largely to the presence of Filipinos. And the group selecting the general "other" option in 1980 was sixty-six times its 1970 strength.

Looked at another way, persons of Spanish origin made up 86.4 percent of the overall "other" total. In 1970 they contributed only 17.0 percent to that category.

Choices by States. If 55.6 percent of individuals of Spanish origin also chose to call themselves "white," while 40.0 percent selected "other," it is not easy to explain those choices by more specific origins. In the 9 states having the largest Spanish-origin populations, the proportions taking the "other" option ranged from 53.8 percent down to 16.7 percent.

Illinois led the list (with 53.8 percent selecting "other"), followed by California (52.0 percent), Arizona (51.7 percent), New York (50.9 percent), and Colorado (49.7 percent). In 4 of these 5 states, most of the persons are of Mexican descent, but in New York they are chiefly of Puerto Rican or other Caribbean origins.

Next came New Jersey (where 40.7 percent picked "other"), followed by New Mexico (39.5 percent), Texas (38.9 percent), with Florida far behind (16.7 percent). Yet these states, where there was less inclination to chose "other," include both New Jersey, where the population is mainly Puerto Rican and Cuban, and New Mexico and Texas, where it is largely Mexican. About the only generalization that is possible is that most of Florida's Cubans prefer to describe themselves as "white."

[4]

BLACK AND HISPANIC POPULATIONS OF THE STATES

	BLACK		HISPANIC	
1.	New York	2,401,842	California	4,543,770
2.	California	1,819,282	Texas	2,985,643
3.	Texas	1,710,250	New York	1,659,245
4.	Illinois	1,675,229	Florida	857,898
5.	Georgia	1,465,457	Illinois	635,525
6.	Florida	1,342,478	New Jersey	491,867
7.	North Carolina	1,316,050	New Mexico	476,089
8.	Louisiana	1,237,263	Arizona	440,915
9.	Michigan	1,198,710	Colorado	339,300
10.	Ohio	1,076,734	Michigan	162,388
11.	Pennsylvania	1,047,609	Pennsylvania	154,044
12.	Virginia	1,008,311	Massachusetts	141,043
13.	Alabama	995,623	Connecticut	124,499
14.	Maryland	958,050	Washington	119,986
15.	South Carolina	948,146	Ohio	119,880
16.	New Jersey	924,786	Louisiana	99,105
17.	Mississippi	887,206	Indiana	87,020
18.	Tennessee	725,949	Virginia	79,873
19.	Missouri	514,274	Hawaii	71,479
20.	Indiana	414,732	Oregon	65,833
21.	Arkansas	373,192	Maryland	64,740
22.	Kentucky	259,490	Kansas	63,333
23.	Massachusetts	221,279	Wisconsin	62,981
24.	Connecticut	217,433	Georgia	61,261
25.	Oklahoma	204,658	Utah	60,302
26.	Wisconsin	182,593	Oklahoma	57,413
27.	Kansas	126,127	North Carolina	56,607
28.	Washington	105,544	Nevada	53,786
29.	Colorado	101,702	Missouri	51,667
30.	Delaware	95,971	Idaho	36,615
31.	Arizona	75,034	Tennessee	34,081
32.	West Virginia	65,051	South Carolina	33,414
33.	Minnesota	53,342	Alabama	33,100
34.	Nevada	50,791	Minnesota	32,124
35.	Nebraska	48,389	Nebraska	28,020
36.	Iowa	41,700	Kentucky	27,403
37.	Oregon	37,059	Iowa	25,536
38.	Rhode Island	27,584	Mississippi	24,731
39.	New Mexico	24,042	Wyoming	24,499
40.	Hawaii	17,352	Rhode Island	19,707
41.	Alaska	13,619	Arkansas	17,873
42.	Utah	9,225	West Virginia	12,707

(continued)

	BLACK		HISPANIC	
43.	New Hampshire	3,990	Montana	9,974
44.	Wyoming	3,364	Delaware	9,671
45.	Maine	3,128	Alaska	9,497
46.	Idaho	2,716	New Hampshire	5,587
47.	North Dakota	2,568	Maine	5,005
48.	South Dakota	2,144	South Dakota	4,028
49.	Montana	1,786	North Dakota	3,903
50.	Vermont	1,135	Vermont	3,304

[2]

BLACK PROPORTIONS OF STATE POPULATIONS

Here are the 50 states, ranked in order of the proportion of black residents in their population.

	PERCENTAGE BLACK POPULATION		PERCENTAGE BLACK POPULATION
Mississippi	35.2%	Nevada	6.4%
South Carolina	30.4%	Kansas	5.3%
Louisiana	29.4%	Massachusetts	3.9%
Georgia	26.8%	Wisconsin	3.9%
Alabama	25.6%	Colorado	3.5%
Maryland	22.7%	Alaska	3.4%
North Carolina	22.4%	West Virginia	3.3%
Virginia	18.9%	Nebraska	3.1%
Arkansas	16.3%	Rhode Island	2.9%
Delaware	16.1%	Arizona	2.8%
Tennessee	15.8%	Washington	2.6%
Illinois	14.7%	New Mexico	1.8%
Florida	13.8%	Hawaii	1.8%
New York	13.7%	Iowa	1.4%
Michigan	12.9%	Oregon	1.4%
New Jersey	12.6%	Minnesota	1.3%
Texas	12.0%	Wyoming	0.7%
Missouri	10.5%	Utah	0.6%
Ohio	10.0%	New Hampshire	0.4%
Pennsylvania	8.8%	North Dakota	0.4%
California	7.7%	Maine	0.3%
Indiana	7.6%	Idaho	0.3%
Kentucky	7.1%	South Dakota	0.3%
Connecticut	7.0%	Vermont	0.2%
Oklahoma	6.8%	Montana	0.2%

[2]

STATES WHERE THE HISPANIC POPULATION EXCEEDS THE BLACK POPULATION

STATE	SPANISH ORIGIN	BLACK	NUMBER OF HISPANICS PER 100 BLACKS
1. New Mexico	476,089	24,042	1980
2. Idaho	36,615	2,716	1348
3. Wyoming	24,499	3,364	728
4. Utah	60,302	9,225	654
5. Arizona	440,915	75,034	588
6. Montana	9,974	1,786	558
7. Hawaii	71,479	17,352	412
8. Colorado	339,300	101,702	334
9. Vermont	3,304	1,135	291
10. California	4,543,770	1,819,282	250
11. South Dakota	4,028	2,144	188
12. Oregon	65,833	37,059	178
13. Texas	2,985,643	1,710,250	175
14. Maine	5,005	3,128	160
15. North Dakota	3,903	2,568	152
16. New Hampshire	5,587	3,990	140
17. Washington	119,986	105,544	114
18. Nevada	53,786	50,781	106

[2]

BLACK PROPORTIONS OF CITY POPULATIONS

According to the 1980 Census, 28 American cities have black populations of more than 100,000. Here is how they rank in absolute numbers and in the black proportion of the total population.

	NUMBER		PERCENTAGE
1. New York	1,784,124	Gary	70.8%
2. Chicago	1,197,000	Washington, D.C.	70.3%
3. Detroit	758,939	Atlanta	66.6%
4. Philadelphia	638,878	Detroit	63.1%
5. Los Angeles	505,208	Newark	58.2%
6. Washington, D.C.	448,229	Birmingham	55.6%
7. Houston	440,257	New Orleans	55.3%
8. Baltimore	431,151	Baltimore	54.8%
9. New Orleans	308,136	Richmond	51.3%
10. Memphis	307,702	Memphis	47.6%
11. Atlanta	282,912	Oakland	46.9%
12. Dallas	265,594	St. Louis	45.6%

(continued)

	NUMBER		PERCENTAGE
13. Cleveland	251,347	Cleveland	43.8%
14. St. Louis	206,386	Chicago	39.8%
15. Newark	191,743	Philadelphia	37.8%
16. Oakland	159,234	Cincinnati	33.8%
17. Birmingham	158,223	Dallas	29.4%
18. Indianapolis	152,626	Houston	27.6%
19. Milwaukee	146,940	Kansas City, Mo.	27.4%
20. Jacksonville	137,324	Jacksonville	25.4%
21. Cincinnati	130,467	New York	25.2%
22. Boston	126,229	Pittsburgh	24.0%
23. Columbus	124,880	Nashville	23.3%
24. Kansas City, Mo.	122,699	Milwaukee	23.1%
25. Richmond	112,357	Boston	22.4%
26. Gary	107,644	Indianapolis	21.8%
27. Nashville	105,942	Columbus	22.1%
28. Pittsburgh	101,813	Los Angeles	17.0%

[12]

THE BLACK PROPORTION OF THE TOTAL POPULATION

Between 1950 and 1980, the black proportion of the population rose from 9.9 percent to 11.7 percent. This growth will probably continue. For example, among children currently under the age of 5—the adults of the future—14.9 percent are black.

In addition, black women are looking forward to having a greater number of children. Among women aged 18 through 34, every 100 white women expected to have 204 children whereas a typical group of 100 black women anticipated having 223.

On the other hand, black infants are less apt to survive: their mortality rate is 23.9 per 1,000—over double the 11.6 per 1,000 rate for white babies.

Moreover, fewer black Americans reach their seventies, with the life expectancy for whites at 74.0 years, as against 69.2 years for blacks.

[29,143]

ETHNICITY AND RESIDENCE

AMERICAN INDIANS

The nation's 1,361,869 American Indians reside in every state of the Union, ranging from 198,095 in California down to 1,555 in West Virginia and 984 in Delaware.

The states with the largest Indian populations are: California (198,095), Oklahoma (169,297), Arizona (152,610), New Mexico (104,634), North Carolina (64,519), Washington (58,159), South Dakota (45,081), Michigan (39,702), Texas (39,374), New York (38,117), Montana (37,153), and Minnesota (34,841).

CHINESE

Of the 806,027 persons of Chinese ancestry, the majority live in the following states: California (322,340), New York (148,104), Hawaii (56,260), Illinois (28,590), Texas (25,459), Massachusetts (25,015), and New Jersey (23,366).

FILIPINOS

Of the 774,640 persons of Filipino origin, the majority live in the following states: California (357,514), Hawaii (133,964), Illinois (43,839), New York (33,956), New Jersey (24,377), and Washington (24,363).

JAPANESE

Of the 700,747 persons of Japanese ancestry, the majority live in the following states: California (261,817), Hawaii (239,618), Washington (26,369), New York (24,524), and Illinois (18,550).

HAWAIIANS

Of the nation's 167,253 native Hawaiians, 115,962 (or 69.3 percent) live in Hawaii. The others reside in every other state, including 46 in North Dakota and 58 in Maine.

The states with the largest numbers of Hawaiians are Hawaii (115,962), California (23,091), Washington (2,974), Texas (2,218), New York (1,566), Oregon (1,488), and Florida (1,377).

KOREANS

Among the 354,529 persons of Korean origin, the majority live in the following states: California (103,891), New York (34,157), Illinois (23,980), Maryland (15,087), Texas (13,997), and Washington (13,077).

VIETNAMESE

Of the 261,714 persons of Vietnamese origin, the majority live in the following states: California (89,587), Texas (29,112), Louisiana

(10,877), Virginia (exactly 10,000), Washington (9,833), and Pennsylvania (9,257).

ASIAN INDIANS

Among the 361,544 persons of Asian Indian ancestry, the majority live in the following states: New York (60,511), California (57,989), Illinois (35,711), New Jersey (29,507), Texas (22,226), and Pennsylvania (15,212).

ESKIMOS

Of the country's 42,149 Eskimos, 34,135 (or 81.0 percent) live in Alaska. The rest reside in all of the other states, including 26 in Nebraska and 57 in North Carolina.

The states with the largest numbers of Eskimos are: Alaska (34,135), California (1,734), Washington (1,251), Oregon (407), Texas (395), and New York (330).

ALEUTS

More than half of the 14,177 Americans of Aleutian ancestry still live in Alaska (8,063). After that, comes California (1,482), Washington (1,361), Oregon (315), and Texas (305).

SAMOANS

The 42,050 persons of Samoan ancestry reside chiefly in California (20,096), Hawaii (14,168), Washington (1,830), Utah (763), and Texas (503).

GUAMANIANS

The 32,132 persons from the island of Guam live mainly in California (17,662), Washington (1,942), Hawaii (1,677), Texas (1,193), and New York (773).

[4]

In light of the choices people made, the nation's population can be divided into the following groups and categories.

| | SPANISH ORIGIN | | NOT OF SPANISH ORIGIN | | TOTAL | |
	Number	Percentage	Number	Percentage	Number	Percentage
White	8,113,648	3.6%	180,227,142	79.6%	188,340,790	83.2%
Black	390,733	0.2%	26,097,485	11.5%	26,488,218	11.7%
Other specific groups	260,854	0.1%	4,657,974	2.1%	4,918,828	2.2%
General "other"	5,840,648	2.6%	916,341	0.4%	6,756,989	3.0%
TOTAL	14,605,883	6.5%	211,898,942	93.6%	226,504,825	100.0%

The expansion of the "other" category means we can no longer classify the total population on a purely "racial" basis, for we now have a sizable number of people who either look on their Spanish origin as their "race" or choose to see themselves as not belonging to any racial group. During the 1970–1980 decade, black Americans barely increased their share of the overall population, going from 11.1 percent of the total figure to only 11.7 percent. At the same time, white Americans who are not of Spanish origin declined from 83.3 percent of the 1970 total to 79.6 percent in 1980.

[4, 11]

FOREIGN-BORN POPULATION

According to the 1980 Census, 13,956,077 of the residents of the United States were born abroad. These persons accounted for 6.2 percent of the total population, representing a noticeable rise over the 1970 figure of 4.7 percent.

Indeed, 1980 marked the first increase in the foreign-born proportion since the 1900–1910 decade. The following were the foreign-born percentages in the Censuses of this century:

1900	13.6%	1930	11.6%	1960	5.4%
1910	14.6%	1940	8.8%	1970	4.7%
1920	13.2%	1950	6.9%	1980	6.2%

In addition, the 1980 Census found that 22,973,410 persons aged 5 years old or over lived in homes where a language other than English was spoken some or all of the time. For 11,117,606 of those persons that language was Spanish; for the other 11,855,804 it was some other language.

[9, 21]

PERCENTAGE OF RESIDENTS BORN OUTSIDE THE UNITED STATES

U.S.A. = 6.2%

California	14.8%	Virginia	3.2%
Hawaii	14.0%	Minnesota	2.7%
New York	13.4%	Ohio	2.7%
Florida	10.9%	Wisconsin	2.7%
New Jersey	10.3%	Idaho	2.3%
Rhode Island	8.8%	Montana	2.3%
Connecticut	8.5%	North Dakota	2.3%
Massachusetts	8.4%	Louisiana	2.1%
Illinois	7.3%	Kansas	2.0%
Nevada	6.7%	Indiana	1.9%
Arizona	6.0%	Nebraska	1.9%
Texas	6.0%	Wyoming	1.9%
Washington	5.8%	Missouri	1.8%
Maryland	4.6%	Oklahoma	1.8%
Michigan	4.4%	Georgia	1.7%
New Hampshire	4.2%	Iowa	1.7%
Oregon	4.2%	North Carolina	1.5%
Vermont	4.2%	South Carolina	1.4%
New Mexico	4.2%	South Dakota	1.4%
Alaska	3.9%	West Virginia	1.1%
Colorado	3.8%	Tennessee	1.0%
Maine	3.8%	Alabama	1.0%
Pennsylvania	3.6%	Arkansas	0.9%
Utah	3.5%	Kentucky	0.9%
Delaware	3.4%	Mississippi	0.9%

[9]

AMERICANS WITH EUROPEAN ANCESTRIES

In March of 1982, the Census Bureau released a report showing the national origins of Americans. The survey simply asked individuals what their "ancestry" was and then recorded the responses. (Racial backgrounds were included, but religious affiliations were not.)

Among the 192,865,000 persons from whom information was obtained, 63,716,000 described themselves as having a single European origin, and the following table shows how many of these Americans fell in the 27 European categories in the Census report.

Due to the incidence of intermarriage, even more people reported having a mixed ancestry—82,582,000 such persons in the country as a whole. Unfortunately, the Census did not specify how many of these individuals had European components in their origins. Instead it recorded the number of European "mentions" given by people with mixed backgrounds. In all, there were 156,802,000 such mentions by the persons in this group. When this number is added to the 63,716,000 persons with a single ancestry, the result is a total of 220,518,000 full or partial European origins among the American population. The second column in the table records the number of mentions for each origin by all individuals of both single and mixed backgrounds.

Generations. The survey covered Americans of all ages, including children, who were counted with their parents. For many the ancestry was quite remote, going back several generations. This span can be seen in the case of five countries—Germany, England, Ireland, Italy, and Poland—which together accounted for 48,029,000 (or 75.4 percent) of the 63,716,000 persons who reported a single European origin. Here is how these groups divided in generational terms.

Among those of German background, 4.0 percent were foreign-born; 10.7 percent were native-born but had one or more foreign-born parents; and 85.3 percent were third or later generation. With individuals of English ancestry, 3.8 percent were foreign-born; 6.2 percent were second generation; and 89.9 percent were third or later generation.

Of the Irish, 2.7 percent were born in Ireland; 10.4 percent had one or more Irish-born parents; and 86.9 percent were later generations.

Among Americans of Italian origin, 13.1 percent were born in Italy; 44.1 percent were second generation; and 42.7 percent were later generations. With persons of Polish ancestry, 10.8 percent were foreign-born; 40.3 percent were second generation; and 48.8 percent were third- or subsequent-generation Americans.

[41]

EUROPEAN ORIGINS

PERSONS WITH A SINGLE EUROPEAN ANCESTRY		MENTIONS OF FULL OR PARTIAL EUROPEAN ANCESTRIES	
German	17,160,000	German	51,649,000
English	11,501,000	Irish	43,752,000
Irish	9,760,000	English	40,004,000
Italian	6,110,000	Scottish	14,205,000
Polish	3,498,000	French	14,047,000
French	3,047,000	Italian	11,751,000
Scottish	1,615,000	Polish	8,421,000
Russian	1,496,000	Dutch	8,121,000
Dutch	1,362,000	Swedish	4,886,000
Norwegian	1,232,000	Norwegian	4,120,000
Swedish	1,216,000	Russian	3,466,000
			(continued)

(continued)

PERSONS WITH A SINGLE EUROPEAN ANCESTRY		MENTIONS OF FULL OR PARTIAL EUROPEAN ANCESTRIES	
Czechoslovakian	794,000	Welsh	2,568,000
Greek	567,000	Czechoslovakian	1,695,000
Hungarian	534,000	Danish	1,672,000
Portuguese	493,000	Hungarian	1,592,000
Welsh	455,000	Swiss	1,228,000
Danish	438,000	Austrian	1,070,000
Austrian	385,000	Greek	990,000
Lithuanian	317,000	Portuguese	946,000
Swiss	312,000	Lithuanian	832,000
General Slavic	300,000	General Slavic	772,000
Yugoslav	283,000	Finnish	616,000
Finnish	255,000	Ukrainian	525,000
Ukrainian	231,000	Yugoslav	467,000
Rumanian	132,000	Belgian	448,000
Belgian	113,000	Rumanian	335,000
General Scandinavian	110,000	General Scandinavian	340,000
	63,716,000		220,518,000

[41]

IMMIGRANTS

In the year ending in September of 1979, a total of 460,348 immigrants—persons allowed to establish permanent residence and eligible to apply for citizenship—were admitted to the United States.

During the decade 1970–1979, a total of 4,336,003 immigrants were admitted, an average of 433,600 per year. (And during 1979, a total of 158,900 immigrants were naturalized as citizens.)

There were also some changes in immigrants' continental origins between 1970 and 1979:

	1970		1979	
	Number	*Percentage*	*Number*	*Percentage*
Europe	116,039	31.1%	60,845	13.2%
Asia	94,883	25.4%	189,293	41.1%
Africa	8,115	2.2%	12,838	2.8%
Latin America	151,087	40.5%	192,923	41.9%
Other	3,202	0.8%	4,449	1.0%
	373,326	100.0%	460,348	100.0%

COUNTRIES OF ORIGIN

In 1979 the major countries from which immigrants were admitted were: Mexico (52,096), Philippines (41,300), Korea (29,248), China and Taiwan (24,264), Vietnam (22,546), Jamaica (19,714), India (19,708), the Dominican Republic (17,519), and Cuba (15,585).

Immigrants from Europe came in the following numbers: Great Britain (13,907), Portugal (7,085), Germany (6,314), Italy (6,174), Greece (5,090), Poland (4,413), Soviet Union (2,543), Yugoslavia (2,171), and Spain (1,933).

And these European countries provided the fewest immigrants: Austria (369), Denmark (414), Switzerland (665), Sweden (750), and Ireland (982).

In addition there were 13,772 immigrants admitted from Canada, 12,838 from all of Africa, 8,476 from Iran, 3,093 from Israel, and 1,400 from Australia.

INTENDED DESTINATIONS

Arriving immigrants were asked where they intended to make their permanent residence. The most popular states were: California (118,800), New York (94,401), Texas (30,520), Florida (26,887), New Jersey (26,465), and Illinois (19,497).

The states least frequently listed were: South Dakota (169), Wyoming (211), North Dakota (271), Vermont (317), New Hampshire (428), and Delaware (510).

[135]

REGISTERED ALIENS: COUNTRY OF ORIGIN

All aliens other than tourists and short-stay visitors are required to register with the Immigration and Naturalization Service. Of course not all do, but most who do are "legal aliens," and they numbered 5,381,107 in 1980. Of these persons, who may have arrived at any time in the past, 100,000 or more came from the following countries:

Mexico (1,058,596), Canada (338,281), Cuba (333,975), Great Britain (312,623), Philippines (247,330), Vietnam (198,540), Korea (182,241), Italy (176,969), Germany (162,190), Portugal (135,495), the Dominican Republic (134,663), India (130,241), China (115,584), and Japan (110,342).

Registrants came from another 148 countries as well, ranging from Afghanistan (1,167) and Albania (1,002) to Zaire (240) and Zambia (699). In between are visitors or residents from such places as:

Bahrain (103), Chad (4), Danzig (11), Estonia (1,479), Fiji (4,364), Guinea (42), Hungary (12,389), Iceland (1,798), Jordan (13,315), Kuwait (846), Liechtenstein (32), Monaco (6), Nepal (402), Oman (73), Paraguay (1,353), Qatar (149), Rwanda (11), Sri Lanka (3,023), Tonga (1,628), Upper Volta (14), Venezuela (18,090), and two Yemens (106 and 1,029).

[135]

REGISTERED ALIENS: BASIS OF ADMISSION

The 5,381,107 aliens who registered in 1980 had been admitted to the United States under the following classifications:

Of the total, 4,532,647 (or 84.2 percent) were admitted as immigrants or are otherwise considered "permanent residents." Another 19,097 were listed as "commuter workers," most of them coming from Canada (4,392) or Mexico (9,214). There were also 59,038 long-stay visitors, with the largest numbers from Poland (7,891), Canada (7,590), Iran (4,358), Japan (3,861), and Great Britain (3,424). And there were 173,440 foreign students, with the most from Iran (20,680), Mexico (10,828), Taiwan (10,590), Great Britain (10,557), Japan (9,464), and Venezuela (6,921).

Another category lists "refugees," of whom there were 217,552, mainly from: Vietnam (90,699), Cuba (37,503), Laos (28,427), Soviet Union (13,725), Cambodia (9,427), Iraq (2,581), plus 13,280 "stateless" persons.

[135]

CHAPTER THREE

BIRTHS, DEATHS, AND HEALTH

Figures on births and deaths are known as "vital statistics." Nowadays virtually all births and deaths are entered on certificates by attending physicians or other qualified personnel. These records are sent to agencies in each state, which then transmit their totals to the National Center for Health Statistics in Hyattsville, Maryland. In a similar manner, reports on 31 "specified notifiable" illnesses are collected by the Centers for Disease Control in Atlanta.

Birth records include such information as the baby's sex and weight, the mother's age and whether she is married, and—in certain states—the parents' education. Death certificates are expected to be as precise as possible about the specific cause. It is not enough, for example, to say that someone simply died from an "accidental fall." The physician is also asked to state whether the fall was "on or from stairs or steps," "from a ladder or scaffolding," "from or out of a building," "into a hole or other opening," "from slipping, stumbling, or tripping," or by "pushing or shoving by another person." Similarly, the exact site of the cancer ("sigmoid colon," "buccal cavity," "lymphosarcoma") must be listed. These and other detailed findings are eventually published in sets of hardbound volumes called "Natality" and "Mortality."

Vital statistics—which also include marriage and divorce—take time to reach the National Center for Health Statistics in final form for publication. Full figures for 1977, for example, did not appear in print until 1981. As a result this chapter contains early, provisional statistics for 1981; more complete figures from 1979 and 1980; and detailed data for 1977.

Rates of Births and Deaths. Births and deaths are usually computed by how many occur each year per 1,000 persons in the population. Thus 1981's birth rate was 15.9 per 1,000; and the rate for deaths came to 8.7 per 1,000. (That there were that many more births than deaths tells us right away that during 1981 the population had a "natural increase" of 7.2 per 1,000, for an annual growth of 0.72 percent.)

The earliest recorded birth rate was in 1820, when there were 55.2 births for every 1,000 persons. By 1860 the rate had fallen to 44.3; and in 1900 it was down at 32.3. During the Depression year of 1936, the figure had declined to 18.4 per 1,000.

Death rates have only been computed since 1900, when the figure was 17.2 per 1,000. Since then it has gradually declined, to 11.7 in 1925 and 9.6 in 1950. The 1981 figure of 8.7 per 1,000 shows that more recent decreases are not apt to be as striking. The main reason the death rate has gone down is that people are living longer. A typical person born in 1900 might expect to live 47.3 years. In 1925 average life expectancy was 59.0 years; by 1950 it was 68.2; and by 1980 the figure had advanced to 73.6 years. With greater longevity a smaller proportion of the population dies each year.

There is one problem with the "per 1,000" rate when it is measured against the total population. Births can only be expected from women of childbearing age, yet from year to year and state to state, the number of women in that range may vary as a proportion of the general population. By the same token, the death rate will change if there are more people at ages when individuals are more apt to die. For this reason statisticians often use narrower-gauged rates, comparing the incidence of certain occurrences—births and deaths, marriages or divorces, and various illnesses—with segments of the population to which they are likely to happen.

BIRTHS

BIRTHS AND RATES

In 1981 a total of 3,633,826 babies were born. This figure represented a birth rate of 15.9 births per 1,000 persons in the population. This rate was part of a gradual increase since 1975, when births were at a low point of 14.8 per 1,000.

Births reached their postwar height, with a rate of 23.7 per 1,000, in

1960. After that the "baby boom" subsided, with the rate down at 18.4 per 1,000 in 1970. Here are the numbers and the rates for 1970 to 1981:

YEAR	BIRTHS	RATE
1970	3,731,386	18.4
1971	3,555,970	17.2
1972	3,258,411	15.6
1973	3,136,965	14.9
1974	3,159,958	14.9
1975	3,144,198	14.8
1976	3,167,788	14.8
1977	3,326,632	15.4
1978	3,333,279	15.3
1979	3,494,398	15.9
1980	3,586,925	15.8
1981	3,633,826	15.9

[142, 144, 145]

Rates and States. In 1980 the states with the highest birth rates were: Utah (31.0 per 1,000 population), Alaska (23.0 per 1,000), Idaho (21.3), Wyoming (20.4), and New Mexico (20.0)

The states with the lowest birth rates were: Connecticut (10.9 per 1,000 population), New Jersey (12.4 per 1,000), Maryland (12.6), Massachusetts (12.7), and New York (13.2).

[142]

BIRTHS BY MONTHS

Among the babies born in 1980, the most frequent month of birth was August; the least was February.

	MONTH	BIRTHS	PERCENTAGE OF BIRTHS	APPROXIMATE MONTH OF CONCEPTION
1.	August	330,000	9.2%	November
2.	October	325,000	9.0%	January
3.	July	313,000	8.7%	October
4.	September	311,000	8.6%	December
5.	December	308,000	8.6%	March
6.	March	302,000	8.4%	June
7.	May	295,000	8.2%	August
8.	June	293,000	8.1%	September
9.	November	286,000	7.9%	February
10.	April	284,000	7.9%	July
11.	January	278,000	7.7%	April
12.	February	272,000	7.6%	May
		3,598,000		

[142]

It took the National Center for Health Statistics until the fall of 1981 to prepare its full report on births in 1979. Some of its findings:

- In 1979, of the 3,494,398 babies that were born, 1,791,267 were boys and 1,703,131 were girls. This works out to a ratio of 1,052 boys for every 1,000 girls.

- In racial terms, 2,808,420 (or 80.4 percent) of the babies were white; 577,855 (or 16.5 percent) were black; and the remaining 108,123 (or 3.1 percent) were of Asian, American Indian, or other origins.

- Of the babies, 1,479,260 (or 42.3 percent) were the first their mothers had had; and 2,015,138 (or 57.6 percent) were second or later children.

- Among the births there were 33,429 sets of twins. And another 1,202 births produced triplets or quadruplets (unfortunately we are not told how many there were of each). Twins arrived in one out of every 104.5 births; and triplets or quadruplets came once with every 2,907 births.

[144]

RACE AND BIRTHS

In 1979 the white birth rate came to 14.8 white babies for every 1,000 white persons in the population. The black birth rate was 22.3 black babies per 1,000 black persons in the population, or a rate which was 50.7 percent higher than that for whites.

Among white babies there were 1,057 boys for every 1,000 girls. For black babies, the ratio was 1,029 boys for every 1,000 girls.

"Multiple deliveries" (the total number of twins, triplets, and quadruplets) accounted for 24.2 babies out of each 1,000 black births, compared with a rate of 18.6 per 1,000 among white births.

And among children of all races born in multiple deliveries, there were 19.8 girls per 1,000 female births, while the rate for boys was 19.1 for each 1,000 male births.

[144]

MOTHERS' AGES AND MARITAL STATUS

The following tables indicate the ages and marital status of the mothers who gave birth in 1979. (The first two columns add up to 100.0 percent. The third column shows the percentage of births in *each* age range in which the mother was not married. Thus the percentage at the bottom is the percentage of total births where the mother was not married.)

	PERCENTAGE ALL BIRTHS	PERCENTAGE FIRST BIRTHS ONLY	PERCENTAGE IN WHICH MOTHER NOT MARRIED
Under 20	16.0%	29.4%	46.9%
20 to 24	34.0%	38.9%	17.7%
25 to 29	30.6%	23.5%	7.5%
30 to 34	14.8%	6.8%	6.0%
35 to 39	3.9%	1.1%	7.8%
40 and over	0.7%	0.2%	10.3%
	100.0%	100.0%	17.1%

Breaking this down further, here are the number of births where the mother was under 20, with the percentage for each age where she was not married:

AGE	BIRTHS	PERCENTAGE MOTHER NOT MARRIED
Under 15	10,699	88.8%
15	28,377	76.8%
16	63,946	64.6%
17	107,814	52.8%
18	153,289	43.3%
19	196,046	34.0% [144]

PAST BIRTHS AND FUTURE EXPECTATIONS

In 1980 the Census Bureau conducted a survey among American women to find out how many children they had had. In addition, they were asked to estimate the total number they thought they would have by the time they finished childbearing.

For every 1,000 women in the age group of 18 to 34, whether married or unmarried, a total of 1,127 babies had already been born. In addition, the women expected to have 932 more, which meant that each 1,000 women anticipated having 2,059 children altogether. This figure is 6.4 percent under the 2,200 children needed to sustain a constant population at a no-growth level. White women said they expected to have 2,036 children on the per 1,000 basis, while the figure for black women was 2,227 per 1,000. Women of Spanish origin expected 2,363 births. Altogether 11.0 percent of all women said they thought they would not have any children at all.

Among young women aged 18 to 24, regardless of marital status, a total of 70.0 percent had not yet had any children. Among those aged 25 to 29, the childless proportion came to 36.8 percent; at ages 30 to 34, a total of 19.8 percent had not yet had any children.

This part of the study also questioned older women. For those 35 to 39, the childless figure was 12.1 percent, and at 40 to 44, usually considered the end of possible childbearing years, 10.1 percent had not had children.

Education and Marital Status. Women who had not completed high school said they expected to have 2,427 children per 1,000 women questioned. In contrast, those who had finished college thought they would have 1,826. This suggests that a substantial proportion would stop with a single child, because 16.0 percent of the college-educated women expected not to have any children at all.

Among the women who were not yet married, the typical group of 1,000 said they expected to have a total of 1,807 children. And within this group, no less than 21.4 percent felt they would not have any children at all.

Of course these statements of "expectations" may reflect flights of fantasy as well as considered judgments. Even so, they offer some insight into attitudes towards childbearing. (The responses might also have been different had the question asked how many children they "wanted"—or "intended" or "planned"—to have. On the other hand, the answers might have been much the same.)

[29]

AVERAGE NUMBER OF CHILDREN BORN TO EACH 1,000 WOMEN AGED 15 TO 44 IN EACH STATE

Utah	1,638	Georgia	1,389
Idaho	1,561	Indiana	1,388
Arkansas	1,514	West Virginia	1,388
Mississippi	1,514	Iowa	1,369
Louisiana	1,483	South Carolina	1,364
New Mexico	1,464	Kansas	1,360
Wyoming	1,464	Tennessee	1,358
Alabama	1,417	Maine	1,356
Montana	1,416	Alaska	1,346
Texas	1,405	Michigan	1,342
Kentucky	1,400	Arizona	1,338
South Dakota	1,395	North Dakota	1,338
Oklahoma	1,392	Missouri	1,334

(continued)

(continued)

Ohio	1,330	Virginia	1,236
Illinois	1,327	Vermont	1,234
Oregon	1,310	Pennsylvania	1,230
Nebraska	1,309	California	1,229
Wisconsin	1,297	Maryland	1,221
Nevada	1,291	New Jersey	1,213
North Carolina	1,288	Colorado	1,195
Minnesota	1,284	New York	1,193
Washington	1,284	Hawaii	1,186
Delaware	1,264	Connecticut	1,183
Florida	1,261	Rhode Island	1,140
New Hampshire	1,241	Massachusetts	1,110

U.S.A. 1,301

[9]

UNMARRIED MOTHERS: RATES AND RACE

In 1979 a total of 17.1 percent of all births were to mothers who were not married. In 1978 the proportion had been 16.3 percent, and in 1960 it was 5.3 percent.

- Among the 597,800 births where the mother was not married, in 44.0 percent of the births the mother was white; in 52.8 percent she was black; and, in the remaining 3.2 percent, she was of another origin.

- Looked at another way, the mother was not married in 9.4 percent of all births to white women. Among the total births to black women, 54.6 percent were to unmarried mothers.

- Where the mother was under 20, 30.9 percent of all white births were to unmarried mothers. Of all black births where the mother was not yet 20, 85.7 percent had mothers who were not married.

- Births to unmarried mothers can be measured per every 1,000 unmarried women aged 15 to 44. For white women the rate was 15.1 unmarried births per 1,000 unmarried women. The black rate came to 85.3 per 1,000 unmarried women, or 5.6 times the white rate.

- At the same time, the rate of *increase* of births to white unmarried mothers between 1978 and 1979 amounted to 12.6 percent, compared with only a 7.6 percent increase for black women. Thus the rate of increase for white unmarried mothers was 65.8 percent higher than for black women.

[144]

OUT-OF-WEDLOCK BIRTHS: 1979

PERCENTAGE OF ALL BIRTHS		PERCENTAGE OF ALL WHITE BIRTHS		PERCENTAGE OF ALL BLACK BIRTHS	
*USA**	*17.1%*	*USA*	*9.4%*	*USA*	*54.6%*
1. Mississippi	27.2%	Arizona	12.9%	Pennsylvania	66.3%
2. Delaware	22.9%	Maine	12.6%	Illinois	65.4%
3. Louisiana	22.8%	Oregon	12.5%	Delaware	63.1%
4. Florida	22.4%	Hawaii	12.4%	Wisconsin	63.0%
5. Illinois	21.9%	Massachusetts	11.9%	Missouri	62.5%
6. Alabama	21.8%	Rhode Island	11.5%	New Jersey	59.6%
7. New Jersey	20.2%	Vermont	11.4%	Nebraska	59.4%
8. Arkansas	19.6%	Washington	11.1%	Florida	58.4%
9. Tennessee	19.0%	Colorado	11.0%	Kentucky	57.6%
10. North Carolina	18.5%	West Virginia	10.4%	Indiana	57.1%
11. Virginia	18.4%	Delaware	10.3%	Tennessee	56.5%
12. Pennsylvania	17.2%	New Jersey	10.2%	Rhode Island	55.3%
13. Arizona	17.1%	South Dakota	9.9%	Arkansas	54.3%
14. Missouri	16.9%	Pennsylvania	9.9%	Iowa	52.8%
15. Hawaii	16.3%	Illinois	9.9%	Minnesota	52.7%
16. Massachusetts	14.8%	Florida	9.6%	Massachusetts	52.1%
17. Indiana	14.6%	Kentucky	9.5%	Kansas	51.6%
18. Rhode Island	14.3%	Indiana	9.4%	Oklahoma	51.6%
19. Oklahoma	14.0%	Wisconsin	9.2%	Virginia	51.4%
20. Kentucky	14.0%	Minnesota	8.8%	Alabama	51.3%
21. Alaska	13.9%	Missouri	8.7%	Mississippi	50.8%
22. Oregon	13.4%	Nebraska	8.5%	West Virginia	50.2%
23. South Carolina	12.9%	Oklahoma	8.4%	Arizona	48.9%
24. Wisconsin	12.8%	Iowa	8.2%	Louisiana	48.6%
25. Maine	12.7%	Kansas	8.1%	Oregon	47.9%
26. Washington	12.6%	Tennessee	8.0%	North Carolina	47.4%
27. Colorado	12.3%	Alaska	7.8%	South Carolina	45.7%
28. West Virginia	11.9%	Arkansas	7.7%	Washington	40.1%
29. Kansas	11.8%	Virginia	7.6%	Utah	39.1%
30. South Dakota	11.8%	Wyoming	6.9%	Vermont	38.8%
31. Vermont	11.5%	Idaho	6.7%	Colorado	38.8%
32. Nebraska	10.8%	Louisiana	6.6%	Wyoming	36.1%
33. Minnesota	10.5%	North Dakota	6.0%	Idaho	20.0%
34. New Hampshire	10.1%	South Carolina	5.9%	Alaska	19.2%
35. Iowa	9.4%	North Carolina	5.7%	North Dakota	14.8%
36. North Dakota	8.3%	Alabama	5.4%	New Hampshire	14.2%
37. Wyoming	7.8%	Mississippi	5.1%	Maine	11.7%
38. Idaho	7.0%	Utah	5.0%	Hawaii	10.8%
39. Utah	5.5%	New Hampshire	1.3%	South Dakota	6.0%

*The following states did not report: California, Connecticut, Georgia, Michigan, Montana, Nevada, New Mexico, New York, Ohio, and Texas.

[144]

THE BOY-GIRL IMBALANCE

Each year a typical crop of births contains 1,052 boy babies for every 1,000 girls.

However, this imbalance begins to even out, starting at an early age. In the first year, the death rate for boys (1,454.8 per 100,000) is 25.5 percent higher than the comparable figure for girls (1,159.3 per 100,000). Between the ages of 1 and 4, boys' deaths (74.0 per 100,000) exceed those of girls (57.1 per 100,000) by 29.6 percent. From 5 to 14, boys die (37.1 per 100,000) at a 45.5 percent greater rate than girls (25.5 per 100,000).

And from 15 to 24 the gap is even more striking: 179.6 of each 100,000 young men die each year, as against 57.3 of every 100,000 young women, making the men's rate 213.4 percent higher.

[142]

A LATER BEGINNING FOR CHILDBEARING

A National Center for Health Statistics study issued in 1982 reported on the ages at which women were having their first babies during the 1970s. In 1970 women under the age of 25 accounted for 81.2 percent of the 1,430,680 first births recorded that year. By 1979 only 68.4 percent of the 1,479,260 first births were to women under 25. In 1970 women in their thirties accounted for 4.0 percent of first births. By 1979 their proportion had doubled, to 8.0 percent of all first births.

Stated another way, in 1979 a total of 116,897 first births were to women in their thirties, while in 1970 only 54,108—half as many—were to mothers of that age. In that period, the birthrate for women aged 20 to 24 declined from 78.2 per 1,000 to 56.4 per 1,000, a dip of 28.9 percent. For women aged 30 to 34, the rate rose from 7.3 per 1,000 to 12.1 per 1,000, an increase of 65.8 percent. In 1970, among the babies born to women aged 30 to 34, in only 10.0 percent of the cases was it a first birth. By 1979 that figure had almost doubled, to 19.5 percent.

Education and Race. In 1970 less than half—44.2 percent—of the first babies born to mothers between 30 and 34 were to women who had attended college. However, by 1979 women who had been to college represented 67.9 percent—more than two thirds—of the first-time births to mothers of that age.

The postponement of childbearing was most evident among white women. Among the first babies born to white women, only 25.8 percent were to mothers under 20, whereas 50.0 percent of first black infants had mothers under 20. By the same token, the proportion of black first births represented by women aged 30 to 34 was 4.4 percent, just about half the 8.5 percent figure for white women that age.

HOW MANY EXPECT TO HAVE CHILDREN?

Still, many married women in their thirties do not yet have children. At the same time, an increasing proportion are saying they do expect to have them. In 1971, of the 253,000 childless wives between 30 and 34, only 26.5 percent said they expected to give birth within the next five years. By 1979, the number of childless wives aged 30 to 34 had grown to 621,000, an increase of 145.5 percent over 1971. But 43.8 percent of them—two thirds more than in 1971—said they expected to have a child before five years had passed.

[29, 147]

HAVING CHILDREN: WHEN AND HOW MANY?

Among women aged 45 to 49 who have passed the age of childbearing, a typical group of 1,000 women had a total of 3,127 children. Among white women in this age range, the rate was 3,047 per thousand, or just about 3 children per woman. For black women, the rate was 3,811 per thousand, or close to 4 per woman.

The following are the figures for women 25 to 29 who are or have been married. While they still may have more children, the figures show difference by race and dates for births per 1,000 women:

	1970	1980	PERCENTAGE DECREASE
White women	1,364	1,918	−28.9%
Black women	1,896	2,536	−25.2%

Among women 25 to 29 who have never been married, the following are the births per 1,000 by race and dates:

	1970	1980	PERCENTAGE DECREASE
White women	161	208	−22.6%
Black women	1,271	1,306	− 2.7%

In 1970, among white women aged 25 to 29 who were or had been married, only 16.1 percent had not yet had a child. By 1979, of this group, 27.4 percent had yet to have a child.

Of black women 25 to 29 in 1970 who were or had been married, 12.3 percent had not had a child. In 1979 the figure was 14.8 percent.

[28]

CONTRACEPTION

In March of 1981, the National Center for Health Statistics released a study on "contraceptive utilization" among American women which analyzed the use of birth control by both married and unmarried women under the age of 45. The study found that 67.7 percent of married couples were using some form of contraception:

- In 22.5 percent of the marriages, the wife used the pill; in 7.3 percent the husband used condoms; and in 19.4 percent some other method was employed.
- In addition, 9.5 percent of the wives and 9.0 percent of the husbands had had surgery for the express purpose of becoming sterile.

The other 32.3 percent of the couples were not using contraception. They fell in the following categories:

- In 11.4 percent of the marriages, either the wife or husband was sterile for reasons *not* intended to ensure contraception. The most common reason (8.9 percent among these cases) was that the wife had had a hysterectomy or some similar operation.
- Another 6.8 percent of the wives were currently pregnant or in the post-partum period.
- A further 6.5 percent of the couples were not using contraception because they wanted to have a child.
- The final 7.6 percent did *not* want a child but still were not using any contraceptive method.

COUPLES NOT USING CONTRACEPTIVES

The proportion of couples which were not using contraceptives even though they did *not* want children varied according to several character-istics. For example, 13.3 percent of black couples fell into this group, as did 10.5 percent of couples of Hispanic origin.

In terms of religion, 9.1 percent of Catholic couples were not using contraceptives; nor were 6.8 percent of Protestants or 5.8 percent of Jewish couples.

By age, in marriages where the wife was 35 or older, 11.4 percent were not practicing birth control. Where the wife was 34 or younger, only 5.7 were leaving pregnancy to chance.

UNMARRIED WOMEN

Women who were widowed, separated, or divorced reported the follow-ing:

- 29.5 percent were either not able to have children, were already pregnant, or wanted to have a baby, so they were not using contraception.
- 40.0 percent used some form of birth control.
- 30.6 percent did not want a child but still were not using contraceptive devices.

However, when it came to women who had never been married, the people conducting the study chose not to question a full cross-section about their contraceptive usage. Instead, they limited their interviews to single women who had "offspring in the household." Among this group:

- 15.2 percent either could not have a child, were already pregnant, or wanted to become pregnant.
- 57.0 percent used contraceptives.
- 27.8 percent did not want to become pregnant but still did not use birth control.

[67]

BIRTH CONTROL METHODS AMONG COUPLES AND INDIVIDUALS WHO DO USE CONTRACEPTIVES

Percentages

	ALL COUPLES	WIFE UNDER 30	WIFE 30–44	WIFE PROTES-TANT	WIFE CATHOLIC	WIFE JEWISH	DIVORCED WIDOWED SEPARATED WOMEN	NEVER-MARRIED WOMEN
Pill	45.8%	57.8%	30.4%	49.4%	41.7%	18.9%	60.8%	64.1%
I.U.D.	12.9%	11.9%	14.1%	12.4%	12.1%	24.1%	20.1%	21.0%
Diaphragm	5.9%	4.4%	7.7%	4.7%	5.0%	17.9%	3.0%	1.8%
Condom	14.8%	10.9%	19.8%	14.4%	15.8%	24.1%	4.1%	4.1%
Foam	6.1%	5.4%	6.9%	6.1%	6.4%	2.8%	3.0%	2.0%
Rhythm	6.9%	4.5%	10.0%	5.2%	11.1%	5.3%	2.6%	1.2%
Withdrawal	4.2%	2.8%	5.9%	3.7%	5.1%	5.5%	0.9%	0.3%
Douche	1.4%	0.7%	2.4%	2.1%	0.5%	0.0%	2.3%	4.3%
Other	2.1%	1.6%	2.7%	2.1%	2.4%	1.4%	3.2%	1.2%
TOTAL	100.0%	100.0%	100.0%	100.0%	100.0%	100.0%	100.0%	100.0%

[67]

NUMBER OF ABORTIONS PER 1,000 BIRTHS: 1979
(ENTIRE U.S.A. = 358 PER 1,000)

1.	New York	666	26.	New Jersey	269
2.	Massachusetts	602	27.	Ohio	255
3.	Washington	539	28.	Maine	252
4.	Nevada	539	29.	Alabama	252
5.	California	515	30.	Montana	250
6.	Maryland	510	31.	Wisconsin*	244
7.	Florida	465	32.	New Hampshire	243
8.	Rhode Island	440	33.	Oklahoma	227
9.	Virginia	426	34.	South Carolina	220
10.	Georgia	409	35.	Missouri	220
11.	Pennsylvania	407	36.	New Mexico	203
12.	Delaware	399	37.	Kentucky	188
13.	Vermont	395	38.	Nebraska	177
14.	Connecticut	385	39.	Arkansas	173
15.	Illinois	376	40.	Arizona	171
16.	Hawaii	351	41.	Louisiana	170
17.	North Carolina	349	42.	Indiana	168
18.	Colorado	345	43.	North Dakota*	168
19.	Oregon	337	44.	Idaho	124
20.	Kansas	332	45.	Iowa	111
21.	Tennessee	324	46.	South Dakota	111
22.	Michigan	313	47.	West Virginia	98
23.	Alaska*	292	48.	Mississippi	96
24.	Texas	290	49.	Utah	87
25.	Minnesota	288	50.	Wyoming	84

[151]

*1978 figure.

ABORTIONS

In 1979 a total of 1,238,987 legally induced abortions were reported to the Department of Health and Human Services, for a ratio of 358 abortions for every 1,000 live births.

Among the states, the abortion-to-birth ratios ranged from 666 per 1,000 in New York to 84 per 1,000 in Wyoming.

More detailed figures on abortion patients are available for 1978, when the national total was 1,157,776, with the ratio 347 per 1,000 births.*

* The Department of Health and Human Services acknowledges that not all abortions are officially reported. For this reason, it also publishes estimates by the Alan Guttmacher Institute, a private organization. The Institute's estimate for 1978 was 1,409,600, while for 1979 it was 1,540,000.

Marital Status. Altogether, 31 states reported on the marital status of the persons having abortions. Of these individuals, 26.4 percent were married and 73.6 percent were unmarried.

The states having the highest proportions of unmarried patients were: Nebraska (80.4 percent), Minnesota (79.3 percent), Utah (79.2 percent), Vermont (77.9 percent), and Virginia (77.4 percent).

Age. In addition, 37 states reported the age of the patients. Of these, 1.0 percent were under the age of 15, 28.7 percent were between 15 and 19, 34.7 percent were from 20 to 24, 18.7 percent were 25 to 29, 14.3 percent were in their thirties; and 2.6 percent were over 40 or did not give an age.

The states having the highest proportions of teenaged patients were: Nebraska (42.1 percent of all patients), Kansas (38.7 percent), New Hampshire (38.3 percent), South Dakota (37.9 percent), and Arkansas (37.7 percent).

Patient's State of Residence. All states reported on whether the patient had the abortion in her state of residence or traveled to another state. Altogether 93.8 percent were performed in the patient's home state; however, in some states a substantial proportion went to a different state: Wyoming (50.5 percent), Kentucky (47.8 percent), South Dakota (47.3 percent), West Virginia (46.0 percent), and Mississippi (45.3 percent).

Length of Pregnancy. Thirty-seven states reported on the weeks of gestation at the time of the abortion. In 52.2 percent of the cases, it was less than 9 weeks; in 27.0 percent it was 9 or 10; in 12.3 percent it was 11 or 12; and in 8.5 percent it was at 13 weeks or more.

Earlier Abortions. In 30 states the patients were asked whether they had had a previous abortion. In all, 70.8 percent said they had not; 22.1 percent said they had had one before; 5.3 percent said they had had two previously; and 1.8 percent said they had had three or more at an earlier time.

The states with the highest percentages of persons who said they had had earlier abortions were: New Jersey (37.1 percent), New York (36.4 percent), Nevada (35.0 percent), and New Hampshire (31.9 percent).

[97]

AN EIGHT-STATE STUDY ON ABORTION

More information on abortion patients is contained in a study by the National Center for Health Statistics issued in 1981, covering 8 sample states. These were: Illinois, Kansas, Nebraska, Oregon, South Carolina, Tennessee, Vermont, and the parts of New York State outside of New York City.

Education. Among the women having abortions, 22.4 percent had not completed high school; 43.8 percent had finished high school; and 33.8 percent had attended college.

Among those aged 25 through 29, however, the group was better educated. Only 11.0 percent had not completed high school; 45.8 percent had; and 43.2 percent had been at college.

Age and Earlier Abortions. Altogether, 25.1 percent had had a previous abortion. In terms of age, of those 19 or younger, 15.1 percent had had at least one earlier abortion. Among women 20 to 24, the proportion was 29.2 percent. For those 25 to 29, the figure was 32.4 percent. At 30 to 34, earlier abortions had been had by 29.3 percent; while at 35 to 39 it was 27.3 percent; and for 40 and over the figure was 23.5 percent.

Abortion Ratios and Race. Overall, there were 308.2 abortions for every 1,000 live births in the states in the study. In racial terms, however, there were some variations. White women had 276.8 abortions for every 1,000 white babies born that year, while for black women the abortion ratio was 386.7 per 1,000 black children who were born. That made the abortion ratio for black women 39.7 percent higher than the figure for white women.

Among white women having abortions, the proportion who were not married was 73.4 percent. For black women the unmarried figure was 77.6 percent. However, among white women, 34.2 percent of the abortions occurred with persons under the age of 20, whereas the comparable figure for black women was 28.4 percent.

[143]

LIFE EXPECTANCY

Life expectancies are statistical estimates, based on past experience and current trends. These probabilities are broken down by sex and race, and comparisons over a period of years can set them in perspective.

Life Spans: 1920 and 1980. Back in 1920 expected life spans for the sexes were only one year apart: 53.6 years for men, and 54.6 years for women. By 1980 the gap had grown considerably: the typical boy born that year would live 69.8 years, compared with 77.5 years for the average girl, or a difference of 7.7 years.

In 1980 black life expectancy was 69.6 years, compared with 74.3 for whites, a gap of 4.7 years. In 1920 the figures were 45.3 years for blacks as against 54.9 for whites, a gulf of 9.6 years.

Race and Sex in 1980: White girl babies born in 1980 were calculated to have a life expectancy of 78.1 years compared with 70.5 years for white boy babies, a difference of 7.6 years or a 10.8 percent longer life span for the girls. Black girl babies were estimated to live 74.0 years, compared with 65.3 years for black boy babies, or a gap of 8.7 years and a 13.3 percent longer life for the girls.

Using the same life expectancy figures, white boys would live 5.2 years or 8.0 percent longer than black boys, and white girls would live 4.1 years or 5.5 percent longer than black girls.

[142]

EXPECTANCY AT VARIOUS AGES

A person born in 1980 had an average expectancy, at time of birth, of living 73.6 years. However, the longer people survive, the more years they can expect to live. Thus for children who reach the age of 5—and 98.5 percent do—life expectancy rises to 74.8 years. After that:

PEOPLE WHO REACH THIS BIRTHDAY	CAN EXPECT TO LIVE TO THIS AGE	PEOPLE WHO REACH THIS BIRTHDAY	CAN EXPECT TO LIVE TO THIS AGE
10	74.9	50	77.8
15	75.0	55	78.7
20	75.3	60	79.9
25	75.6	65	81.4
30	75.9	70	83.3
35	76.3	75	85.4
40	76.6	80	88.2
45	77.1	85	91.5

[142]

LIFE EXPECTANCY BY STATES

Life expectancies on a state-by-state basis are only published every ten years. This is because the probabilities for each state must be computed separately, based on age-distribution figures from the last decennial Census.

The most recent figures, which appeared in 1975, showed that people could expect to live the longest in Hawaii (73.6 years), Minnesota (73.0 years), Utah (72.9), North Dakota (72.8), and Nebraska (72.6).

The states whose population had the shortest expected life spans were: South Carolina (68.0 years), Mississippi (68.1), Georgia (68.5), Louisiana (68.8), and Nevada (69.0).

Expectancies in these and other states are now considerably longer. However, we will not have the exact figures until 1985, when the next report appears.

[69]

DEATHS

A total of 1,986,000 persons died during 1980, a rate of 8.7 per 1,000 people in the population, while in 1970 the death rate had been 9.4 per 1,000.* The decline is due mainly to the fact that people are living longer. Fewer people die each year, in proportion to the population, as more years are added to individuals' lives.

Thus between 1970 and 1980, the death rate for persons aged 65 to 74 fell from 36.7 to 29.7 per 1,000 people in that age range. Among those 75 to 84, the rate dropped from 77.7 to 71.7, and for those 85 or older, the rate declined from 178.7 to 144.5.

An additional cause for the overall fall is that the death rate for infants under one year declined from 20.4 per 1,000 in 1970 to 12.5 per 1,000 in 1980.

[142]

DEATHS AT VARIOUS AGES

Of the persons who died during 1980, infants under the age of 1 accounted for 2.3 percent of the deaths and people 65 and over comprised 67.2 percent.

The following were the ages at which Americans died, and the death rate for each age group. The rate represents the percentage of each 1,000 persons in that age group who died during the year. For example, assuming there were 25,631,247 Americans aged 35 to 44, if 58,210 of

*The 1980 death rate was originally reported as being 8.9 per 1,000, based on an estimate of the total population. However when the 1980 Census showed that the population was larger than that estimate, the 1980 figure was adjusted downward to 8.7 per 1000.

them died in 1980, that rate would be 2.3 per 1,000 individuals in that age range. (Rates can also be computed on a per 100,000 basis.)

AGE GROUP	NUMBER OF DEATHS	PERCENTAGE OF YEAR'S DEATHS	DEATH RATE FOR AGE GROUP
Under 1 year	45,000	2.3%	13.1
1–4 years	8,270	0.4%	0.7
5–14 years	10,680	0.5%	0.3
15–24 years	49,100	2.5%	1.2
25–34 years	50,840	2.6%	1.4
35–44 years	58,210	2.9%	2.3
45–54 years	134,450	6.8%	5.9
55–59 years	127,260	6.4%	11.2
60–64 years	166,010	8.4%	16.9
65–69 years	214,810	10.8%	24.6
70–74 years	247,640	12.5%	36.2
75–79 years	263,780	13.3%	60.7
80–84 years	252,440	12.7%	88.6
85 and over	356,010	17.9%	144.9
TOTAL	1,984,500	100.0%	8.9

[142]

MEN AND WOMEN

Of the persons who died in 1980, a total of 54.3 percent were men and 45.7 percent were women. The death rate was 10.0 per 1,000 for men and 7.9 per 1,000 for women. Looked at another way, 1.00 percent of all American men died during the year, whereas only 0.79 percent of all women did.

Women enjoy a lower death rate because they live longer, 77.5 years, compared with 69.8 for men. Because their deaths are spread out over 7.7 more years, a smaller percentage of the nation's women die during any given year.

[142]

The most recent detailed figures on deaths by age and sex are for 1977. Here are the sexual distributions for the deaths in each age group, and also each age group's percentage of deaths for each sex.

Age Group	SEXUAL DISTRIBUTION PERCENTAGES		AGE DISTRIBUTION PERCENTAGES	
	Male	Female	Male	Female
Under 1	57.2%	42.8%	2.6%	2.4%
1–14	60.4%	39.6%	1.2%	1.0%
15–24	74.2%	25.8%	3.4%	1.4%
25–34	70.3%	29.7%	3.0%	1.6%
35–44	63.6%	36.4%	3.5%	2.5%
45–54	63.5	36.5%	8.8%	6.2%
55–64	63.8%	36.2%	17.9%	12.4%
65–74	60.2%	39.8%	25.6%	20.8%
75–84	49.3%	50.7%	23.1%	29.2%
85 and up	37.0%	63.0%	10.8%	22.6%
			100.0%	100.0%

[60]

INFANT DEATH RATES BY RACE

Between 1950 and 1980, the infant death rate (babies dying in their first year) declined quite markedly, but at different rates for the races.

For white babies, the death rate fell from 29.9 per 1,000 to 11.2 per 1,000, or a drop of 62.5 percent.

For babies who were black or of other races, the rate began at 53.7 per 1,000 in 1950, and declined to 22.1 per 1,000 by 1980, comprising a decrease of 58.8 percent, or 3.7 points less than the drop for whites.

[142]

CAUSES OF DEATHS

Each year the National Center for Health Statistics releases figures on the various causes of all the deaths that have occurred in the country. The list is very long, containing very detailed subdivisions, but at the same time, it should be noted that "old age" and "natural causes" are not among the categories.

It is easy to see why. Many people who do die at the age of, say, 85 cannot necessarily be said to have died of "old age." They may have had serious medical conditions that did not get suitable treatment; had they received such attention, they might have lived to, say, 88. At this point we can only speak of "natural causes" if we are sure nothing further could be done to keep a person alive. However, that kind of information is not easily expressed in the form of statistics.

What statistics can show are the ages of the individuals who have died from various listed causes. In 1977, the most recent detailed figures in this area, 14.5 percent of the persons who died were under the age of 50; another 20.1 percent were between 50 and 64; and 65.4 percent were 65 or over.

The following 13 "causes" accounted for 86.8 percent of the year's deaths. The figures show which causes are more apt to be associated with old age, and which ones are likely to strike earlier.

| | PERCENTAGES OF DEATHS AT VARIOUS AGES | | |
	Under 50	*50 to 64*	*65 and over*
All causes	14.5%	20.1%	65.4%
Heart disease	4.3%	17.1%	78.6%
Cancer	9.7%	30.3%	60.0%
Pneumonia	10.8%	11.4%	77.8%
Diabetes	7.4%	21.1%	71.5%
Cirrhosis of liver	27.4%	44.7%	27.9%
Emphysema	2.7%	22.3%	75.0%
Nephritis and nephrosis	11.2%	20.3%	68.5%
Septicemia	24.7%	17.0%	58.3%
Tuberculosis	15.7%	27.2%	57.1%
Suicide	61.8%	21.6%	16.6%
Homicide	81.3%	12.8%	5.9%
Motor vehicle accident	76.4%	12.0%	11.6%
All other accidents	49.6%	16.2%	34.2%

[60]

CAUSES OF DEATHS: 1961 AND 1981

The following are some of the principal causes of deaths in 1981, with comparable figures for 1961. The "Percentage Change" column has been adjusted to reflect the fact that the overall death total in 1981 was 15.5 percent higher than it was in 1961.

	1961	1981	PERCENTAGE CHANGE
Cardiovascular disease	731,670	964,520	+ 14.1%
Neoplasm (cancer)	278,250	425,010	+ 32.2%
Pneumonia	53,040	50,550	− 17.5%
Diabetes	30,100	34,230	− 1.5%
Congenital anomaly	21,920	13,240	− 47.4%
Cirrhosis of the liver	20,740	29,100	+ 21.5%
Nephritis and nephrosis	13,180	17,300	+ 13.6%
Ulcers	11,540	6,840	− 48.7%
Emphysema	10,270	13,410	+ 13.0%
Tuberculosis	9,940	1,780	− 84.5%
Abdominal hernias	9,180	4,750	− 55.2%
Asthma	4,910	3,120	− 45.0%
Bronchitis	4,060	4,500	− 4.0%
Anemias	3,280	3,510	− 7.3%
Syphilis	2,850	1,900	− 42.3%
Meningitis	2,260	1,250	− 52.1%
Influenza	2,140	3,170	+ 28.2%
Nutritional deficiencies	1,750	2,010	− 0.6%
Motor vehicle accidents	38,090	49,910	+ 13.4%
Other accidents	54,160	49,200	− 21.3%
Suicides	19,000	26,010	+ 18.5%
Homicides	8,580	23,250	+134.7%
All other causes	370,610	237,340	− 44.6%
TOTAL	1,701,520	1,965,900	+ 15.5%

[61, 146]

Deaths from Cancer. These were the sites of the cancers associated with deaths from that disease in 1960 and 1980:

	1960	1980
Number of deaths	272,520	414,320

	Percentages	
Digestive organs	33.4%	26.5%
Respiratory organs	14.6%	26.1%
Genital organs	14.2%	11.2%
Breasts	8.8%	8.4%
Lymphatic tissues	4.8%	5.1%
Urinary organs	4.7%	4.2%
Leukemia	4.7%	4.1%
Lip, mouth, pharynx	2.3%	2.1%
Other or unspecified	12.6%	12.3%
	100.0%	100.0%

[61, 142]

DEATHS FROM "EXTERNAL CAUSES"

The National Center for Health Statistics uses the phrase "external causes" for deaths not attributable to diseases or other bodily malfunctionings. The most recent figures for such deaths, for 1977, come from a detailed report published in 1981.

The general categories include: motor vehicle and water transport deaths, falls, poisonings, "medical misadventures," homicides, and suicides.

MOTOR VEHICLE AND WATER TRANSPORT DEATHS

Among 47,038 deaths in motor vehicle accidents, the largest single number (16,002) involved colliding with another vehicle, followed by accidents on streets or highways but where another vehicle was not hit (7,536). Next came pedestrians killed by vehicles (7,467), deaths in collisions with trains (1,033), and accidents where the vehicle was not in traffic (1,026). However, for a very substantial number (13,974) no specific causes were listed.

A total of 1,371 persons died in water transport accidents, of whom 1,182 met their deaths by "drowning or submersion." Among other causes were fires or explosions (16), falls within the vessel (14), and machinery accidents (4).

Among those dying in motor vehicle accidents, 34,049 (or 72.4 percent) were men, and 12,989 (or 27.6 percent) were women. And of the deaths in water transport accidents, 1,237 (or 90.2 percent) were men, and 134 (or 9.8 percent) were women.

[60]

FALLS

Of the 14,136 fatal accidental falls, those where the circumstances were recorded included: falls "on or from stairs or steps" (1,411), from ladders or scaffolding (363), falls on a level surface from "slipping, stumbling, or tripping" (483), falling into a hole "or other opening in the surface" (140), and falls out of a building or some other structure (687).

Of those who died from falls, 7,325 (or 51.8 percent) were men; and 6,811 (or 48.2 percent) were women.

[60]

POISONINGS

A total of 4,161 poisoning deaths came from ingesting "solid and liquid substances." Among the specific incidents recorded were: "opiates and synthetic analogues" (854), alcohol (337), barbiturates (224), "cardiac tonics" (132), tranquilizers (92), "salicylates and congeners" (79), anti-depressants (65), "petroleum products and other solvents" (45), local anesthetics (35), "hormones and synthetic substitutes" (26), and "corrosives and caustics" (22).

Another 1,569 accidental poisonings were caused by "gases and vapors," of which the largest number came from "motor vehicle exhaust gas" (789).

Among victims of poisoning fatalities, 3,915 (or 68.3 percent) were men; and 1,815 (or 31.7 percent) were women.

[60]

MEDICAL "MISADVENTURES"

A total of 3,009 deaths occurred due to "surgical and medical complications and misadventures." In these cases 1,669 (or 55.5 percent) of those dying were men, and 1,340 (or 44.5 percent) were women.

The causes included: deaths during surgical treatment (1,884); those due specifically to anesthesia (57); from "drugs and biologicals" (296); from X rays and radioactive substances (48); and "complications and misadventures" during diagnostic procedures (327).

[60]

OTHER CAUSES

A total of 6,338 deaths were caused by fires of which 425 were due to "ignition of clothing." Of the victims, 3,878 (or 61.2 percent) were men and 2,460 (or 38.8 percent) were women.

There were 1,299 accidental deaths from "natural and environmental factors." These included fatalities due to "excessive heat" (100) and "excessive cold" (424), "hunger, thirst, exposure, and neglect" (247), lightning (81), and bites and stings of venomous animals and insects (53). Among the victims were 929 (or 71.5 percent) men and 370 (28.5 percent) women.

Among other causes were: drownings that did not involve boating (5,645); "inhalation and ingestion of food or other objects causing obstruction or suffocation" (3,033); suffocations in cribs or cradles (159);

being hit by falling objects (1,060); accidental self-inflicted deaths by firearms (448); accidental gas explosions (203); and accidental electrocutions (1,041).

[60]

HOMICIDES

Of 19,260 murder victims, 14,853 (or 77.1 percent) were men and 4,407 (or 22.9 percent) were women.

The principal means of death were: firearms or explosives (12,766 cases); "cutting and piercing instruments" (3,304); hanging or strangulation (717); "fights, brawls, or rapes" (80); poisoning (43); drowning (70); and "pushing from high places" (15).

In addition, 294 persons (of whom 5 were women) died from "legal intervention," which means their deaths were caused by law enforcement officers.

[60]

SUICIDES

Of the 26,832 recorded suicides, 19,493 (or 72.6 percent) of the victims were men, and 7,339 (or 27.4 percent) were women. The following were the means they utilized:

| | PERCENTAGES | |
	Men	Women
Firearms	62.2%	35.4%
Strangulation or suffocation	14.5%	11.7%
Poisoning by gas	8.4%	11.1%
Solid or liquid poisons	7.3%	30.7%
Jumping	2.8%	4.3%
Cutting or piercing	1.6%	1.6%
Drowning	1.4%	3.0%
Other or unspecified	1.8%	2.2%
	100.0%	100.0%

[60]

HOMICIDE, SUICIDE, AND RACE

The chances of being murdered are more than 5 times as high for black men (52.6 per 100,000 every year) as they are for white men (9.2 per 100,000).

Black women have a higher chance of becoming homicide victims (11.8 per 100,000) than do white men, and 4 times greater a chance than white women (2.9 per 100,000).

In contrast, white men have a suicide rate (20.2 per 100,000) almost twice the figure for black men (11.1 per 100,000). The suicide rate for white women is even lower (6.9 per 100,000), and for black women it is lower still (3.1 per 100,000).   [60]

SUICIDES, HOMICIDES, AND VEHICLE DEATHS BY MONTHS

The following were the percentages of suicides, homicides, and motor vehicle deaths occurring in the various months of the year. (If the deaths were spread evenly, each month would have 8.3 percent of the annual total.)

PERCENTAGES

Suicides		Homicides		Vehicle deaths	
May	9.0%	July	9.5%	July	10.1%
August	8.8%	October	8.7%	August	9.6%
July	8.7%	August	8.7%	October	9.1%
June	8.6%	December	8.7%	May	9.0%
April	8.4%	January	8.4%	September	8.8%
March	8.4%	September	8.3%	June	8.8%
September	8.4%	February	8.3%	December	8.5%
October	8.1%	May	8.2%	November	7.8%
December	8.1%	June	8.1%	April	7.8%
January	8.1%	November	8.0%	March	7.1%
November	7.8%	April	7.8%	January	6.8%
February	7.7%	March	7.5%	February	6.5%
	100.0%		100.0%		100.0%

[60]

DEATHS AMONG YOUNG MEN

Among young men between the ages of 15 and 24, these were the principle causes of death in a typical year:

	PERCENTAGES	
	15–19	20–24
Cancer	6.6%	4.5%
Heart disease	2.5%	2.9%
Motor vehicle accident	42.8%	35.6%
All other accidents	19.2%	16.5%
Suicide	9.7%	14.8%
Homicide	9.1%	12.8%
All other causes	10.1%	12.9%
	100.0%	100.0%

[60]

TRANSPORTATION FATALITIES: 1980

The following figures are available for transportation fatalities in 1980. During the year, a total of 56,186 persons were victims of deaths involving vehicles. By far the largest proportion, 51,900 deaths, involved motor vehicles. Among those killed were 480 bicyclists; 4,672 motorcyclists; 7,103 persons in vans or pickup trucks; and 7,622 pedestrians. The remaining 32,023 were in cars, larger trucks, or buses.

Altogether, 1,378 persons died in railroad accidents, of whom 850 were killed at a grade crossing. Another 1,408 were in fatal airplane crashes, of whom 33 were on scheduled or commuter airlines. A further 1,480 died on the water, 1,285 in recreational boats and 195 on commercial vessels, and a final 20 lost their lives in pipeline accidents, which are classed as transportation deaths.

[136]

RAILROAD-CROSSING ACCIDENTS

In 1980 detailed information was available on 708 people who were killed in railroad-highway crossing accidents. Among this group:

- 485 were in cars, 197 were in trucks, and 26 were on motorcycles.
- 562 of the accidents involved freight trains, 59 involved passenger trains, and 87 switching engines.
- 46 deaths came when the vehicle had stopped on the crossing, 21 when it stalled on the crossing, and 641 while it was moving over the crossing.
- 532 of the deaths were caused when the train struck the vehicle, and the other 176 came as the vehicle ran into the train.

[125]

CASES OF DISEASES: 1961 AND 1981

The following were the numbers of cases of various diseases reported to the U.S. Public Health Service in 1961 and 1981. (The percentage change has been adjusted to take account of the fact that the 1961 population was 20.8 percent smaller than in 1981.)

	1961	1981	PERCENTAGE CHANGE
Measles	423,919	3,032	− 99.4%
Gonorrhea	264,158	984,330	+ 195.1%
Syphilis	124,658	30,970	− 80.3%
Hepatitis	72,651	56,581	− 38.3%
Tuberculosis	53,726	27,412	− 59.6%

(continued)

	1961	1981	PERCENTAGE CHANGE
Whooping Cough	11,468	1,189	− 91.8%
Meningitis	5,162	9,027	+ 38.5%
Encephalitis	2,248	1,481	− 47.8%
Poliomyelitis	1,312	12	− 99.3%
Typhoid Fever	814	589	− 42.7%
Undulant Fever	636	159	− 80.2%
Diphtheria	617	4	− 99.5%
Trichinosis	306	145	− 62.5%
Rocky Mountain			
Spotted Fever	219	1,165	+ 321.3%
Malaria	73	1,304	+ 1314.8%
Leprosy	63	244	+ 206.7%
Botulism	14	79	+ 346.9%

[150, 152]

OTHER ILLNESSES IN PEOPLE AND ANIMALS

During 1981 the Centers for Disease Control also received reports of 2,060 cases of German measles; 9,027 cases of meningitis; 4,729 of mumps; and 195,061 of chicken pox.

In addition, 1981 brought notification of 7,211 cases of rabies in animals. Detailed breakdowns on rabid animals are available for 1980, when the total came to 6,477. On that year's list were 4,100 skunks, 738 bats, 396 cattle, 393 raccoons, 241 dogs, 217 foxes, 211 cats, 62 horses, 54 mongooses, 27 sheep, plus 8 coyotes and 8 bobcats, 5 pigs, 4 opossum, 3 badgers, 2 woodchucks, and 1 squirrel. (However, not all these animals bit people. In fact, the Centers for Disease Control were not notified of a single case of rabies in humans in 1980.)

[150, 152]

VENEREAL DISEASES

The Centers for Disease Control collect figures on venereal disease rates by states and cities, and also by sex and age. The following table ranks the states by their incidence of syphilis and gonorrhea.

VENEREAL DISEASE RATES: 1980
NUMBER OF REPORTED CASES PER
100,000 PERSONS

	SYPHILIS		GONORRHEA	
U.S.A.		12.0	U.S.A.	443.3
1.	Louisiana	33.9	Alaska	1016.5
2.	Georgia	33.8	Nevada	886.6
3.	Texas	26.9	Georgia	866.7
4.	Mississippi	26.7	South Carolina	754.3
5.	Florida	23.2	Florida	671.9
6.	Tennessee	20.1	North Carolina	651.9
7.	California	19.6	Tennessee	646.2
8.	New York	15.5	Maryland	640.0
9.	South Carolina	13.0	Alabama	617.5
10.	Hawaii	12.4	Mississippi	613.6
11.	Alabama	12.3	Delaware	608.6
12.	Illinois	12.0	Texas	564.4
13.	Nevada	11.6	California	554.7
14.	Virginia	10.9	Louisiana	537.2
15.	Arkansas	9.5	Missouri	447.9
16.	Maryland	9.4	Arkansas	443.1
17.	Arizona	8.9	Virginia	434.9
18.	New Mexico	8.6	Oregon	423.8
19.	North Carolina	8.4	Oklahoma	420.6
20.	Colorado	6.6	Illinois	410.8
21.	Washington	6.3	Ohio	400.1
22.	New Jersey	6.0	Arizona	389.1
23.	Massachusetts	5.5	Michigan	377.5
24.	Pennsylvania	4.8	New York	372.3
25.	Connecticut	4.3	Colorado	366.4
26.	Michigan	4.3	New Mexico	350.9
27.	Oregon	4.1	Kansas	348.1
28.	Indiana	3.7	Washington	344.2
29.	Oklahoma	3.7	Hawaii	338.6
30.	Kentucky	3.5	Connecticut	333.5
31.	Ohio	3.5	Kentucky	323.4
32.	Missouri	3.4	Indiana	317.2
33.	Rhode Island	3.4	Wisconsin	305.7
34.	Delaware	3.2	New Jersey	278.6
35.	Minnesota	3.1	Nebraska	236.9
36.	Alaska	2.5	Wyoming	232.7
37.	Wisconsin	2.2	Pennsylvania	232.5
38.	Wyoming	1.9	South Dakota	197.3
39.	Idaho	1.8	Minnesota	194.5
40.	Kansas	1.6	Massachusetts	188.2

(continued)

(continued)

SYPHILIS		GONORRHEA	
41. Utah	1.2	Montana	186.7
42. Iowa	1.1	Idaho	183.7
43. West Virginia	1.0	Iowa	174.8
44. South Dakota	0.9	West Virginia	171.5
45. Vermont	0.8	Rhode Island	171.1
46. Nebraska	0.8	Utah	134.3
47. Maine	0.5	Maine	129.8
48. New Hampshire	0.5	Vermont	104.3
49. Montana	0.3	North Dakota	104.1
50. North Dakota	0.3	New Hampshire	96.4

[149, 152]

VENEREAL DISEASES

GONORRHEA RATES FOR CITIES

The 25 cities with the largest numbers of reported cases of gonorrhea (per 100,000 population) in 1980 were:

Atlanta (3114.7 per 100,000 persons), San Francisco (2810.7), Washington, D.C. (2730.4), Baltimore (2324.9), St. Louis (1938.9), Cincinnati (1750.0), Charlotte, N.C. (1729.6), Newark (1723.3), Cleveland (1712.5), Milwaukee (1564.6), New Orleans (1534.2), Memphis (1524.7), Richmond (1487.0), Norfolk, Va. (1454.8), Columbus (1387.5), Kansas City, Mo. (1386.9), Rochester (1285.7), Detroit (1242.4), Oklahoma City (1239.0), Dayton (1228.3), Nashville (1177.0), Dallas (1128.6), Houston (1111.2), Denver (1090.2), and Indianapolis (1019.1).

The rates for some other large cities were: New York (615.4 per 100,000), Chicago (1000.2), Philadelphia (814.5), Los Angeles (739.4), Miami (935.1), Boston (911.8), and San Diego (400.0).

[152]

Gonorrhea: Sex and Age. The 1980 gonorrhea rate for men was 538.8 reported cases per 100,000 men in the population. For women the rate came to 353.1 cases for every 100,000 women.

The highest rate (2102.2 per 100,000) was for men aged 20 to 24. Next came women 20 to 24 (1458.6), followed by men 25 to 29 (1449.8) and women 15 to 19 (1414.5). There were somewhat lower rates for men aged 15 to 19 (930.0), women 25 to 29 (636.3), and men 30 to 39 (613.7). After that the rate fell off sharply, with men 40 to 49 (195.7) and women 30 to 39 (191.6).

[152]

SYPHILIS

Syphilis, a much more serious disease, is less prevalent than gonorrhea. Still, there were 27,204 cases reported in 1980, a rise of 23.8 percent from the 21,982 cases in 1970.

The cities with the highest rates per 100,000 population were: San Francisco (153.2 per 100,000), Atlanta (138.9), New Orleans (95.6), Memphis (87.1), and the District of Columbia (77.3).

Men and Women. The highest rates tended to be among men. Of men aged 20 to 24, there were 5,605 reported syphilis cases for each 100,000 in that age range. For those 30 to 39, the rate was 5,286 per 100,000. And at 25 to 29, there were 5,136 cases per 100,000.

The highest rate for women was in the 20-to-24 group, at 2,027 per 100,000. After that came the 15-to-19 range, with 1,562 cases per 100,000.

Altogether, men accounted for 20,767 of the syphilis cases, and women, 6,437.

[149, 152]

HEALTH CARE

VISITS TO PHYSICIANS AND DENTISTS

In 1979 Americans paid a total of 1,021,986,000 visits to physicians and 366,270,000 visits to dentists.

Among those visiting physicians, 41.3 percent were men and 58.7 percent were women. Women on the average made 5.4 visits a year, compared with 4.1 for men.

Of those visiting dentists, 44.2 percent were men and 55.8 percent were women; women averaged 1.8 visits a year as against 1.3 for men.

The following were the times since people had last seen a physician or a dentist.

Last Visit Was:	Physician	Dentist
Less than 6 months ago	58.5%	35.6%
6 to 11 months ago	16.5%	14.5%
Approximately 1 year ago	10.9%	13.1%
2 to 4 years ago	9.3%	12.7%
5 or more years ago	3.5%	13.6%
Never	0.2%	9.1%
Not known	1.1%	1.4%
	100.0%	100.0%

[68]

HOSPITAL TREATMENT

According to a study released in April of 1981, a total of 30,070,000 in-patients were treated in American hospitals. (The number of persons is actually lower, as some people were in the hospital more than once.)

Of these patients, 12,125,000 (or 40.3 percent) were men, and 17,945,000 (or 59.7 percent) were women. Also, 6,301,000 (or 21.0 percent) of the total number were persons 65 or over.

During the year 11.6 percent of the nation's male population underwent hospital treatment, as did 16.1 percent of the female population. Among those 65 or over, 27.0 percent were patients at least once, including 28.7 percent of the men and 25.8 percent of the women.

The average hospital stay was 5.8 days for all men and 5.3 days for all women. Among those 65 and over, it was 10.7 days for the men and 10.9 days for the women.

[68]

HOSPITALS

The most recent statistics on general hospitals appeared in March of 1981, with figures for the end of 1978. At that time there were 6,270 hospitals with a total of 1,074,733 beds.

On an average day there were 791,060 patients in residence, and total admissions for the year came to 36,359,395.* The hospitals had the equivalent of 2,879,734 full-time employees. This worked out to 268 employees for every 100 beds, and 364 employees for every 100 patients.

*This figure is based on information provided by the hospitals. The lower figure of 30,700,000, cited earlier, comes from the responses of individuals who were interviewed in a national health survey, which suggests that some persons may not want to admit that they have had hospital treatment.

Among the hospitals, 5.5 percent were operated by the federal government, 29.5 percent by state or local governments, 11.3 percent were under religious auspices, 41.7 percent by other nonprofit organizations, and 12.1 percent were profit-making businesses.

The states with the largest numbers of patients per 100,000 population on an average day were: North Dakota (498 daily patients per 100,000 population), Missouri (456 per 100,000), West Virginia (453), Kansas (451), and Nebraska (446).

The states with the fewest daily patients per 100,000 population were: Alaska (220 per 100,000), Utah (240), Hawaii (247), Wyoming (250), and Idaho (252).

Altogether, the hospitals attended to 252,427,553 out-patient visitors. Of these, 32.7 percent were emergency calls and the other 67.3 percent came in for clinic treatments.

[66]

Where Babies Were Born. The following figures show where babies were born and who was in attendance:

| | PERCENTAGES | | |
	Physician in Hospital	*Physician at Home*	*Midwife Either Place*
1940	55.8%	35.0%	9.3%
1950	88.0%	7.1%	5.0%
1960	96.6%	1.2%	2.2%
1970	99.4%	0.1%	0.5%
1979	97.1%	1.3%	1.6%

[59, 144]

OPERATIONS

According to a study published in March of 1980, a total of 20,754,000 operations were performed in American short-stay hospitals.

Of the patients in these operations, 62.3 percent were women. However, if gynecological and obstetrical operations are subtracted from the total, women then comprise 49.4 percent of the patients.

The following operations made up 95.2 percent of the total:

		PERCENTAGE WOMEN	
Gynecological	3,824,000	100.0%	
Abdominal	2,830,000	52.3%	
Orthopedic	2,821,000	48.1%	
Otorhinolaryngological	1,668,000	50.7%	*(continued)*

(continued)

		PERCENTAGE WOMEN
Urological	1,572,000	27.6%
Obstetrical	1,469,000	100.0%
Biopsies	1,172,000	62.0%
Vascular and cardiac	1,143,000	38.0%
Plastic	1,078,000	48.7%
Ophthalmological	881,000	58.1%
Proctological	548,000	45.3%
Neurosurgical	396,000	50.8%
Breast operations	365,000	94.2%

[63]

NURSING HOMES

The most recent report on nursing homes appeared in March of 1981, with statistics for the end of 1978. In that year there were 18,722 nursing homes, with an overall total of 1,348,794 beds.

On an average day there were 1,240,373 patients in residence. The homes had a full-time equivalent of 809,543 employees, or 65 employees for every 100 patients.

Of the homes, 6.2 percent were operated by state or local governments, 0.3 percent were federally controlled, 18.6 percent were nonprofit institutions, and the other 74.9 percent were profit-making businesses.

The states with the most nursing home beds per 1,000 persons aged 65 or over were: Alaska (110.8 beds per 1,000 persons), South Dakota (97.2 per 1,000), Minnesota (96.0), Wisconsin (93.8), and Iowa (89.9).

The states with the fewest beds per 1,000 persons aged 65 or over were: Florida (22.6 per 1,000), Arizona (25.2), New Mexico (25.4), West Virginia (27.4), and Nevada (30.1).   [66]

CHANGES IN FOOD CONSUMPTION: 1970–1980
(Pounds per Capita)

	1970	1980	PERCENTAGE CHANGE
Dairy products	335.0	308.0	− 8.1%
Meat	164.7	159.7	− 3.0%
Flour and cereal products	142.0	150.0	+ 5.6%
Fresh vegetables	141.4	149.9	+ 6.0%
Sugar and other sweeteners	121.4	133.4	+ 9.9%
Potatoes	83.2	81.0	− 2.6%

(continued)

(continued)

	1970	1980	PERCENTAGE CHANGE
Fresh fruits	78.6	84.0	+ 6.9%
Processed fruits	55.5	56.4	+ 1.6%
Canned vegetables	51.1	49.8	− 2.5%
Fats and oils	50.4	54.7	+ 8.5%
Poultry	48.8	60.9	+24.8%
Eggs	39.2	34.6	−11.7%
Melons	25.1	20.9	−16.7%
Fish	15.8	16.8	+ 6.3%
Coffee, tea, and cocoa	14.2	11.2	−21.1%
Frozen vegetables	9.6	10.4	+ 8.3%
All foods	1,402.0	1,408.0	+ 0.4%
All animal products	619.0	592.0	− 4.4%
All crop products	783.0	816.0	+ 4.2%

[108]

SMOKING HABITS: 1965–1980

In 1965 altogether 52.4 percent of all men aged 20 or over described themselves as "smokers." By 1980 only 38.3 percent answered to this description.

Between 1965 and 1980, the proportion of women who called themselves "smokers" dropped by a somewhat lesser rate: from 34.1 percent to 29.2 percent.

Stated another way, among the 1965 smokers there were 651 women for every 1,000 men. By 1980, of the people who still smoked, the ratio had risen to 762 women for every 1,000 men.

Heavier Smokers. Of the men who considered themselves smokers in 1965, only 25.4 percent said they smoked 25 or more cigarettes per day. In 1980, of the men who said they were smokers, 34.1 percent were smoking at least 25 a day.

Among the women who were smokers in 1965, only 14.2 percent smoked 25 or more a day. By 1980, of those who still were smokers, 34.1 percent were smoking at least 25 a day.

[70]

RECREATIONAL ACCIDENTS

During the one-year period going from July 1, 1980 to June 30, 1981, the Consumer Product Safety Commission estimated that the following numbers of accidents ("that required medical treatment or resulted in some limitation of normal activity") occurred during recreational activities:

Bicycling (518,000); baseball (478,000); football (470,000); basketball (434,000); skating (225,000); swimming (126,000); soccer (96,000); volleyball (75,000); tennis, badminton, or squash (67,000); wrestling (66,000); fishing (64,000); gymnastics (62,000); hockey (50,000); exercising with equipment (48,000).

Also: snow skiing (45,000); horseback riding (44,000); boating (37,000); sledding (32,000); waterskiing (29,000); skateboarding (28,000); dancing (26,000); golf (23,000); martial arts (19,000); bowling (19,000).

And: off-road vehicles (13,000); lacrosse (10,000); boxing (10,000); snowmobiling (8,000); trampolining (8,000); billiards or pool (6,000); and cheerleading (5,000).

[131]

HOUSEHOLD ACCIDENTS

The Consumer Product Safety Commission also computed that there were the following numbers of accidents involving objects or appliances in or around American households:

Stairs (763,000); glass doors (208,000); cutlery and knives (140,000); glass bottles and jars (140,000); home power tools (101,000); ladders and stools (99,000); bathtubs and showers (83,000); lawnmowers (68,000); chain saws (64,000); and guns (60,000).

Also: carpets and rugs (51,000); pencils, pens, and desk supplies (45,000); cooking ranges or ovens (40,000); pins and needles (40,000); electrical fixtures (38,000); razors, shavers, and blades (38,000); cleaning agents (36,000); hatchets and axes (29,000); television sets (27,000); baby carriages, walkers, and strollers (24,000).

And: paints, solvents, and lubricants (23,000); mirrors (19,000); scissors (17,000); screwdrivers (14,000); irons and ironers (13,000); rope and string (12,000); bars and bar stools (12,000); icepicks and skewers (11,000); pressurized containers (10,000); fireworks (10,000); matches (8,000); clothes hangers (7,000); blenders and mixers (7,000); ashtrays (6,000); coffeemakers and teapots (6,000); and musical instruments (6,000).

[131]

HEALTH CARE PERSONNEL

In the 4-year period from March of 1977 to March of 1981, the number of persons in health care occupations rose from 4,083,000 to 4,849,000, an increase of 18.8 percent. This also meant that health care employment rose from 4.6 percent to 5.0 percent of total national employment. The following were the major occupational categories in the health care field:

	MARCH 1977	MARCH 1981	PERCENTAGE CHANGE
Medical and osteopathic physicians	369,000	424,000	+14.9%
Dentists	105,000	142,000	+35.2%
Pharmacists	126,000	126,000	no change
Registered nurses	1,013,000	1,293,000	+27.6%
Practical nurses	381,000	381,000	no change
Nursing aides and attendants	994,000	1,086,000	+ 9.3%
Dental assistants	123,000	137,000	+11.4%
Therapists	169,000	228,000	+34.9%
Laboratory technicians	190,000	247,000	+30.0%
X-ray technicians	81,000	99,000	+22.2%

[178]

PHYSICIANS' SPECIALTIES

The Graduate Medical Education National Advisory Committee of the Department of Health and Human Services listed the following as the fields of specialization among physicians in private practice in 1981:

FIELD	NUMBER
General family practice	54,350
General internal medicine	48,950
General surgery	30,700
General psychiatry	25,250
General pediatrics	23,800
Radiology	18,550
Anesthesiology	14,850
Osteopathic medicine	13,550
Pathology	12,650
Orthopedic surgery	12,350
Cardiology	7,700
Urology	7,100
Preventive medicine	6,100
Otolaryngology	6,100
Emergency medicine	5,000
Neurology	4,850
Child psychiatry	3,050
Gastroenterology	2,900
Plastic surgery	2,600
Nephrology	1,450

[101]

In June of 1980, the National Center for Health Statistics issued a study on "visits to female and male physicians." The report stated that while women comprised 6.2 percent of physicians "engaged in office-based patient care," only 4.0 percent of patients' visits were to women practitioners.

Among male physicians, 60.1 percent of their visits were from women and 39.9 were from men. Among women physicians, women patients accounted for 71.5 percent of their visits and 28.6 percent came from men.

With women physicians the average time spent in "face-to-face encounter" with patients was 17.8 minutes; with men the figure was 15.3 minutes. However, the times varied by specialities. In general or family practice, women physicians averaged 17.6 minutes with their patients, as opposed to 12.7 minutes for men.

In pediatrics, women saw their patients for 11.4 minutes as against 13.0 minutes by men, and in obstetrics and gynecology, women spent about the same time with their patients: 14.4 minutes, compared with 14.7 minutes by men. With psychiatric patients, women averaged 48.3 minutes, while men allowed 43.9 minutes.

[64]

PUBLIC HEALTH

FLUORIDATED WATER SYSTEMS

Just under half of all Americans—49.3 percent—drink from 9,425 community water systems that are fluoridated.

The states in which the greatest proportions of the residents are served by fluoridated systems are: Illinois (86.2 percent), Colorado (83.8 percent), Connecticut (79.4 percent), Michigan (76.1 percent), and Minnesota (71.5 percent).

The states with the lowest proportions are: Utah (2.4 percent), Nevada (3.0 percent), Hawaii (6.4 percent), Oregon (10.7 percent), and New Hampshire (13.3 percent).

Of the 9,425 systems, 2,630 have water that is naturally fluoridated. The states with the largest number of these systems are: Texas (500), Illinois (191), Iowa (175), Oklahoma (158), and Ohio (122).

[98]

During 1980, inspectors from the Department of Agriculture examined the following numbers of animals to see if they were fit for consumption:

	ANIMALS EXAMINED	ANIMALS CONDEMNED	CONDEMNED PER 100,000
Pigs	90,037,586	318,650	354
Cattle	30,882,588	108,216	350
Sheep	5,087,112	31,887	627
Calves	2,218,907	32,991	1,487
Horses	339,410	1,681	495
Goats	115,467	948	821

[109]

CHAPTER FOUR

HOUSEHOLDS AND FAMILIES

DEFINITIONS, DISTRIBUTION, COMPOSITION

According to the 1980 Census, the nation had a total of 80,376,609 households, which are defined by the Census Bureau as taking one of three general forms.

First, there are *family households,* which consist of two or more persons living together who are related by birth or marriage. The most common family household is still a married couple, with or without children in the home. A single parent with one or more children also comprises a family household. There can be other family variations as well, such as two sisters who share a residence.

Second, there are *nonfamily households.* These consist of two or more unrelated individuals who share living quarters. They can be nonmarried couples, of the same or opposite sex. Or the household can contain three or more persons "who occupy a single room or a group of rooms" where "the occupants live and eat separately from other persons in the building and have direct access from the outside of the building or through a common hall."

Third, there are *single-person households,* individuals who live alone in their own separate residential units.

Altogether, 220,762,922 persons, or 97.5 percent of the population, resided in one of these three kinds of households. The other 5,741,903, or 2.5 percent, lived in "group quarters," which could be military barracks, college dormitories, hospitals, prisons, or other institutional settings.

HOUSEHOLD SIZE

The average 1980 household contained 2.75 persons, compared with 3.14 persons in 1970 and 3.33 members in 1960. There are three main reasons for this decline in household size: (1) families now have fewer children; (2) more families now have only one spouse in residence; and (3) there are more single-person households, which have swelled the overall total and helped decrease the average size.

The states with the smallest-size households were: Florida (average: 2.55), Nevada (2.59), Oregon (2.60), Washington (2.61), and Kansas and Oklahoma (both 2.62).

Those with the largest households were: Utah (3.20), Hawaii (3.15), Mississippi (2.97), South Carolina and Alaska (both 2.93), and Louisiana (2.91).

[26]

HOUSEHOLDS AND FAMILIES: THEIR CHANGING COMPOSITION

For further statistics on the country's households in 1980, we must draw on the Census Bureau's Current Population Survey, which was conducted in March of that year. Full household information from the 1980 Census will not be available until late 1983 or early 1984, nor will all its findings be released in printed form.

The Current Population Survey is based on interviews with approximately 65,000 households in all parts of the nation. The responses from that sample are then extrapolated so that they reflect the entire population. Thus the March 1980 survey reported its results as representing a total of 79,108,000 households. It should be noted that this figure is somewhat smaller than the 80,379,609 households found by the full 1980 Census that was carried out in April. A discrepancy of this kind—it comes to 1.6 percent—is usual between a good sample survey and a complete count.

Most of the information in this chapter is from the Current Population Survey. This is true as well for Chapter Five on "Marriage and Divorce," and Chapter Seven on "Income and Expenditures."

The following figures highlight what happened to American households during the 1970–1980 decade.

- From 1970 to 1980 the total number of households rose from 63,401,000 to 79,108,000. This amounted to an increase of 24.8 percent, more than double the general population rise of 11.5 percent. During the decade the number of persons in the average household declined from 3.14 to 2.75. This drop was due to fewer children in each family, more single-parent households, and—most important—more people living alone.

- During the decade family households fell from 81.2 percent of the total to 73.9 percent. By the same token, nonfamily households rose from 18.8 percent of the total to 26.1 percent.

- Within the family household category, families containing a married couple declined from 86.9 percent of that group to 82.5 percent. Put another, more graphic way, the actual number of married couples increased by only 7.7 percent, one-third less than the general population rise. On the other hand, families with nonmarried heads grew by 52.3 percent.

- Of the 8,540,000 families headed by women, 5,918,000 (or 69.3 percent) contained at least one child under the age of 18. This represented a 71.7 percent rise from 1970, when 3,447,000 homes with children had women as their heads. (As it happened, the number of solo fathers remained fairly constant, changing from 716,000 in 1970 to 736,000 in 1980.)

- By 1980 altogether 23.4 percent of all children aged 17 or under were living with one parent, another relative, or some nonrelative. This was the situation for 17.3 percent of white children and 57.8 percent of black children.

- Between 1970 and 1980, families where the head was a widow dropped by 49.6 percent. So did those headed by separated women, with a drop of 18.7 percent. On the other hand, the proportion of divorced women as family heads rose by 33.2 percent. Even more striking were single women ("never married" in Census terminology) whose share increased by 90.6 percent.

- Among married couples, the proportion with no children rose by 24.2 percent, while those with 3 or more declined by 39.5 percent. However, the Census counts as "childless" older couples whose children have left home. If we focus on younger couples, we find that in 1970 among those where the husband was under 25, only 44.6 percent did not yet have any children. By 1980 the childless group had grown to 52.0 percent. And where the husband was 30 to 34, the proportion without children rose from 10.2 percent to 17.6 percent.

- Nonfamily households, taken together, increased from 11,919,000 to 20,682,000 between 1970 and 1980, a growth of 73.5 percent, which was more than six times that for the overall population.

- Altogether, 6,965,000 more people were living by themselves in 1980 compared with 1970. This increase came from several sources, all of them associated with the trend away from family living. First, young people are not only marrying later, but they are living on their own while in the single state. Among those the Census calls the "never married," the number of men with residences of their own grew by 118.3 percent, while the comparable figure for women went up 89.3 percent.

- Next, came persons who were separated or divorced and no longer living with their former mates. The number of men in this category rose by 121.8 percent, with the parallel figure for women 79.4 percent. The sexual discrepancy derives from the fact that when divorced and separated women have children they generally get custody. Given that arrangement, these women fall in the category of "single heads of families" whereas their former husbands are classed as "living alone."

- For some time, more widowed men and women have been living by themselves rather than with their adult children. The number of widows living alone rose by 31.9 percent during the decade, with the figure for widowers up 16.4 percent. But these growth rates were not as sharp as those for the other groups.

- A total of 2,866,000 households consisted of unrelated persons sharing quarters. This group broke down as follows: 25.1 percent were 2 men living together; 19.2 percent were 2 women; and 55.8 percent were mixed-sex arrangements. In this third group, 31.5 percent had children on the premises, in most cases from the woman's previous marriage. Indeed, in only 37.2 percent of the mixed-sex households had both partners never been married. (It should be noted that these figures do not include people who spend a lot of time together but keep their own apartments.)

- Altogether, 1970 to 1980 saw the creation of 15,707,000 new households. Of these, 55.6 percent were of the nonfamily variety. And among the 44.4 percent that were counted as family households, there were 3,518,000 new ones with single heads as opposed to 3,452,000 containing married couples. This means that only 22.0 percent of total household growth came from couples who were married. Moreover, whereas in 1970 couples with 2 or more children accounted for 28.1 percent of all households, by 1980 they were down to 19.0 percent.

[30, 31]

The following table shows the changes in the numbers and proportions of various kinds of households. The column called "Change in Proportion" shows the changes in percentage share. Thus the growth of single person households from having a 17.1 percentage share in 1970 to 22.5 percent in 1980 works out to a 31.6 percent growth in the percentage represented by those households.

THE CHANGING CHARACTER OF HOUSEHOLDS: 1970–1980

| | 1970 | | 1980 | | Percentage |
	Number	Percent- age	Number	Percent- age	Change in Proportion
All households	63,401,000	100.0%	79,108,000	100.0%	
Family					
households	*51,456,000*	*81.2%*	*58,426,000*	*73.9%*	*– 9.0%*
Married couples	44,728,000	70.6%	48,180,000	60.9%	– 13.7%
Women heads only	5,500,000	8.7%	8,540,000	10.8%	+ 24.1%
Men heads only	1,228,000	1.9%	1,706,000	2.2%	+ 15.8%
Nonfamily					
households	*11,945,000*	*18.8%*	*20,682,000*	*26.1%*	*+ 38.8%*
Single person	10,851,000	17.1%	17,816,000	22.5%	+ 31.6%
Two people	877,000	1.4%	2,316,000	2.9%	+107.1%
Three or more	217,000	0.3%	550,000	0.7%	+133.3%

[31]

MARRIED COUPLE HOUSEHOLDS

WITH AND WITHOUT CHILDREN

The Census Bureau defines "children" as family members who are under the age of 18. Using this definition, the proportion of married couples who had *no* children grew from 42.5 percent in 1970 to 49.0 percent in 1980.

And the proportion with three or more children fell from 21.2 percent to 11.9 percent, which meant that more couples who were having children were having only one or two.

| | 1970 | 1980 | PERCENTAGE CHANGE IN PROPORTION |
	Percentage		
No children	42.5%	49.0%	+15.3%
With children	*57.5%*	*51.0%*	*−11.3%*
One child	18.4%	19.7%	+ 7.1%
Two children	17.9%	19.4%	+ 8.4%
Three or more	21.2%	11.9%	−43.9%

[16, 31]

"CHILDLESS" COUPLES

Of course, many of the couples in the "no children" category are older couples who have sons and daughters, all of whom are over 18. Unfortunately, the Census figures do not distinguish younger childless couples from those whose children are all grown.

However, we do have figures showing the number of married-couple households with no children under 18, tabulated according to the husband's age. If he is under 35, it seems likely that he has no children over 18 so that the couple is truly "childless."

Between 1970 and 1980, in marriages where the husband was under 25, the proportion of couples without children rose from 44.6 percent to 52.0 percent. Among marriages where the husband was between 25 and 29, the childless contingent increased from 22.9 percent to 32.2 percent. And when he was in the 30 to 34 age-range, 17.6 percent of the 1980 couples still had no children, compared with 10.2 percent in 1970.

[16, 31]

WORKING WIVES

Among all married couples, the wife is in the "labor force" in 50.3 percent of the marriages.*

Among couples who have one or more children under the age of 18, a total of 54.3 percent of the wives are in the labor force.

And, among couples with one or more children under the age of 6, the wives are in the labor force in 45.2 percent of the marriages.

However, among couples with *no* children under 18, only 46.1 percent of the wives are in the labor force. This is because the total contains women whose children are all grown, and they are less likely to work than younger wives. Thus among couples where the husband is aged 45 or older, only 35.9 percent of the wives are in the labor force.

[31]

---

*A person is considered to be a member of the "labor force" if he or she: (a) is working at a full-time or part-time job; (b) has been laid off from a job but expects to be called back; or (c) is not currently employed but is looking for a full-time or part-time job. Figures are not available on how many wives and mothers fall in each of these separate categories.

FAMILIES WITH SINGLE HEADS

In the 8,540,000 families that are headed by women who are not living with husbands, 62.5 percent have at least one child under the age of 18. In the remaining 37.5 percent there may be children of 18 or over, or she may be sharing quarters with another relative.

Among the 1,706,000 families that are headed by men who are not living with wives, 35.7 percent contain one or more children under 18. In the other 64.3 percent there are children aged 18 or over, or he may be sharing the household with some other relative.

The women and men who head households on their own have the following marital status:

PERCENTAGES		
	Women	*Men*
Single	15.6%	32.4%
Separated	20.3%	15.6%
Divorced	34.7%	28.0%
Widowed	29.5%	24.0%
	100.0%	100.0%

[31]

Educational Levels. Among women who head families, 40.3 percent did not finish high school, 38.4 percent completed high school, and 21.3 percent attended college.

Changing Composition. In 1960 a majority (61.4 percent) of the women who headed families were over the age of 45, a majority (53.3 percent) had no children under 18, and a majority (51.7 percent) were widows.

By 1980 most of the women who headed families (56.5 percent) were under 45, most had children under 18 (62.5 percent), and the majority (70.5 percent) were single, separated, or divorced.

Women Heads and Race. Between 1970 and 1980 the proportion of families with children under 18 that were headed by women grew from 10.2 percent to 17.5 percent. Among white families, the proportion with women as heads went from 7.8 percent to 13.4 percent, and with black families the women's proportion rose from 30.6 percent to 46.8 percent.

[30, 31, 36]

CHILDREN AND PARENTS

From 1970 to 1980, the proportion of children aged seventeen or younger who were living with both parents fell from 85.2 percent to 76.6 percent. During this period the proportion living only with their mother rose from 10.8 percent to 18.0 percent.

In 1980 a total of 82.7 percent of all white children were residing with two parents, while only 42.2 percent of black children had two parents present.

Altogether, 13.5 percent of white children were living only with their mother, whereas for black children the comparable figure was 43.8 percent. Moreover, the marital status of the mothers differed considerably by race:

	PERCENTAGES	
Mothers' Marital Status	White	Black
Single	7.3%	29.3%
Separated	28.6%	36.7%
Widowed	12.4%	9.2%
Divorced	51.7%	24.8%
	100.0%	100.0%

In all, 3.8 percent of white children were living only with their fathers, with other relatives, or persons to whom they were not related. For black children that proportion came to 14.1 percent.

[30]

CHILD SUPPORT PAYMENTS

In recent years the Census Bureau has sought to ascertain how many women who head families are receiving child support payments from the fathers of the children.

The latest survey discovered that only 48.3 percent of these mothers were supposed to receive such payments, either by a court order or an informal agreement. Of those who were supposed to receive payments, 48.9 percent received the full amount, 22.7 percent got less than the expected sum, and 28.4 percent received no payments at all during the year.

Among those who received some support, the average monthly payment came to $149.92. White mothers received, on average, $155.08, and black mothers averaged $107.83.

Mothers with one child who received some payment received a monthly average of $107.33. Mothers with two children received

$166.25, an average of $83.13 per child, and women with three children averaged $210.67 per month, or $70.22 per child.

In terms of marital status, among mothers who were divorced but *not* remarried, 70.8 percent were supposed to receive child support and 51.9 percent actually did, with the average monthly payment amounting to $162.58.

Among those who had been divorced and *were* remarried, 57.1 percent were supposed to receive support from the children's fathers and 39.0 percent actually did, with the payments received averaging $133.50 per month.

Of women who were separated, 45.1 percent were supposed to receive child support and 26.7 percent actually did, with average monthly payments of $158.83.

And of mothers who had never been married, 10.6 percent were supposed to receive payments, while 6.3 percent in fact did, with payments averaging $81.33 per month.

Divorce and Alimony. At the time of the most recent study, conducted in the spring of 1979, there were 2,309,000 separated women and 5,311,000 divorced women who had not remarried.

Among the divorced women, 8.9 percent were supposed to receive alimony; 6.4 percent did, with their monthly sums averaging $263.50.

Of the separated women, 5.8 percent were supposed to receive alimony or maintenance payments, and 4.8 percent actually did, with the monthly check averaging $193.92.

[38]

NONFAMILY HOUSEHOLDS

NONMARRIED COUPLES

In 1980 there were 2,798,000 households that included two unrelated adults. Of these, 1,238,000 (or 44.2 percent) contained housemates of the same sex. Within this group, 56.6 percent were pairs of men and 43.4 percent were pairs of women.

The other 1,560,000 (or 55.8 percent) had housemates of different sexes. Within this group, 59.5 percent listed the man as the "householder," while 40.5 percent gave that designation to the woman.

Of the men in these households, 52.8 percent were single, 31.1 percent were divorced, 9.8 percent were widowed, and 6.3 percent were separated.

Among the women, 52.4 percent were single, 32.7 percent were divorced, 3.7 percent were widowed, and 11.3 percent were separated.

And among the households having housemates of different sexes, 491,000 (or 31.5 percent) had children under 18 living with them.

However, only 37.2 percent of these households consisted of single men and women living together. And of the 3,120,000 unmarried persons of different sexes sharing quarters, 99,000 of the men and 92,000 of the women were aged 65 or over.

Note: In fact, the Census counts those with children present as "family households" because a mother (or a father) plus a child constitutes a family unit even if another nonmarried person is also in residence. If there are no related children present, then a nonmarried couple is a "nonfamily household."

[30]

ONE-PERSON HOUSEHOLDS

Between 1970 and 1980, the number of individuals living alone (as one-person households) rose from 10,851,000 to 17,816,000. This came to an increase of 64.2 percent, or more than 5 times the 11.5 percent rise for the population as a whole. The number of women living by themselves grew from 7,319,000 to 11,022,000 (a rise of 50.6 percent), while the number of men living alone went from 3,532,000 to 6,793,000 (an increase of 92.3 percent).

Here is the composition of persons living alone, according to their sex and marital status, comparing 1970 and 1980. Widows and widowers account for a declining share of one-person households, with single and divorced people assuming larger proportions.

	PERCENTAGES			
	Men		*Women*	
	1970	1980	1970	1980
Single	40.1%	45.5%	18.3%	23.0%
Separated	13.8%	13.0%	6.5%	5.6%
Widowed	26.6%	16.1%	64.4%	56.4%
Divorced	19.5%	25.4%	10.8%	15.0%
	100.0%	100.0%	100.0%	100.0%

[30]

SOURCES OF INCREASE

In terms of numbers, 6,965,000 more people were living alone in 1980 compared with 1970. Here were the rates of increase for the groups within this total, plus each group's percentage share of the 1970–1980 growth.

	ADDITIONAL PERSONS LIVING ALONE	PERCENTAGE GROUP'S GROWTH 1970–1980	PERCENTAGE SHARE OF 1970–1980 GROWTH
Single men	1,676,000	+118.1%	24.0%
Widowed women	1,504,000	+ 31.9%	21.6%
Single women	1,196,000	+ 89.2%	17.2%
Divorced men	1,036,000	+150.9%	14.9%
Divorced women	862,000	+109.3%	12.4%
Separated men	396,000	+ 18.1%	5.7%
Widowed men	154,000	+ 16.5%	2.2%
Separated women	141,000	+ 30.7%	2.0%
TOTAL	6,965,000	+ 64.2%	100.0%

[30]

FARM HOUSEHOLDS

In 1980 a total of 6,051,000 Americans lived on farms, comprising 2.7 percent of the total population. They belonged to 1,631,000 families, which also works out to 2.7 percent of the nation's total.

* The farm population is 94.4 percent white, as opposed to 83.2 percent of the rest of the country.

* It has a median age of 35.5 years, compared with 30.0 years for the remainder of the country.

* Farm women had a fertility rate of 1,911 (the number of children thus far born to every 1,000 women aged 18 to 44) as against 1,529 for women not on farms. However, only 16.5 percent of farm women were 20 to 34, the chief childbearing years, as against 25.3 percent of women elsewhere.

* Among farm women who had ever been married, 87.8 percent are still living with their husbands, whereas the same figure for nonfarm women is 71.0 percent. Only 2.1 percent of farm women are divorced or separated, in contrast to 9.6 percent of other women.

* Farm families had a median income of $15,755 in 1980, compared with $21,151 for families elsewhere. And 26.6 percent had incomes of over $25,000, as against 39.7 percent for nonfarm homes.

* Out of 1,642,000 resident agricultural workers, 1,316,000 (or 80.1 percent) were self-employed, which meant they owned their own farms or rented some or all of the land on which they worked.

- An additional 1,399,000 farm residents had their principal employment outside of agriculture. Of these workers, 50.8 percent were men and 49.2 percent were women.

- Back in 1960 black families comprised 16.4 percent of the farm population. By 1980 the black proportion had declined to 4.0 percent.

- In 1960 children under 14 accounted for 31.9 percent of the farm population. In 1980 they constituted 18.9 percent. In this period also, persons 65 or over rose from 8.5 percent of the farm population to 12.3 percent.

[44, 47]

CHAPTER FIVE

MARRIAGE AND DIVORCE

Statistics on marital status deal with the experience of *individuals* as opposed to households. Figures on this subject come from two main sources. First, there are the findings of the Census Bureau's Current Population Survey for 1980. Second, there are figures on marriage and divorce compiled by the National Center for Health Statistics. Some of these statistics are for 1980, but in other cases, we will have to satisfy ourselves with figures from earlier years due to delays in collection and publication.

So far as definitions are concerned, "single" refers to persons who have never been married. "Married" means individuals who are married and currently living with their spouses. "Separated" can mean either a legal separation prior to divorce or married persons living apart for any other reason. "Divorced" means that legal proceedings have been completed and the person has not remarried. "Widowed" means the couple was still married when one of the spouses died. Thus a person stays in the "divorced" category even if his or her ex-spouse dies.

MARITAL STATUS: NUMBERS AND RATIOS

The following was the marital status of American men and women who were aged 20 and over in 1980:

| | MEN | | WOMEN | |
	Number	Percentage	Number	Percentage
Single	13,626,000	19.5%	10,512,000	13.5%
Married	48,545,000	69.3%	48,013,000	61.7%
Separated	2,046,000	2.9%	3,065,000	3.9%
Widowed	1,972,000	2.8%	10,476,000	13.5%
Divorced	3,869,000	5.5%	5,805,000	7.4%
	70,058,000	100.0%	77,871,000	100.0%

Among persons aged 20 and over, there are 1,296 single men for every 1,000 single women, because more women get married before they are 20. For the same reason, there are slightly more married men than married women: 1,011 to 1,000.

However, there are 668 separated men for every 1,000 separated women, 666 divorced men for every 1,000 divorced women, and only 188 widowers for every 1,000 widows. If these three groups are considered together, there are 408 unattached men for every 1,000 women of similar status.

[30]

Are There More Separated Women Than Men? In theory, the number of "separated" men and women should be precisely equal. After all, "separation" means both spouses are still legally married to each other, and they cannot marry someone else until a divorce has been decreed. How, then, are we to explain the fact that 1,019,000 more women than men say that they are "separated"?

Officials at the Census give three general explanations. First, some men may have married again without bothering with a divorce. Second, some separated men may choose to describe themselves as single. Third, women who have never been married but have children may prefer to say they are separated rather than single. Insofar as this is so, the number of women who really belong in the "single" category should be somewhat larger.

MARRIAGE

The "Marriage Rate." One way to measure the marriage rate is by comparing the number of weddings with the number of unmarried women aged 15 to 44. (In this age range, 93.5 percent of all women's marriages and remarriages occur.)

In 1960 there were 148.0 marriages for every 1,000 unmarried women between 15 and 44. By 1970 the rate was down to 140.2 per 1,000, and in 1979 only 107.9 women got married for every 1,000 in their potential pool.

For 1980 and 1981 we only have marriage rates as measured against the total population. For both those years the rate was 10.6 per 1,000.

[141, 145]

MARRIAGE RATES BY STATES

Marriage rates by states are computed on the basis of the overall population. The state with the highest marriage rate is Nevada, which had 156.8 marriages performed in 1980 for every 1,000 persons living in the state.

However, this is a highly inflated figure, because most of the couples marrying there come to Nevada simply for the ceremony and are not residents of the state. (In 1980 there were 121,874 marriages in Nevada, more than the 110,667 in Illinois or the 110,875 in the six New England states together.)*

Among the rest of the states, those with the highest marriage rates in 1980 were: South Carolina (18.2 per 1,000 population), Oklahoma (15.8 per 1,000), Wyoming (14.6), Idaho (14.3), and Texas (13.6).

The states with the lowest marriage rates were: New Jersey (7.5 per 1,000), Delaware (7.6), Rhode Island (7.8), New York (8.0), and Pennsylvania and North Carolina (both 8.1).

[142]

MARRIAGE AND REMARRIAGE

In 1979, of the persons getting married, 70.1 percent were doing so for the first time, and within this group, 50.6 were women and 49.4 percent were men.

Another 26.3 percent of the brides and grooms had been previously divorced, of which 48.1 percent were women and 51.9 percent were men.

And 3.6 percent of the marriage partners were widows or widowers. In this group, 52.2 percent were women and 47.8 percent were men. However, among widowed persons aged 65 or over who remarried, 60.6 percent were men and only 39.4 percent were women.

[141]

*Nevada also has an abnormally high divorce rate of 18.6 (measured against each 1,000 of its residents), because many people still travel there to dissolve their marriages. Indeed, a considerable number remarry there the same day their decree comes through.

MONTH OF MARRIAGE

The following are the percentage of marriage ceremonies occurring in each month, according to whether it is the bride's first marriage or if she is remarrying.

If marriages were spread evenly throughout the year, the average would work out to 8.3 percent in every month. Also, these figures vary somewhat from year to year, depending on how many Fridays and Saturdays (when most weddings occur) there are in each month.

BRIDE'S FIRST MARRIAGE	Percentage	BRIDE REMARRYING	Percentage
June	12.3%	December	10.2%
August	11.1%	July	10.2%
July	10.7%	June	9.7%
September	9.6%	August	8.7%
May	8.9%	April	8.5%
October	8.8%	October	8.5%
April	7.9%	May	8.4%
December	7.4%	November	8.3%
November	7.0%	September	8.1%
March	5.8%	March	6.8%
February	5.4%	February	6.7%
January	5.1%	January	5.9%
	100.0%		100.0%

[62]

DAY OF THE WEEK

Here are the percentage of marriages occurring on the various days of the week: Saturdays (53.0 percent), Fridays (19.7 percent), Sundays (8.0 percent), Thursdays (5.6 percent), Mondays (5.2 percent), Tuesdays (4.3 percent), and Wednesdays (4.2 percent).

[62]

RELIGIOUS OR CIVIL CEREMONIES

When it is the *first* marriage for the bride, 79.2 percent of the weddings are religious ceremonies and 20.8 percent are civil. (When the bride is getting *remarried*, 60.6 percent of the ceremonies are religious and 39.4 percent are civil.)

The following are the states in which the highest proportions of brides' *first* marriages are religious ceremonies: West Virginia (97.9 percent), Indiana (91.0 percent), Missouri (90.0 percent), Delaware (89.6 percent), and Montana (89.0 percent).

Those states that have the lowest percentages of religious ceremonies at brides' *first* marriages are South Carolina (43.7 percent), Georgia (59.1 percent), Alaska (62.9 percent), Florida (65.3 percent), and Wyoming (66.7 percent).

[62]

AGE AT MARRIAGE

The median age of first marriages is 22.1 for the bride and 24.6 for the groom, a difference of 30 months.

The median age at remarriage where the bride has been divorced is 31.9, and for the groom it is 35.3, a difference of 41 months.

And at remarriages for people who have been widowed, the median age for the bride is 55.2 and for the groom is 61.7, a difference of 78 months.

[141]

MEDIAN AGE AT MARRIAGE: 1890–1980

The following were the median ages at first marriages for men and women from 1890 through 1980:

	MEN	WOMEN	AGE DIFFERENCE (YEARS)
1980	24.6	22.1	2.5
1970	23.2	20.8	2.4
1960	22.8	20.3	2.5
1950	22.8	20.3	2.5
1940	24.3	21.5	2.8
1930	24.3	21.3	3.0
1920	24.6	21.2	3.4
1910	25.1	21.6	3.5
1900	25.9	21.9	4.0
1890	26.1	22.0	4.1

[30]

AGE OF MARRIAGE FOR WOMEN: 1970 AND 1980

In 1970 altogether 86.0 percent of all women had been married at least once by the age of 25. By 1980 the proportion of women married by 25 was down to 71.6 percent.

Here are figures on how many women were married at various ages in 1970 and 1980:

Age	PERCENTAGES 1970	1980
18	18.0%	12.0%
19	31.2%	22.5%
20	43.1%	33.5%
21	56.1%	40.3%
22	66.5%	51.9%
23	77.6%	58.2%
24	82.1%	66.5%
25	86.0%	71.6%
26	87.8%	77.3%
27	90.9%	77.9%
28	91.1%	84.1%
29	92.0%	85.5%
30–34	93.8%	90.5%
35–39	94.6%	93.8%
40–44	95.1%	95.2%

[30]

AGE DIFFERENCES IN MARRIAGES

Among American marriages, the husband is younger than the wife among 14.4 percent of the couples; both partners are the same age in another 12.1 percent of the marriages. (This means the same age in terms of years—statistics are not divided by months. Needless to say, except in some very rare cases, one spouse is always older or younger than the other.)

In the 73.4 percent of the marriages where the husband is older, he is 1 to 4 years older among 46.6 percent of the couples; 5 to 9 years older with 19.6 percent; and 10 or more years the wife's senior in 7.2 percent.

[62]

INTERRACIAL MARRIAGES

In 1980 there were 166,000 married couples in which the partners were black and white.

In 120,000 of these marriages (or 72.3 percent) the husband was black and the wife was white. In the other 46,000 (or 27.7 percent) the wife was black and the husband was white.

[31]

DIVORCE

In 1980 a total of 1,182,000 divorces were granted, the highest number in the nation's history. This worked out to a rate of 5.2 divorces for every 1,000 persons in the population. Previous divorce rates had been:

1970: 3.5 per 1,000   1940: 2.0 per 1,000
1960: 2.2 per 1,000   1930: 1.6 per 1,000
1950: 2.6 per 1,000   1920: 1.6 per 1,000

[62, 142]

COMPUTING THE "DIVORCE RATE"

Official agencies calculate the incidence of divorce in two different ways. The first method computes the number of divorces per 1,000 population in a given year. Thus in 1980 there were 5.2 divorces for each 1,000 Americans. In 1970 the rate was 3.5 per 1,000. And back in 1960 it was 2.2 per 1,000. So we can say that the divorce rate rose by 140.9 percent between 1960 and 1980.

The second method counts the number of divorces for every 1,000 marriages. In 1980 the ratio came to 490 divorces for each 1,000 marriages. In 1970 it was 328 per 1,000. And in 1960 the ratio was 258 per 1,000. With this method, the divorce rate only rose by 89.9 percent from 1960 to 1980.

How come this discrepancy? The reason is that each rate's "base" has different characteristics. For example, the number of divorces per 1,000 population will vary with changes in the country's age distribution. Thus the years 1960 to 1980 saw an increase in the age group in which divorces generally take place, which in turn inflates the rate. On the other hand, the ratio of divorces per 1,000 marriages is complicated by the fact that the marriage total includes remarriages. So the divorces are also matched against the marriages of people who had been divorced before, and that tends to deflate the rate.

The difference is even more striking if we compare the rates for states. In 1980 Oklahoma had 8.2 divorces for every 1,000 persons in the state. For Wisconsin the comparable rate was 3.7 per 1,000. Thus Oklahoma's rate was more than double—221.6 percent—that of Wisconsin.

In the same year Oklahoma granted 521 divorces for every 1,000 marriages that took place in the state. Wisconsin's ratio was 436 for each 1,000 marriages. In this case Oklahoma's divorce rate was only about one-fifth higher—19.5 percent—than Wisconsin's.

The first method is obviously more striking if we wish to highlight the differences between states. The second method tends to suggest that states do not vary terribly much.

There is also a third method, which tries to compute how many marriages will end in divorce. This "rate" is really a forecast, because many of the divorces have not yet taken place. In addition, marriages that occurred some time ago are less likely to end in divorce because couples in older generations are more apt to stick together. Thus one study concluded that of marriages contracted back in 1952, a total of 32.1 percent would end in divorce. However, among those marrying in 1977, the total would reach 49.6 percent.

DIVORCE RATES: 1980
U.S.A. = 5.2

DIVORCE–MARRIAGE RATIOS: 1980
U.S.A. = 490

		DIVORCES PER 1,000 POPULATION		DIVORCES PER 1,000 MARRIAGES
1.	Nevada	18.6	Arkansas	864
2.	Arkansas	9.9	Oregon	775
3.	Wyoming	8.5	Alaska	677
4.	Alaska	8.4	Arizona	659
5.	Oklahoma	8.2	Florida	646
6.	New Mexico	8.1	New Mexico	640
7.	Arizona	7.8	California	615
8.	Florida	7.8	Washington	610
9.	Idaho	7.3	North Carolina	608
10.	Alabama	7.1	Montana	593
11.	Texas	7.1	Ohio	585
12.	Washington	7.0	Wyoming	582
13.	Oregon	7.0	West Virginia	568
14.	Tennessee	6.8	New Hampshire	562
15.	Colorado	6.4	Alabama	548
16.	Georgia	6.4	Kansas	537
17.	Montana	6.3	Colorado	533
18.	California	5.8	Delaware	523
19.	New Hampshire	5.8	Oklahoma	521
20.	Maine	5.7	Texas	519
21.	Missouri	5.7	Tennessee	512
22.	Kansas	5.6	Idaho	508
23.	Utah	5.6	Rhode Island	503
24.	Mississippi	5.5	Missouri	500
25.	Ohio	5.4	Kentucky	495
26.	West Virginia	5.3	Vermont	486
27.	North Carolina	5.0	Georgia	485
28.	Vermont	5.0	Mississippi	480
29.	Kentucky	4.8	New Jersey	470

(continued)

DIVORCE RATES: 1980

U.S.A. = 5.2

DIVORCE–MARRIAGE RATIOS: 1980

U.S.A. = 490

		DIVORCES PER 1,000 POPULATION		DIVORCES PER 1,000 MARRIAGES
30.	South Carolina	4.7	Utah	466
31.	Hawaii	4.7	Nebraska	457
32.	Illinois	4.5	Michigan	456
33.	Virginia	4.5	Illinois	456
34.	Michigan	4.4	Connecticut	444
35.	Nebraska	4.1	Wisconsin	436
36.	South Dakota	4.1	Maine	435
37.	Delaware	4.0	Iowa	427
38.	Iowa	4.0	Minnesota	400
39.	Maryland	3.9	Virginia	392
40.	Rhode Island	3.9	New York	384
41.	Connecticut	3.8	Hawaii	376
42.	Minnesota	3.7	Pennsylvania	365
43.	Wisconsin	3.7	Maryland	354
44.	New Jersey	3.5	North Dakota	349
45.	North Dakota	3.3	Massachusetts	336
46.	New York	3.1	South Dakota	316
47.	Pennsylvania	3.0	South Carolina	256
48.	Massachusetts	2.9	Nevada	118

[142]

Note: Indiana and Louisiana did not report divorce figures for 1980.

DIVORCE-MARRIAGE RATIO

In 1980 a total of 2,413,000 marriages were performed and 1,182,000 divorces were granted. This works out to a ratio of 490 divorces for every 1,000 marriages.

The preceding table gives the divorce-marriage ratios for the 48 states reporting this information. (Louisiana and Indiana are the two exceptions.) It should be noted that in many cases the divorces granted by a state are of marriages that were contracted in some other state. This is especially so with states having large numbers of newcomers.

Nevada is also a special case. Because so many people go there just to get married, its marriage side of the ratio is considerably inflated. If its divorces were only measured against marriages of native Nevadans, then the state would have a much higher ratio. (Nevada ranks first in divorces per 1,000 population.)

[142]

WHICH MARRIAGE WAS DISSOLVED?

Among divorces granted in 1977, the marriages which were terminated divided as follows:

	PERCENTAGE	
	Husbands'	*Wives'*
First marriage	75.1%	75.4%
Second marriage	19.2%	18.7%
Third or subsequent marriage	5.7%	5.9%
	100.0%	100.0%

[62]

LENGTH OF MARRIAGE AT DIVORCE

The duration of marriages at the time of divorce decrees were:

	PERCENTAGE	CUMULATIVE PERCENTAGE
Under one year	4.4%	4.4%
One year	8.1%	12.5%
Two years	9.0%	21.5%
Three years	9.2%	30.7%
Four years	8.4%	39.1%
Five years	7.2%	46.3%
Six years	6.2%	52.5%
Seven years	5.7%	58.2%
Eight years	4.7%	62.9%
Nine years	4.1%	67.0%
10–14 years	13.5%	80.5%
15–19 years	8.0%	88.5%
20–24 years	5.4%	93.9%
25–29 years	3.3%	97.2%
30 or more years	2.8%	100.0%
	100.0%	

Median (1979)   6.8 years

[62. 139]

MARRIAGE LENGTH AND CHILDREN

Thirty states reported the median length of marriages at the time they were ended by divorce. The 5 states where marriages had lasted longest were: Massachusetts (8.9 years), Connecticut (8.5 years), Maryland (8.4), New York (8.3), and Rhode Island (8.5).

Those where marriages were briefest were: Wyoming and Utah (both 4.8 years), Kansas (4.9), Idaho (5.0), and Alaska (5.2).

The same 30 states also reported the number of children in marriages ending in divorce: 44.6 percent had no children involved, 25.5 percent had 1 child, 19.7 percent had 2, 7.2 percent had 3, and 3.1 percent had 4 or more.

[139]

AGE AT TIME OF DIVORCE

The following were the ages of divorcing husbands and wives at the time their decree was handed down:

| | HUSBANDS | | WIVES | |
	Percentage	Cumulative Percentage	Percentage	Cumulative Percentage
Under 20	0.9%	0.9%	3.8%	3.8%
20–24	14.7%	15.6%	22.3%	26.1%
25–29	24.0%	39.6%	24.5%	50.6%
30–34	19.8%	59.4%	17.9%	68.5%
35–39	13.4%	72.8%	11.3%	79.8%
40–44	9.4%	82.2%	7.7%	87.5%
45–49	6.9%	89.1%	5.3%	92.8%
50–54	4.8%	93.9%	3.4%	96.2%
55–59	2.9%	96.8%	2.0%	98.2%
60–64	1.6%	98.4%	1.0%	99.2%
65 and up	1.6%	100.0%	0.8%	100.0%
	100.0%		100.0%	

Among husbands who got divorced, the median age at the time of decree was 32.4 years. For wives, the median age was 29.9 years.

[62]

RATIOS OF DIVORCED TO MARRIED PERSONS

In 1960 there were only 28 divorced men for every 1,000 married men; by 1980 that ratio had risen to 79 per 1,000.

Again, in 1960 there were 42 divorced women for every 1,000 married women, but by 1980 that ratio had climbed to 120 per 1,000.

And in 1980 among white women there were 110 who were divorced for every 1,000 who were married; for black women that ratio was 257 per 1,000.

[30]

In November of 1980, the National Center for Health Statistics released a study giving the chances for "marriage dissolution and survivorship" in the United States.

The analysis began by ascertaining how many of the marriages contracted in three different years—1952, 1962, and 1972—had ended in divorce by 1977. The study then projected how many more divorces would occur after 1977. These were the results:

| | PERCENTAGES | | |
| | YEAR OF MARRIAGE | | |
	1952	1962	1972
Already divorced by 1977	28.9%	29.7%	19.6%
Likely post-1977 divorces	3.2%	10.3%	29.6%
Total to be divorced	32.1%	40.0%	49.2%

The general finding is that the more recent the marriage, the greater the likelihood of divorce. Older couples, who married in 1952, will end up with a final divorce rate of 32.1 percent. Younger couples, marrying in 1962 and 1972, stand less chance of having their marriages survive. Indeed, of those who married in 1962, a total of 29.7 percent were divorced 15 years later. And of those who married in 1972, no less than 19.6 percent got divorces within 5 years of their weddings.

The Outlook for 1977 Marriages. The report then projected the outcomes of marriages contracted in 1977, assuming the continuation of current trends. From these figures, it concluded that within the first 3 years (1977–1980) a total of 10.8 percent of the 1977 marriages would end in divorce. In the fourth year (1981) another 5.4 percent would be dissolved, as would a further 4.0 percent in the fifth year (1982), adding up to a 19.2 percent rate for the first 5 years.

Here are the overall projections for 1977 marriages:

	PERCENTAGE MARRIAGES DIVORCED	CUMULATIVE PERCENTAGE MARRIAGES DIVORCED	CUMULATIVE PERCENTAGE OF DIVORCES
1977–1982	19.2%	19.2%	38.7%
1983–1987	13.7%	32.9%	66.3%
1988–1992	7.3%	40.2%	81.0%
1993–1997	4.2%	44.4%	89.5%
1998–2007	4.0%	48.4%	97.6%
After 2007	1.2%	49.6%	100.0%

While it is true that two-thirds of the divorces are likely to occur in the first 10 years of marriage, dissolutions will keep coming at a steady rate. Moreover, these projections do not count either desertions or separations which never bother with divorce proceedings. If those cases are added in then the real dissolution rate will be higher than 49.6 percent.

The study also projected that 47.8 percent of first marriages (defined as those where it is the first time for the wife) will have ended 30 years after the wedding. With remarriages (where it is the second or subsequent marriage for the wife) 55.4 percent will have dissolved by their thirtieth year.

This difference is expected because all first marriages include a pool of people who are unwilling to get divorced, regardless of the circumstances. So the divorce rate for first marriages will always be lower than that for remarriages. Among persons who remarry, everyone in the group (apart from some widows and widowers) has shown him- or herself willing to go through a divorce. As this group contains fewer conscientious objectors, its divorce rate will inevitably be higher.

[65]

REMARRIAGE

Of women who get divorced before they reach the age of 30, 76.3 percent remarry.

Of those who get divorced while in their thirties, 56.2 percent remarry, and for those divorced in their forties, 32.4 percent remarry. For women whose divorce comes when they are 50 or older, only 11.5 percent remarry.

The Census has not published comparable figures for divorced men.

[22]

CHILDREN AND REMARRIAGE

Among divorced women under 30 who have no children, 79.6 percent remarry. Of those who have 1 child, 75.0 percent remarry, for those who have 2 the proportion is 74.9 percent, and with 3 children it is 71.5 percent.

For a woman, youth is a more important determinant of remarriage than whether she has children. Thus among divorced women in their twenties who have 3 children, 71.5 percent will remarry. Whereas among divorced women in their thirties who are childless, only 59.7 percent will remarry.

[22]

Most divorced persons remarry—according to the most recent Census study, 73.0 percent do so. However, the prospect of remarriage is not the same for the sexes. Altogether, 68.8 percent of divorced women remarry, whereas the figure for men is 78.3 percent.

This imbalance begins to set in when people reach their thirties. Here is the information on divorced people who do remarry, showing how many are men and how many women in each group:

	DIVORCED PERSONS WHO REMARRY		
Age Group	*Percentage Men*	*Percentage Women*	*Women per 100 Men*
30–35	52.5%	44.8%	86
35–44	57.9%	42.1%	73
45–54	61.9%	38.1%	62
55–64	67.6%	32.4%	48
65 and up	74.4%	25.6%	34

At the later ages, the imbalance is even greater than these figures suggest. Due to the fact that more men die earlier, by ages 55 to 64 there are only 88 men left for every 100 women. And by 65 and over, only 67 men remain for every 100 women. So, even though there are fewer older men, they participate in more of the remarriages than do women their own age. The chief reason is that divorced men are more apt to choose younger women as their second brides, including women who have not been married before.

Thus of divorced men aged 30 and older who remarry, 26.1 percent marry women who have not been married before. (The rest remarry widows or women who have also been divorced.) However, among the divorced women 30 and older who remarry, only 17.5 percent marry men who have not been married earlier.

But because not as many divorced women remarry as do divorced men, it works out that among the marriages where a divorced person weds someone who has not been married earlier, in 67.3 percent of those cases it is a man marrying a hitherto single bride.

Men Remarry Younger Women. In first marriages, the husband is typically 2.5 years older than the wife. However, with remarriages following divorce the man wants a bride not quite so close to his own age. The most recent figures giving median ages come from the 1970 Census, and they show that when it is a remarriage for the woman and the first time for the man, the man is generally only eleven months older. When both spouses are on a second or later marriage, he is usually 3.7 years her senior. And when it is his second or later marriage and the first one for her, he tends to be 6.2 years older.

If we look at all divorced persons aged 35 through 44 who remarry, here are the ages of their new spouses. (These figures, also the most recent, are from the National Center for Health Statistics' report on 1977 marriages.)

| | PERCENTAGE | |
| | Remarrying Men | Remarrying Women |
Age of New Spouse	Aged 35–44	Aged 35–44
Under 25	12.8%	2.2%
25–29	21.9%	6.3%
30–34	26.2%	13.2%
Same age range	33.2%	44.6%
45–54	5.4%	27.3%
55 and up	0.5%	6.5%
	100.0%	100.0%

What emerges is that 60.9 percent of the remarrying husbands choose younger partners, whereas only 21.7 percent of remarrying wives do so. Indeed, 34.7 percent of the men want brides at least 5 years their junior. Similarly, 33.8 percent of the women marry older husbands, compared with 5.9 percent of the men who remarry older spouses. Partners' ages within the "same age range" of 35 to 44 can only be guessed at, as detailed figures are not available. Such marriages could include as much as a 9-year difference, with a husband of 44 and a bride of 35. The accompanying percentages suggest that this would often be the case.

Here are the comparable figures for a somewhat older group, remarriages of divorced persons aged 45 through 54.

| | PERCENTAGE | |
| | Remarrying Men | Remarrying Women |
Age of New Spouse	Aged 45–54	Aged 45–54
Under 25	3.5%	0.4%
25–34	21.3%	4.1%
35–44	39.2%	16.2%
Same age range	30.6%	45.4%
55–64	5.0%	28.5%
65 and up	0.4%	5.4%
	100.0%	100.0%

[17, 62]

REMARRIAGES BY STATES

The states with the highest proportions of marriages with participants who have been divorced before were: Wyoming (40.8 percent of the brides and 40.3 percent of the grooms), Georgia (39.7 percent for the brides and 41.3 percent of the grooms), Florida (37.6 percent and 39.9 percent), Alaska (39.1 percent and 38.9 percent), and Idaho (38.1 percent of the brides and 39.1 percent of the grooms).

The states with the lowest proportions were: Utah (15.6 percent of the brides and 16.8 percent of the grooms), Wisconsin (17.3 percent and 19.2 percent), Minnesota (17.5 percent and 20.1 percent), New Jersey (18.6 percent and 22.6 percent), and New York (19.2 percent of the brides and 22.5 percent of the grooms).

[62]

WIDOWS

Among the 10,479,000 widowed women, 4.3 percent were under the age of 45; 7.8 percent were between 45 and 54; 19.9 percent were between 55 and 64; and 67.9 percent were 65 or older.

[30]

Just under a third—32.9 percent—of all women who become widows lose their husbands before they themselves reach the age of 40.

Among widows in their twenties who have two children, 76.6 percent remarry, while of those in their thirties who also have two children, 44.8 percent remarry.

[22]

CHAPTER SIX

EMPLOYMENT AND OCCUPATIONS

The "Labor Force." The Bureau of Labor Statistics bases its analysis of employment on a pool of people it calls the "labor force."

This group includes everyone currently *employed* in full-time or part-time jobs. In addition, the labor force includes *unemployed* persons who meet one of two conditions. Individuals are still counted as belonging to the labor force if they have been laid off from jobs, but are not looking for other employment because they are waiting to be called back. Second, they are listed as being in the labor force if they say they are "available for work" and have "looked for jobs" over the past several weeks. This category includes people who want employment for the first time, or who have worked in the past and say they now wish to reenter the job market.

As of 1980 the labor force so defined averaged 106,821,000 persons during the year. Of these, 2,102,000 were members of the armed services, so the "civilian labor force" averaged 104,719,000. And of these persons, 7,448,000—or 7.1 percent—were considered unemployed in the two senses just described.

"EMPLOYED" AND "UNEMPLOYED"

As for those considered to be "employed," the Bureau of Labor Statistics does not distinguish part-time from full-time employment. So far as its figures are concerned, "employed persons comprise all civilians who did a minimum of an hour's work for pay or profit during the reference week"—that is, during the week the BLS conducts its study. Consequently, the total of "employed persons" includes individuals who spent 5 hours each week delivering newspapers. Thus the finding that average annual employment in 1980 totaled 97,270,000 must be construed as a rather liberal figure.

It is important to add that individuals are classed as "unemployed" even if all they want is a part-time job. By the same token, people who have given up looking for a job are no longer counted as "unemployed," and are no longer numbered in the "labor force."

According to the Census Bureau, during 1980 a total of 116,849,000 persons had some kind of earnings. This means that the people in that pool of 116,849,000 persons "took turns" holding the 97,270,000 full-time or part-time jobs that were available on an average day.

FULL-TIME VS. PART-TIME

According to Census Bureau definitions, persons who are employed fall into four general categories:

Full-Time Year-Round Workers. These individuals worked at least 35 hours per week during 50 or more weeks of the year (paid vacations are counted as working weeks). This is a fairly rigorous definition. There are many people who have been fully and steadily employed for most of their lives, but who have had periods between jobs of more than two weeks at various times during their careers. Moreover, there are many well-paid jobs that do not involve 35 hours of work every week. In 1980 a total of 64,948,000 persons (or 55.6 percent of all those employed) met the Full-Time Year-Round criteria.

Part-Time Year-Round Workers. These persons worked for 50 or more weeks during the year, but at jobs that required them to be present for 34 or fewer hours. In 1980 a total of 9,139,000 persons (or 7.8 percent) were in this category.

Full-Time Part-Year Workers. These workers had jobs that called for 35 or more hours of weekly work, but they held them for fewer than 50 weeks. A total of 26,120,000 persons (or 22.4 percent) were in this group.

Part-Time Part-Year Workers. This final group worked for fewer than 50 weeks at jobs requiring less than 35 hours. Overall, 16,643,000 people (or 14.2 percent) were in this category.

[44]

Of the women who worked in 1980, a total of 44.3 percent had full-time year-round jobs. The other 55.7 percent worked less than that schedule.

Among the men, 64.6 percent held full-time year-round jobs, with the remaining 35.4 percent working less than that schedule.

And as it happens, among the persons who were employed on a full-time year-round basis, 64.6 percent were men and 35.4 percent were women.

Of those working at less than full-time year-round jobs, 44.2 percent were men and 55.8 percent were women.

[44]

RACE AND SEX

Altogether, 82.3 percent of white men had some kind of employment, as did 72.1 percent of black men. Among white women, 58.2 percent were employed during the year, as were 55.8 percent of black women.

The proportion of black men who were employed was 87.6 percent of that for white men. However, the proportion of black women who worked stood at 95.9 percent of the figure for white women.

Moreover, black women were more apt to have full-time jobs than were white women as the following breakdowns for employed persons show:

	White Men	Black Men	White Women	Black Women
	PERCENTAGES			
Full-time—full-year	67.3%	59.3%	43.3%	47.2%
Full-time—part-year	20.5%	26.1%	23.8%	27.8%
Part-time—full-year	4.3%	3.7%	11.2%	8.3%
Part-time—part-year	7.9%	10.9%	21.7%	16.7%
	100.0%	100.0%	100.0%	100.0%

In addition, 48.2 percent of black women who are married work a full schedule, whereas only 34.6 percent of white married women do.

[162]

Race and Family Work Experience. Among white couples where the husband had full-time year-round employment, 57.1 percent of the wives were in the labor force. Among black couples where the husband had the same work experience, 68.8 percent of the wives were in the labor force.

Of white women who headed families, 37.5 percent worked at full-time year-round jobs. Among black women who headed families, 31.3 percent had full-time year-round jobs.

[44]

MARITAL STATUS

During a typical week in 1980, a total of 72,023,000 persons were employed at full-time jobs. Of these 44,775,000 (or 62.2 percent) were men and 27,248,000 (or 37.8 percent) were women. By marital status:

- 32,390,000 (or 45.0 percent) were married men.
- 14,913,000 (or 20.7 percent) were married women.
- 8,646,000 (or 12.0 percent) were single men.
- 6,484,000 (or 9.0 percent) were single women.
- 5,851,000 (or 8.1 percent) were women who were separated, widowed, or divorced.
- 3,739,000 (or 5.2 percent) were men who were separated, widowed, or divorced.

Thus among the nonmarried persons in full-time jobs, the sexual ratio is almost equal: 12,385,000 men and 12,335,000 women.

[79]

EMPLOYMENT AND THE POPULATION

The Bureau of Labor Statistics prepares figures on the proportion of employed persons in the population as a whole. In 1980, for example, 73 percent of all men aged 20 or over were employed. Back in 1948, when fewer people were in college and retirements came later, the figure was 85 percent. However, for women of 20 and over, the employment-population ratio rose from 30 to 48 percent between 1948 and 1980.

The figures for breadwinners by states are available for 1979, and indicate that the following states had the highest proportions of men 20 or over employed: Wyoming (85.4 percent), Colorado (81.8 percent), Nevada (81.5 percent), and Texas and South Dakota (both 80.7 percent).

These states had the lowest ratios for men: Florida (67.3 percent), West Virginia (69.0 percent), Maine (70.3 percent), Arkansas (70.5 percent), and Mississippi (71.5 percent).

The following states had the highest employment-population ratios for women 20 and over: Alaska (56.9 percent), Nevada (54.8 percent), Hawaii (54.3 percent), and Minnesota and Kansas (both 54.1 percent).

And these had the lowest rates for women: Louisiana (42.3 percent),

Florida (42.5 percent), Pennsylvania (42.6 percent), Alabama (42.9 percent), and Arizona (44.2 percent).

[164]

YOUNG PEOPLE: EDUCATION OR EMPLOYMENT

Of the 24,346,000 young men and women aged 16 to 21, a total of 9,421,000 (or 38.7 percent) said that "going to school" was their "major activity." Of the remainder, 10,089,000 (or 41.4 percent) were employed, 1,776,000 (or 7.3 percent) said they were looking for work, and 3,060,000 (or 12.6 percent) were neither at school nor employed nor looking for work.

Here is how these 12,015,000 young men and 12,331,000 young women were apportioned:

	PERCENTAGES	
	Young Men	*Young Women*
Going to school	40.0%	37.5%
Employed	44.3%	38.7%
Looking for work	8.3%	6.3%
Not looking for work	7.4%	17.5%
	100.0%	100.0%

Among those going to school, 2,719,000 (or 28.9 percent) also had some kind of employment; another 643,000 (or 6.8 percent) said they were looking for jobs; and the remaining 6,060,000 (or 64.3 percent) were not working or looking for work.

[79]

EMPLOYMENT OF OLDER PERSONS

In 1950 a total of 45.8 percent of all men aged 65 and over belonged to the labor force. By 1960 the proportion had fallen to 33.1 percent, and by 1970 to 26.8 percent. In 1979 only 20.0 percent remained in the labor force.

However, for women the picture was rather different. In 1950 of those 65 and over, 9.7 percent belonged to the labor force. In 1960 the proportion was up to 10.8 percent, and in 1970 it was down to 9.7 percent again. In 1979 it had fallen again, but only slightly, to 8.3 percent.

Figures for persons aged 60 through 64 are available for 1960 on. In that year, 81.1 percent of the men were in the labor force; by 1970 the figure was down to 75.0 percent; and in 1979 it had declined to 61.8 percent.

For women 60 through 64, a total of 31.4 belonged to the labor force in 1960; in 1970 the proportion was up to 36.1 percent; and by 1979 it had decreased a bit to 33.9 percent.

[162]

LENGTH OF EMPLOYMENT

In May of 1979, the Bureau of Labor Statistics obtained information on how long full-time workers in private industry had been employed in their current jobs:

	PERCENTAGES	
Years	Men	Women
25 or more	8.5%	3.3%
20 to 24	4.5%	2.4%
15 to 19	6.1%	4.3%
10 to 14	11.3%	9.0%
5 to 9	19.0%	17.9%
1 to 4	30.2%	36.2%
Less than 1	20.3%	26.8%
	100.0%	100.0%

[154]

WORKWEEK

Wage and salaried employees in full-time occupations put in an average workweek of 42.3 hours. (In some cases, some of these hours are counted and paid for as overtime; in other cases they are not.)

Among these workers, 83.5 percent had a 5-day workweek. Another 3.5 percent worked 5.5 days, 8.9 percent were on the job for 6 days, and 1.9 percent for 7. The other 2.2 percent completed their hours in fewer than 5 days.

[161]

Work Attendance. During an average week in 1980, of the 97,270,000 persons who had jobs, 5,785,000 (or 5.9 percent) were not at work. Of these, 3,268,000 were on vacation, 1,404,000 were sick, 153,000 could not get to their jobs because of the weather, 104,000 were involved in industrial disputes, and the remaining 856,000 had various other reasons. (This last category included family obligations or emergencies, as well as people who simply didn't feel like going to work.)

[79]

EARNINGS

In 1980 average hourly earnings for all production workers came to $6.66—or $266.40 for a 40-hour week.

Among those most highly paid were workers in basic steel production ($11.39 per hour), motion picture production ($11.13), petroleum refining ($10.94), coal mining ($10.83), construction ($9.94), motor vehicle manufacturing ($9.89), and utility services ($9.64).

At the other end of the scale were workers in: variety stores ($3.87 per hour), children's outerware ($4.15), hotels and motels ($4.42), shoe stores ($4.46), knitting mills ($4.76), toys and sporting goods ($4.98), household furniture ($5.11), and watches, clocks, and watch cases ($5.24).

[78]

EARNINGS: SEX AND OCCUPATIONS

For every $1,000 made by men in these occupations during 1981, women received the following amounts:

Postal clerks	$939	Waiters and waitresses	$720
Cashiers	$920	Accountants	$712
Security guards	$907	Lawyers	$710
Packers and wrappers	$854	Real estate agents	$709
Editors and reporters	$850	School administrators	$699
Bartenders	$844	Bookkeepers	$694
High school teachers	$829	Manufacturing assemblers	$690
Elementary school teachers	$822	Office machine operators	$688
Nursing aides and orderlies	$822	Engineers	$678
Textile operatives	$813	Sales clerks	$674
Stock handlers	$812	Insurance agents	$671
Physicians and dentists	$809	Health administrators	$655
College teachers	$803	Office managers	$655
Social workers	$799	Personnel workers	$643
Cleaning service workers	$756	Blue-collar supervisors	$642
Social scientists	$749	Buyers	$623
Computer programmers	$736	Advertising workers	$617
Cooks	$734	Bank officers and financial managers	$602

[169]

Each $100.00 in compensation paid to the average employee divides out as follows: Straight-Time Pay, $74.80; Premium Pay and Bonuses, $3.00; Vacations and Holidays, $5.70; Sickness and Other Leaves, $1.40.

The remaining $15.10 is paid into various accounts on the employee's behalf: Social Security, $4.10; Private Pensions and Savings Plans, $5.20; Health and Other Insurance, $3.60; and Workmen's Compensation and Unemployment Funds, $2.20.

[73]

UNEMPLOYMENT

As of July 1982, a total of 10,790,000 persons were unemployed, an overall unemployment rate of 9.8 percent. (In 1969, the lowest postwar year, the rate was 3.5 percent.) The rates for various groups in the labor force follow (some individuals can be counted within several of these groups). While the overall unemployment rate fluctuates with changing economic conditions, the various groups' relation to the total rate remains comparatively constant.

	GROUPS' PERCENTAGE RATES	TIMES THE OVERALL RATE
Black teenagers	49.7%	5.07
White teenagers	21.0%	2.14
All black persons	18.5%	1.89
Young men aged 20–24	15.9%	1.62
Blue-collar workers	14.4%	1.47
Persons of Hispanic origin	13.9%	1.42
Young women aged 20–24	12.9%	1.32
Women heads of households	12.0%	1.22
Part-time workers	11.5%	1.17
Workers in private industry	10.2%	1.04
Full-time workers	9.5%	0.97
All white persons	8.7%	0.89
Service workers	8.0%	0.82
Men aged 25 and over	7.5%	0.77
Married women	7.4%	0.76
Women aged 25 and over	7.4%	0.76
Married men	6.6%	0.67
Farm workers	6.1%	0.62
White-collar workers	4.9%	0.50
Government workers	4.6%	0.47

[170]

OCCUPATIONS

Unemployment rates by occupational areas were as follows in July 1982: managers and administrators, 3.7 percent; professional and technical workers, 3.3 percent; sales workers, 5.4 percent; clerical workers, 6.9 percent; craft workers, 10.9 percent; transport operatives, 11.6 percent; factory workers, 17.4 percent; general laborers, 18.6 percent; and construction workers, 20.3 percent.

DURATION AND REASONS

Among the unemployed, 37.2 percent had been out of work for less than 5 weeks; 29.5 percent had been unemployed for 5 to 14 weeks; 16.7 percent had not had jobs for 15 to 26 weeks; and another 16.7 percent had not worked for 27 or more weeks. The average duration of unemployment was 15.6 weeks.

Those listed as unemployed fell into two principal groups. The first consisted of persons who had been working, which amounted to 64.9 percent of all the unemployed. In this group were individuals who had been laid off by their employers (19.3 percent of all unemployed); those who had lost their jobs for other reasons (38.1 percent); and those who had quit their jobs voluntarily (7.5 percent). The second group included persons who were seeking their first job (11.6 percent of the unemployed total) and individuals who wished to gain employment after a period of not working (23.5 percent).

[170]

Who is Considered to be "Unemployed"? The Bureau of Labor Statistics does not count among the "unemployed" those persons who have given up looking for work. Although there are no precise figures for these "discouraged" individuals, the Bureau estimated that there were 1,497,000 people in this group as of July of 1982. It might be noted that women accounted for approximately two thirds of the "discouraged" category.

In addition, the figure for unemployment does not include people who are employed in part-time jobs, but who would prefer full-time work if they could find suitable positions. In July 1982 there were 2,001,000 persons listed as working "part-time for economic reasons" but who "usually work full-time." (These individuals could be considered "partially unemployed," but the Bureau does not have such a category.)

On the other hand, the unemployment total includes people who only want—and are only looking for—part-time employment. In July 1982 there were 2,325,000 such individuals, and they made up 21.5 percent of the total unemployment rate.

[172]

[172]

UNEMPLOYMENT BENEFITS

Throughout 1980 a total of 10,000.851 workers applied for and received some unemployment benefits. In an average week, 2,843,885 persons were on the benefit rolls. In addition, during 1980 a total of 3,076,371 individuals exhausted the benefits to which they were entitled.

For the nation as a whole, the average weekly unemployment check came to $105.66. The states with the highest average benefits were: Illinois ($132.52 per week), Minnesota ($127.53), Ohio ($127.05), Wisconsin ($125.06), and Iowa ($120.37).

The states with the lowest average benefits were: Mississippi ($72.88 per week), Alabama ($76.61), Georgia ($78.44), Florida ($79.33), and Tennessee ($80.88).

[168]

OCCUPATIONAL CHANGES

Between 1970 and 1980, occupational changes continued trends which have been visible for a generation. During the decade, the number of employed persons rose from 78,627,000 to 97,270,000, an increase of 23.7 percent. The Bureau of Labor Statistics divides occupations into ten general categories. These groups had the following proportions of the employment force in 1970 and 1980:

| | PERCENTAGES | | Percentage Change in Proportion |
	1970	1980	
Professional and technical	14.5%	16.1%	+11.0%
Managers and administrators	8.1%	11.2%	+38.3%
Sales	7.1%	6.3%	−11.3%
Clerical	17.8%	18.6%	+ 4.5%
Craft workers	13.9%	12.9%	− 7.2%
Factory operatives	14.1%	10.6%	−24.8%
Transport operatives	3.8%	3.6%	− 5.3%
Laborers	4.7%	4.6%	− 2.1%
Service workers	12.9%	13.3%	+ 3.1%
Farm workers	3.1%	2.8%	− 9.7%
TOTAL	100.0%	100.0%	− 9.0%

[15, 78]

EXPANDING OCCUPATIONS

Between 1970 and 1980, employment as a whole rose by 23.7 percent. The following occupations were among those that increased at a greater rate than the total figure:

	1970	1980	PERCENTAGE INCREASE
Computer operators	117,000	522,000	346.2%
Teachers' aides	132,000	383,000	190.2%
Social scientists	109,000	278,000	155.0%
Health administrators	84,000	210,000	150.0%
Roofers	58,000	139,000	139.7%
Sales demonstrators	38,000	91,000	139.5%
Real estate agents	262,000	582,000	122.1%
Bank tellers	249,000	531,000	113.3%
Restaurant and bar managers	322,000	672,000	108.7%
Receptionists	304,000	629,000	106.9%
Educational administrators	209,000	431,000	106.2%
Lawyers	272,000	547,000	101.1%
Nursery and kindergarten teachers	125,000	243,000	94.4%
Social workers	267,000	499,000	86.9%
Cashiers	832,000	1,554,000	86.8%
Building superintendents	83,000	154,000	85.5%
Insurance adjusters	96,000	174,000	81.3%
Vocational counselors	107,000	181,000	69.2%
Nurses, dieticians, and therapists	945,000	1,574,000	66.6%
Foresters and conservationists	40,000	65,000	62.5%
Architects	56,000	90,000	60.7%
Personnel workers	291,000	452,000	55.3%
Statistical clerks	250,000	387,000	54.8%
Librarians	129,000	199,000	54.3%
Bus drivers	236,000	356,000	50.8%
Machinists	379,000	567,000	49.6%
Accountants	704,000	1,047,000	48.7%
Secretaries	2,705,000	3,876,000	43.3%
Carpenters	844,000	1,185,000	40.4%
Miners	155,000	215,000	38.7%
Electricians	469,000	648,000	38.2%
Truck drivers	1,381,000	1,844,000	33.5%

[15, 78]

DECLINING OCCUPATIONS

But while employment as a whole increased by 23.7 percent between 1970 and 1980, the following occupations actually declined in numbers:

	1970	1980	PERCENTAGE DECREASE
Tailors	67,000	26,000	−61.2%
Stenographers	128,000	64,000	−50.0%
Newspaper vendors	182,000	110,000	−39.6%
Barbers	167,000	108,000	−35.3%
Textile operatives	430,000	323,000	−24.9%
Garage workers	437,000	337,000	−22.9%
Telephone operators	408,000	316,000	−22.5%
Tool and die makers	202,000	176,000	−12.9%
File clerks	360,000	324,000	−10.0%
Sewers and stitchers	869,000	788,000	− 9.3%
Delivery drivers	625,000	584,000	− 6.6%
Household workers	1,089,000	1,041,000	− 4.4%
Garbage collectors	72,000	69,000	− 4.2%
Mail carriers	253,000	244,000	− 3.6%
Key punch operators	273,000	266,000	− 2.6%
Elementary school teachers	1,415,000	1,383,000	− 2.3%

[15, 78]

FEMALE- AND MALE-DOMINATED OCCUPATIONS

The following were the most pronounced "female" *occupations:*

	PERCENTAGE
Secretaries	99.1%
Dental assistants	98.6%
Nursery and kindergarten teachers	98.4%
Child care providers	97.4%
Practical nurses	97.5%
Dressmakers	97.2%
Chambermaids	97.0%
Maids and servants	96.9%
Typists	96.9%
Sales demonstrators	96.7%
Private housekeepers	96.6%
Registered nurses	96.5%
Receptionists	96.3%

The following were the most pronounced "male" *occupations:*

	PERCENTAGE
Stonemasons	99.9%
Plumbers	99.4%
Auto mechanics	99.3%
Roofers	99.3%
Cutters and loggers	99.0%
Electricians	98.8%
Carpet installers	98.7%
Firefighters	98.7%
Carpenters	98.5%
Truck drivers	97.8%
Tool and die makers	97.2%
Garbage collectors	97.1%
Sheetmetal workers	96.9%
Surveyors	96.6%

(continued)

(continued)

The following were the most pronounced "female" *occupations:*

	PERCENTAGE
Keypunch operators	95.9%
Sewers and stitchers	95.7%
Bank tellers	92.7%
Telephone operators	91.8%
Bookkeepers	90.5%
Billing clerks	90.2%

The following were the most pronounced "male" *occupations:*

	PERCENTAGE
Cabinetmakers	96.3%
Engineers	96.0%
Clergy	95.8%
Dentists	95.7%
Welders	94.7%
Police officers	94.5%
Office machine repairers	93.7%
Architects	93.3%

[78]

Men in "Women's" Occupations. Between 1970 and 1980 more men entered several occupations traditionally associated with women.

They rose from being 5.6 percent of nurses, dieticians, and therapists to 6.7 percent; from 5.6 percent of telephone operators to 8.2 percent; and from 9.9 percent of hairdressers to 11.7 percent. Men also increased their proportion among stenographers from 6.3 percent to 10.9 percent; and among library assistants, from 21.3 percent to 22.4 percent.

[15, 78]

RACE AND OCCUPATIONS

Black Americans accounted for 11.2 percent of all employed persons in 1980. Here are some exceptions to that average, where they comprised more than that percentage:

	PERCENTAGE
Registered nurses	11.4%
Clerical supervisors	12.0%
Barbers	13.0%
Meat cutters	13.3%
Nursery and kindergarten teachers	13.6%
Computer operators	14.0%
Shipping clerks	14.1%
Factory assemblers	15.2%
Typists	15.5%
Telephone operators	15.8%
Dressmakers and seamstresses	15.9%
Security guards	16.8%
Farm laborers	16.9%

(continued)

	PERCENTAGE
Vocational counselors	17.7%
Cooks	18.4%
Social workers	18.5%
Bus drivers	19.9%
File clerks	21.6%
Keypunch operators	21.8%
Textile operators	22.6%
Postal clerks	24.2%
Taxi drivers	25.3%
Nursing aides and orderlies	28.8%
Garbage collectors	34.8%
Clothing pressers	40.4%
Household servants	53.4%

[78]

And here are some occupations in which blacks comprised less than that percentage:

	PERCENTAGE
Earth drillers	1.8%
Real estate agents	2.1%
Surveyors	2.2%
Tool and die makers	2.3%
Foresters and conservationists	3.1%
Newspaper vendors	3.6%
Sales managers	4.4%
Sales demonstrators	4.4%
Photographers	4.5%
Legal secretaries	5.4%
Bartenders	6.0%
Window dressers	6.1%
Sheetmetal workers	6.2%
Clergy	6.8%
Typesetters	6.9%
Bill collectors	7.7%
Telephone installers	7.8%
Firefighters	7.9%
Receptionists	8.1%
Accountants	8.2%
Police and detectives	8.4%
Bank tellers	8.7%
Aircraft mechanics	9.1%
Plumbers	9.2%

[78]

WOMEN AND EMPLOYMENT

In 1960 the labor force was composed 33.4 percent of women and 66.6 percent of men, but by 1980 women accounted for 42.4 percent and men were 57.6 percent.

Looked at another way, labor force participation of women rose from 37.7 percent in 1960 to 51.4 percent in 1980. During this time, the rate for men actually fell, from 83.3 percent to 77.6 percent.

[71]

PROPORTION OF POSITIONS HELD BY WOMEN

The states where women formed the largest proportions of the workforce were: Hawaii (45.9 percent), North Carolina (44.4 percent), Arkansas (44.3 percent), Rhode Island and South Carolina (both 44.0 percent), and Virginia (43.7 percent).

The states where women had the lowest representation were: West Virginia (36.8 percent), Wyoming (39.3 percent), Idaho (39.6 percent), and Oregon and Louisiana (each 39.8 percent).

[75]

PROPORTIONS OF WOMEN WHO ARE WORKING

The states that had the highest proportions of working women were: Alaska (55.8 percent of all women worked), Minnesota (54.8 percent), Kansas (54.5 percent), Nevada (54.2 percent), and South Dakota (53.1 percent).

The states where women were least likely to work were: West Virginia (35.6 percent of all women worked), Louisiana (41.1 percent), Alabama (41.3 percent), Pennsylvania and Florida (both 42.4 percent), and Mississippi (43.5 percent).

[75]

SEXUAL COMPOSITION

Changing proportions of occupations were closely related to the sexual makeup of the workforce. Between 1970 and 1980 the number of women who were employed rose from 30,286,000 to 41,281,000, an increase of 36.3 percent. In the same period male employment went from 49,441,000 to 55,989,000, a rise of only 13.2 percent.

Here are the percentages for the positions held by women in each occupational group in 1970 and 1980:

	PERCENTAGES	
	1970	*1980*
Professional and technical	40.2%	44.3%
Managers and administrators	16.7%	26.1%
Sales	40.0%	45.3%
Clerical	73.6%	80.1%
Craft workers	5.0%	6.0%
Factory operatives	39.2%	40.1%
Transport operatives	4.4%	8.0%
Laborers	9.0%	11.6%
Service workers	60.5%	62.0%
Farm workers	10.0%	18.0%
TOTAL	38.0%	42.4%

[15, 78]

CHANGES IN WOMEN'S EMPLOYMENT

Women's employment also changed in distribution during the decade. Here are the changes in proportions among the occupational groups in 1970 and 1980:

	PERCENTAGES		PERCENTAGE CHANGE IN PROPORTION
	1970	*1980*	
Professional and technical	15.3%	16.7%	+ 9.2%
Managers and administrators	3.6%	6.9%	+91.7%
Sales	7.4%	6.8%	− 8.1%
Clerical	34.5%	35.1%	+ 1.7%
Craft workers	1.8%	1.8%	No change
Factory operatives	14.6%	10.0%	−31.5%
Transport operatives	0.5%	0.7%	+40.0%
Laborers	1.0%	1.3%	+30.0%
Service workers	20.5%	19.5%	− 4.9%
Farm workers	0.8%	1.2%	+50.0%
TOTAL	100.0%	100.0%	

[15, 78]

ADVANCES IN WOMEN'S REPRESENTATION

In the decade between 1970 and 1980, women's representation in the nation's labor force grew from 38.1 percent to 42.4 percent.

While in terms of percentage *points* this was a rise of only 4.3 points, the women's *proportion* of the work force increased by 11.1 percent.

The following were some occupations at which the proportionate rise of women exceeded 11.1 percent:

	1970	1980	Rise in Women's Proportion
Barbers	4.7%	15.7%	234.0%
Lawyers	4.8%	12.8%	166.7%
Compositors and typesetters	15.0%	34.5%	130.0%
Insurance adjusters	26.7%	57.5%	115.4%
Advertising agents	19.5%	41.8%	114.4%
Computer operators	29.2%	59.8%	104.8%
Bank and financial managers	17.6%	33.6%	90.9%
Social scientists	19.2%	36.0%	87.5%
Stock and bond sales agents	9.1%	16.4%	80.2%
Bus drivers	28.0%	44.9%	60.4%
Real estate agents	31.9%	50.7%	58.9%
Shipping clerks	14.5%	21.6%	49.0%
Bakers	29.8%	42.9%	44.0%
Educational administrators	26.4%	37.1%	40.5%
Accountants	26.0%	36.2%	39.2%
Decorators and window dressers	57.6%	71.1%	23.4%

[15, 78]

DOMESTIC SERVANTS

In 1870, of the 1,836,000 women who were employed, 52.3 percent were domestic servants. By 1880 the proportion had fallen to 40.7 percent, and by 1910, it was down to 22.1 percent.

In 1940 the figure was still at 20.4 percent. But by 1960 household servants had dropped to 8.9 percent of all women workers, and by 1970 they were down to 5.1 percent.

In 1979, of 40,446,000 employed women, 1,062,000—or 2.6 percent—were domestic servants.

In 1979, among women working as domestic servants, 41.3 were under the age of 35. Of these, 92.5 percent were white, 6.7 percent were black, and 0.8 percent were of other races. Among the 58.7 percent aged 35 or over, exactly equal proportions were black and white—49.1 percent—with the remaining 1.8 percent of other races.

[161]

In 1960 only 34.5 percent of all women were in the labor force. By 1980 that proportion had grown to 51.4 percent.

- Among married women living with their husbands, those in the labor force rose from 30.5 percent in 1960 to 50.2 percent in 1980.
- For women who had never been married, labor force participation increased even more sharply: from 44.1 percent to 62.7 percent.
- On the other hand, among women who were widowed, the proportion actually declined, from 29.8 percent to 22.6 percent, largely because by 1980 widows tended to be older.
- Among all married women with children under 18, membership in the labor force rose from 27.6 percent to 54.2 percent between 1960 and 1980. For those who had children under 6, the figure rose from 18.6 percent to 45.0 percent.

However, as was indicated earlier, labor force participation includes part-time workers and persons who may not work the entire year, plus individuals who are unemployed and others seeking to enter the job market.

[71, 167]

WORK EXPERIENCE OF MARRIED WOMEN

Another Bureau of Labor Statistics study, issued in 1981, uses "work experience" as its measure rather than "labor force participation." The "work experience" rate tends to be somewhat higher, as it includes everyone who held a job at any time during the year. ("Labor force participation" counts only those in the labor market during a specific—or an average—week.)

Using this criterion, the study found that 56.5 percent of all married women had had some work experience during the previous year. Interestingly, among those who had children under 18, the work experience rate was even higher: 60.7 percent. And of the women who had children under the age of 6, 55.5 percent had held a job.

As it happens, the lowest proportion of working wives was among women whose husbands were aged 55 or over. Only 34.5 percent of these wives worked, and only 16.5 percent had full-time year-round jobs.

Mothers Who Work Full-Time. While 60.7 percent of all married mothers had some work experience, only 21.8 percent had full-time year-round employment. For mothers with children under 6, the full-time year-round figure was down at 15.0 percent.

However, among black married women with children under 6, 29.1 percent had full-time year-round jobs. The comparable figure for white mothers was 13.6 percent.

[77]

CHILDREN OF WORKING MOTHERS

As of March of 1981, there were 59,148,000 American children under the age of 18, and of these, 31,785,000—or 53.7 percent—had mothers in the labor force. Of the 18,306,000 children under the age of 6, 8,216,000—or 44.9 percent—had mothers in that group.

Among the children under 18 who lived with both parents, 53.0 percent had mothers in the labor force. Of those who lived only with their mother, 62.8 percent of the children had mothers in the labor force.

Mothers' Marital Status and Race. Among white children under 18 who lived with two parents, 51.9 percent had mothers in the labor force. However, for black children in two-parent families the figure was considerably higher: 63.6 percent.

At the same time, if white children lived only with their mother, 66.5 percent had that parent in the labor force. But for black children in comparable households, the proportion with labor-force mothers was 52.7 percent.

[164]

MARRIED WORKING MOTHERS AND HUSBANDS' INCOMES

Among families with children under 18, the following percentages of wives are in the labor force when their husbands' incomes are in these ranges:

	PERCENTAGE
$15,000–$20,000	54.6%
$20,000–$25,000	49.1%
$25,000–$35,000	46.2%
$35,000–$50,000	38.9%
$50,000 and over	29.3%

[77]

The most recent figures on daycare arrangements for children of working mothers are for 1977. In that year, 2,669,000 children under the age of 6 had mothers who worked at full-time jobs. Their arrangements can be compared with those prevailing in 1958, when 2,039,000 children had full-time working mothers.

	PERCENTAGES	
	1958	*1977*
In the child's own home:		
Cared for by the father	14.7%	10.6%
By another relative	27.7%	11.4%
By a nonrelative	14.2%	6.6%
	56.6%	28.6%
In another home:		
By a relative	14.5%	20.8%
By a nonrelative	12.7%	26.6%
	27.2%	47.4%
Group care center	4.5%	14.6%
"Child cares for self"	0.6%	0.4%
Mother takes child to work	11.2%	9.0%
	16.3%	24.0%

[42]

WORKING COUPLES

In marriages where both spouses work and the husband has a professional position, the wives are in the following fields: professional (39.7%), managerial (6.4%), clerical (33.7%), sales (6.6%), other (13.6%).

Among husbands with managerial positions, the wives are in the following fields: professional (21.0%), managerial (13.1%), clerical (41.1%), sales (8.2%), and other (16.6%).

Altogether, in marriages with professional husbands, 46.1 percent of the wives have professional or managerial positions. In marriages with managerial husbands, 34.4 percent of the wives have professional or managerial positions.

[164]

In 1970 the Census analyzed husbands who had earnings of $15,000 or over to see how many had wives who worked. The following percentages of husbands with these occupations also had working wives:

	PERCENTAGE
Physicians	17.7%
Stock and bond salesmen	20.6%
Dentists	20.7%
Bank officers	20.9%
Welders	22.0%
Lawyers	22.2%
Sales managers	23.1%
Engineers	25.1%
Advertising executives	26.8%
Accountants	27.8%
Carpenters	28.0%
Truck drivers	28.1%
Architects	29.5%
Insurance agents	29.8%
Realtors	30.9%
Pharmacists	31.4%
College professors	34.3%
Editors and reporters	34.7%
Bar and restaurant managers	43.9%

Note: The Census Bureau has said that because of budgetary cutbacks it will not be able to publish comparable computations from its 1980 records.

[18]

SELF-EMPLOYMENT

Between 1949 and 1959 the proportion of self-employed persons in the nonagricultural labor force fell from 12.0 percent to 10.4 percent.

From 1959 to 1969 the percentage dropped even further, from 10.4 percent to 7.0 percent.

However, during 1969 through 1979, the self-employed proportion had stopped dropping, and was still at 7.0 percent. Indeed, along with the rise of the overall labor force, the number of self-employed persons increased from 5,253,000 to 6,652,000 between 1969 and 1979.

[274]

Of the 11,345,616 proprietorships, 8,598,763 (or 75.8 percent) were held by men and 2,158,365 (or 19.0 percent) were owned by women, with the remaining 588,488 (or 5.2 percent) jointly owned.

The following kinds of businesses were among those most likely to be owned by women:

Direct sales operations	296,023
Farms	277,093
Real estate agencies	210,285
Beauty shops	196,305
Eating or drinking places	57,296
Private nurses	48,832
Accountants and bookkeepers	41,049
Management and public relations	32,227
Apparel shops	30,311
Entertainers and producers	23,275
Gift shops	22,221
Food stores	20,842
Home furnishings	18,089
Hotels and lodging places	16,736
Construction companies	16,129
Florists	15,930
Insurance agencies	13,405
Trucking companies	9,399
Gas stations	4,023

The average receipts for businesses owned by women came to $12,826, whereas businesses owned by men averaged $41,558.

[106]

UNION MEMBERSHIP

In 1980 a total of 20,095,000 Americans, or 23.0 percent of all employed workers, belonged to labor unions.

Among white-collar workers, 15.3 percent were union members; in blue-collar employment, union membership totaled 39.1 percent; and in service industries, 16.2 percent of the workers belonged to unions.

Of all employed men, 28.4 percent were union members. For employed women, the proportion was 15.9 percent.

Among workers who were white, 22.2 percent belonged to unions. Of those who were black or other races, 29.0 percent were members.

Black men were 21.6 percent more likely to belong to unions than were white men. And black women were 64.4 percent more apt to be union members than were white women. Among the men who belonged to unions, 12.7 percent were black; whereas among women union members, 20.1 percent were black.

[80]

UNIONS AND INDUSTRIES

The following are the percentages of unionized workers in various areas of employment.

Railroads, 81.8 percent; U.S. Postal Service, 73.7 percent; automobile manufacturing, 61.2 percent; primary metals, 58.4 percent; paper manufacturing, 49.1 percent; aircraft manufacturing, 42.4 percent; food processing, 37.5 percent; local governments, 36.9 percent; fabricated metals, 36.1 percent.

Education, 34.3 percent; petroleum processing, 34.1 percent; mining, 32.1 percent; construction industry, 31.6 percent; rubber and plastics, 29.6 percent; furniture manufacturing, 27.0 percent; electrical equipment, 26.9 percent; state governments, 26.0 percent; chemicals processing, 25.8 percent.

Apparel, 25.1 percent; printing, 20.2 percent; federal government, 19.3 percent; hospitals, 17.7 percent; textiles, 14.9 percent; insurance and real estate, 5.5 percent; eating and drinking places, 4.9 percent; agriculture, 3.5 percent; banking and finance, 1.6 percent.

Altogether, 21.7 percent of workers in private employment are represented by unions. In government employment, the proportion is 43.4 percent.

[80]

UNIONS AND EARNINGS

Among workers represented by unions, average weekly earnings came to $320 in 1980. For workers not represented by unions, average weekly earnings were $278.

The following were the respective average earnings for union and nonunion workers in various industries.

Where Union Workers Received More. Constuction, $405 and $284; retail trade, $292 and $222; local governments, $316 and $251; transportation, $381 and $326; education, $303 and $261; federal government, $395 and $366; hospitals, $266 and $256.

Where Union Workers Received Less. Food processing, $301 and $308; metals industries, $317 and $322; wholesale trade, $300 and $314; communications, $344 and $369; automotive manufacturing, $347 and $385; chemicals and petroleum processing, $310 and $382.

[80]

MEMBERSHIP BY STATES

The states with the highest proportions of workers who were union members were: New York (39.2 percent), West Virginia (36.8 percent), Michigan (34.6 percent), Pennsylvania (34.2 percent), and Washington (33.1 percent).

The states with the lowest union percentages were: North Carolina (6.5 percent), South Carolina (6.7 percent), South Dakota (10.3 percent), Mississippi (11.0 percent), and Florida (11.7 percent).

[72]

UNION RECOGNITION ELECTIONS

During the year ending September 30, 1980, a total of 7,905 elections were held in which employees decided whether or not they wished to be represented by a union.

The numbers of elections ranged from 1,024 in California and 579 in Ohio, down to 10 in Wyoming and 13 in Vermont.

In 3,543 of these ballotings (or 44.8 percent) the workers decided to have a union. In the other 4,362 (or 55.2 percent) they voted against a union.

Altogether, 506,040 workers cast ballots in union representation elections. Of this group, 246,424 workers (or 48.7 percent) voted for a union, and 259,616 (or 51.3 percent) voted against having one.

The states where the highest proportions of workers voted in favor of having a union were: Virginia (82.3 percent), Nebraska (60.5 percent), Delaware (58.8 percent), South Dakota (58.6 percent), New Mexico (55.6 percent), Nevada (54.6 percent), New York (54.2 percent), Kansas (53.8 percent), Rhode Island (53.4 percent), and Hawaii (52.7 percent).

States where the lowest percentages of votes were cast for a union were: Arkansas (34.7 percent), North Dakota (36.2 percent), Colorado (39.7 percent), Maine (40.3 percent), Louisiana (40.4 percent), Oregon (40.8 percent), Georgia (41.1 percent), Washington (41.1 percent), South Carolina (41.2 percent), and Pennsylvania (41.2 percent).

[137]

Between 1960 and 1980 the country experienced a total of 93,572 "work stoppages"—either strikes or lockouts—involving 40,975,000 workers. The overall number of workdays lost came to 669,289,000, or an annual average of 33,464,000 days during the 20-year period.

- 1970 had the largest number of workers (3,305,000) involved in stoppages (5,716) and the most days lost (66,414,000).

- 1963 had the fewest workers (941,000) involved in stoppages (3,362) and the fewest days lost (16,100,000).

- The year running from December of 1980 through November of 1981 had 3,759 stoppages, involving 1,163,000 workers, resulting in 25,635,000 days lost from work.

[168]

CHAPTER SEVEN

INCOME AND EXPENDITURES

Every March the Census Bureau asks a nationwide sample of people for information about the income they received the previous year. This means that the first reports on the 1980 incomes appeared late in 1981. More complete studies take even longer to prepare, so in some cases the most recent statistics are for incomes of 1979.

Analysis of income can be approached in several different ways. First comes *family* income, which means the total amount from all members of the family who are living together.

Second are the incomes of persons the Census calls *unrelated individuals*. These are people who live alone or with individuals to whom they are not related. Generally speaking, the incomes of these persons are considered as separate sums regardless of the arrangement they have with their living mates.

Incomes of individuals can also be analyzed without reference to their living arrangements, and here the Census simply speaks of the incomes of *persons*. Moreover, those incomes can be divided into earnings from employment and money coming from other sources.

In 1980 the country had 60,309,000 family units, which the Census defines as two or more related persons sharing living quarters. The incomes of these families had the following distribution:

	NUMBERS	PERCENTAGE
Over $75,000	948,000	1.6%
$50,000–$75,000	3,079,000	5.1%
$25,000–$50,000	19,684,000	32.6%
$20,000–$25,000	8,263,000	13.7%
$15,000–$20,000	8,414,000	14.0%
$10,000–$15,000	8,537,000	14.2%
$5,000–$10,000	7,646,000	12.7%
Under $5,000	3,736,000	6.2%
TOTAL	60,309,000	100.0%

The median income for these families came to $21,023; the average was $23,974. (The "median income" is the income of the one family at the exact midpoint when all 60,309,000 families are ranked in order of their incomes. The "average income" is computed by taking the aggregate income received by all the families (in this case, $1,445,847,966,000) and dividing that figure by the number of families.

[44]

INCOMES OF "UNRELATED INDIVIDUALS"

The country's 27,133,000 "unrelated individuals" had incomes distributed as follows:

	NUMBERS	PERCENTAGE
Over $75,000	66,000	0.2%
$50,000–$75,000	171,000	0.6%
$25,000–$50,000	1,641,000	6.0%
$20,000–$25,000	1,761,000	6.5%
$15,000–$20,000	3,000,000	11.1%
$10,000–$15,000	4,864,000	17.9%
$5,000–$10,000	7,283,000	26.8%
Under $5,000	8,346,000	30.8%
	27,133,000	100.0%

Their median income came to $8,315; the average worked out to $10,815.

Among unrelated individuals, almost three in ten—29.4 percent—were persons aged 65 or over. These older individuals had a median income of $5,096, and they accounted for almost half—46.9 percent—of all the unrelated people with incomes under $5,000.

[44]

INCOMES OF OVER $75,000

The Census Bureau's top income category of "$75,000 and over" included 948,000 families and 66,000 individuals in 1980, for a total of 1,014,000 households.

More detailed breakdowns above that level can be obtained from Internal Revenue Service reports compiled from income tax returns. But it should be noted that tax returns are not fully comparable with Census reports on household incomes. For example, some married couples file separate returns. Moreover, the "adjusted gross income" figure declared on a tax return may exclude some of the income an individual received.

Still, there were 1,071,521 returns for 1980 with incomes of $75,000 or over, and they were distributed as follows:

INCOME RANGE	NUMBER OF RETURNS	
Over $1 million	4,112	
$500,000–$1 million	12,105	
$200,000–$500,000	97,232	
$100,000–$200,000	434,041	
$75,000–$100,000	524,031	
TOTAL	1,071,521	[175]

INCOME DISTRIBUTION: 1960–1980

Here is how family incomes were distributed in 1960, 1970, and 1980, using dollars with a 1980 value (that is, 1960 and 1970 incomes were adjusted to express their 1980 purchasing power). In 1960 the highest bracket was $25,000 and over, and in 1970 it was $50,000 and over.

	PERCENTAGE		
	1960	*1970*	*1980*
Over $50,000	{18.9%}	5.5%	6.7%
$25,000–$50,000		32.0%	32.6%
$20,000–$25,000	10.6%	11.3%	13.7%
$15,000–$20,000	22.8%	19.7%	14.0%
$10,000–$15,000	20.2%	13.6%	14.2%
$5,000–$10,000	16.1%	11.7%	12.7%
Under $5,000	11.4%	6.1%	6.2%
	100.0%	100.0%	100.0%
Median income	$15,637	$20,926	$21,023

[44]

THE OVERALL DISTRIBUTION OF FAMILY INCOME

America's 60,309,000 families had an aggregate income of $1,445,847,966,000 in 1980. If these households are divided into five equal groups of 12,061,800 each, the following distributions can be seen:

- The wealthiest 12,061,800 families had incomes of $34,534 or over, and received an aggregate income of $601,472,768,000, which worked out to 41.6 percent of the overall figure.

- The next wealthiest 12,061,800 families had incomes falling between $24,630 and $34,534, which gave them an aggregate income of $351,341,064,000, which came to 24.3 percent of the total sum.

- The middle 12,061,800 families had incomes going from $17,390 to $24,630, which totaled $253,023,400,000, or 17.5 percent of the national figure.

- The fourth 12,061,800 families went from $10,286 to $17,390, and their aggregate income was $167,718,368,000, or 11.6 percent of the total family figure.

- The bottom 12,061,800 families all had incomes below $10,286, which gave them $73,738,248,000, or 5.1 percent of the aggregate sum.

The aggregate income of the top 12,061,800 families was thus 8.2 times that of the bottom 12,061,800 families.

[44]

HOUSEHOLDS HEADED BY WOMEN

Among the 60,309,000 families, 9,082,000 (or 15.1 percent) had a woman as the principal householder and no man in residence.

The median income for these families was $10,408, which comes to 54.9 percent of the $18,972 median for married couple households in which the wife was not working, and 38.7 percent of the $26,879 median of married households which had both spouses working.

Of the women who headed households, 3,245,000 (or 35.7 percent) worked year-round at full-time jobs. Their median family income was $15,947, or 63.7 percent of the median for married couples in which the husband worked full-time but the wife was not employed.

[44]

INCOME AND RACE

The median income of all white families came to $21,904 in 1980. For black families, it was $12,674, or 57.9 percent of the white figure.

However, the income gap between black and white families varied with household composition and work experience:

	WHITE MEDIAN	BLACK MEDIAN	BLACK AS PERCENTAGE OF WHITE
All families with two earners	$25,108	$20,360	81.1%
Married couple families	$23,501	$18,593	79.1%
Married families where husband has full-time year-round employment	$27,795	$24,059	86.6%
Married families where husband has full-time year-round employment and wife is in the labor force	$29,842	$26,432	88.6%
Families headed by women	$11,908	$7,425	62.4%
Families headed by women with full-time year-round employment	$16,988	$13,214	77.8%

[44]

BLACK-WHITE DIFFERENCES: 1970 AND 1980

Between 1970 and 1980 white median family income remained relatively stable when measured in dollars with 1980 purchasing power, moving from $21,722 in 1970 to $21,904 in 1980.

However, black median family income declined from $13,325 in 1970 to $12,674 in 1980. This means that black income fell from 61.3 percent of the white figure to 57.9 percent of that sum.

Moreover, white families with incomes under $10,000 remained relatively stable, going from 15.9 percent to 16.2 percent of the white total, but black families with incomes under $10,000 rose from 36.5 percent of the 1970 black total to 40.4 percent of that total in 1980.

On the other hand, while the proportion of white families with incomes of $35,000 and over rose by 31.6 percent during the decade, black families in that bracket increased by 56.9 percent.

[44]

PERSONS WITH AND WITHOUT INCOMES

The Census counts a person as having an income if he or she receives some money, no matter how small the amount, from earned or other sources. Thus of the 174,082,000 persons aged 15 or older, 159,487,000 (or 91.6 percent) were listed as having incomes.

In this group, for example, were 7,161,000 young men and 6,780,000 young women between 15 and 19, whose respective median incomes during 1980 were $1,801 and $1,673.

Of the 14,595,000 persons with no income of their own, 5,879,000 (or 40.3 percent) were married women living with their husbands, and 6,257,000 (or 42.9 percent) were young people between 15 and 19.

And of the 159,487,000 persons with incomes, 43,309,000 (or 27.2 percent) received all their money from sources other than earnings. Of this group, 13,931,000 (or 32.2 percent) were men, and 29,378,000 (or 67.8 percent) were women.

[44]

INDIVIDUALS' INCOME AND MARITAL STATUS

These are the median incomes (from all sources) of all persons aged 18 or over, classified by marital status:

	MEN	WOMEN	WOMEN AS PERCENTAGE OF MEN
Married	$16,462	$4,551	27.6%
Separated	$10,561	$6,083	57.6%
Divorced	$12,907	$9,059	70.2%
Widowed	$6,799	$5,052	74.3%
Single	$7,024	$5,561	79.2%
TOTAL	$13,355	$5,232	39.2%

[44]

INDIVIDUALS' INCOMES AT VARIOUS AGE LEVELS

The following are the median incomes (from earnings or other sources) of men and women at various age levels:

AGE	MEN'S MEDIAN	WOMEN'S MEDIAN	WOMEN'S INCOMES AS PERCENTAGE OF MEN'S
15–19	$1,801	$1,673	92.9%
20–24	$7,923	$5,286	66.7%
25–34	$15,580	$6,973	44.8%
35–44	$20,037	$6,465	32.3%
45–54	$19,974	$6,403	32.1%
55–64	$15,914	$4,926	31.0%
65 and up	$7,342	$4,226	57.6%

[44]

Each year the government computes a series of figures called the "poverty thresholds." Persons with incomes under these levels are classified as "poor." These individuals are eligible for food stamps, Medicaid services, and other government benefits.

Single individuals under the age of 65 were counted as poor in 1981 if their annual income was less than $4,729. If they were 65 or over, the threshold figure fell to $4,359.

For a family of 2 the poverty line was $5,917; for a family with 3 persons it was $7,250; and for 4 it came to $9,287.

These figures apply to "nonfarm" households. For families or persons who live on farms, the figure tends to be 16.2 percent to 19.1 percent lower.

In 1981 the Census Bureau computed that 11.2 percent of all families were below the poverty line. For persons aged 65 or over, the figure was 15.3 percent. Among those families headed by a woman where there was no husband present, 34.6 percent were beneath the poverty level, and of all children in the nation under the age of 18, 19.8 percent were in households under the poverty line.

[44, 160]

EARNINGS FROM EMPLOYMENT

While a total of 116,178,000 people worked at some kind of job in 1980 and earned some income from that employment, only 64,740,000 (or 55.7 percent) of the persons in that group had full-time year-round jobs. Here were the income distributions for both sets of individuals:

	SOME EMPLOYMENT DURING THE YEAR		FULL-TIME YEAR-ROUND EMPLOYMENT	
	Number	*Percentage*	*Number*	*Percentage*
Over $75,000	495,000	0.4%	454,000	0.7%
$50,000–$75,000	1,236,000	1.1%	1,140,000	1.8%
$25,000–$50,000	11,260,000	9.7%	10,505,000	16.2%
$20,000–$25,000	9,967,000	8.6%	8,964,000	13.8%
$15,000–$20,000	14,318,000	12.3%	12,262,000	18.9%
$10,000–$15,000	20,792,000	17.9%	16,455,000	25.4%
$5,000–$10,000	23,419,000	20.2%	12,186,000	18.8%
Under $5,000	34,688,000	29.8%	2,771,000	4.3%
TOTAL	116,178,000	100.0%	64,740,000	100.0%
Median for men	$14,010		$18,611	
Median for women	$6,623		$11,196	

[44]

SEX AND FULL-TIME EMPLOYMENT

In the nation as a whole, 22,859,000 women held full-time year-round jobs, as opposed to 41,881,000 men. This works out to a ratio of 546 women for every 1,000 men.

Here are the numbers of men and women in various income ranges, along with the ratio of women to every 1,000 men:

	MEN	WOMEN	WOMEN PER 1000 MEN
Over $75,000	442,000	12,000	27
$50,000–$75,000	1,103,000	37,000	34
$35,000–$50,000	2,644,000	128,000	48
$25,000–$35,000	7,133,000	600,000	84
$20,000–$25,000	7,550,000	1,414,000	187
$15,000–$20,000	8,571,000	3,691,000	431
$10,000–$15,000	8,366,000	8,089,000	967
$5,000–$10,000	4,574,000	7,612,000	1,664
Under $5,000	1,495,000	1,276,000	854
TOTAL	41,881,000	22,857,000	546

[44]

SEX, OCCUPATIONS, AND EDUCATION

Here are median incomes for men and women, broken down by occupational categories and educational levels of full-time year-round workers:

	MEN	WOMEN	WOMEN'S INCOMES AS PERCENTAGE OF MEN'S
Professional	$23,026	$15,285	66.4%
Managerial	$23,558	$12,936	54.9%
Sales	$19,910	$9,748	49.0%
Clerical	$18,247	$10,997	60.3%
Craft	$18,671	$11,701	62.7%
Operatives	$15,702	$9,440	60.1%
Laborers	$12,757	$9,747	76.4%
Service workers	$13,064	$7,853	60.1%
5+ years college	$27,690	$18,100	65.4%
4 years college	$24,311	$15,143	62.3%
1–3 years college	$20,909	$12,954	61.9%
4 years high school	$19,469	$11,537	59.3%
1–3 years high school	$16,101	$9,676	60.1%
Less than high school	$13,117	$8,216	62.6%

[44]

Here are the median income figures of full-time year-round workers, classified by sex and race (these sums include both earnings from employment and income from other sources).

All men	$19,173	All women	$11,591
White men	$19,720	White women	$11,703
Black men	$13,875	Black women	$10,915

The median income for all women workers is 60.5 percent of the amount for men. However, the median for black women comes to 78.7 percent of the figure for black men, while the white women's median is 59.3 percent of the white men's.

Moreover, while the median for black men is 70.4 percent of that for white men, the figure for black women is 93.3 percent of the sum for white women.

[44]

EDUCATION, OCCUPATIONS, AND RACE

The gap between the earnings of black and white workers varies when education, occupations, and periods of employment are taken into consideration. (It should be noted that the following figures are for men only.)

In terms of *annual* earnings for all occupations, black workers' earnings are 69 percent of those received by white workers. However, the gap in average *weekly* earnings has black workers at 72 percent of whites. This difference occurs because black workers work fewer weeks per year than do whites.

So far as high school graduates are concerned, in annual terms, black workers make 70 percent of what whites do. In weekly terms, they receive 74 percent.

With men who have attended college, black workers get 78 percent of white earnings on an annual basis, and 80 percent by weekly calculations.

With respect to average weekly earnings, black farm laborers make 75 percent of the white figure; clerical workers earn 78 percent; transportation operators get 79 percent; managers and administrators make 81 percent; and factory operatives get 91 percent of the average white paycheck.

[165]

FAMILY INCOME

The grand total of $1,307,350,000,000 in family income in 1979 came from the following sources:

	TOTAL INCOME	PERCENTAGE
Wages and salaries	$1,000,255,000,000	76.5%
Self-employment income from farming	14,697,000,000	1.1%
Self-employment from nonfarm sources	82,744,000,000	6.3%
Property income*	67,581,000,000	5.2%
Social Security	66,114,000,000	5.1%
Public assistance	8,645,000,000	0.7%
Veterans, workmen's, and unemployment compensation	15,692,000,000	1.2%
Private and civil servants' pensions	38,121,000,000	2.9%
Alimony and child support	13,487,000,000	1.0%
	$1,307,050,000,000	100.0%

*Includes dividends, interest, rents, estates, trusts, and royalties.

[46]

AGGREGATE FAMILY INCOME

In 1979 all families taken together had incomes totaling $1,307,350,080,000. Here are the percentages of families in various income ranges; the percentage of aggregate income received by the families in each range; and the ratio between those percentages:

	PERCENTAGE OF FAMILIES	PERCENTAGE OF AGGREGATE INCOME	PROPORTIONATE SHARE OF AGGREGATE
Over $75,000	1.3%	6.1%	469.2%
$50,000–$75,000	3.8%	10.1%	265.8%
$25,000–$50,000	29.5%	43.8%	148.5%
$20,000–$25,000	14.4%	14.3%	99.3%
$15,000–$20,000	15.0%	11.6%	77.3%
$10,000–$15,000	15.6%	8.7%	55.8%
$5,000–$10,000	13.6%	4.5%	33.1%
Under $5,000	7.0%	0.9%	12.9%
	100.0%	100.0%	100.0%

[46]

Altogether, 56.2 percent of all families have two or more people bringing in earnings from employment. Only 30.9 percent have a single earner, and the remaining 12.9 percent obtain all their income from sources other than employment.

At the highest income level ($75,000 and over), 32.5 percent of the families get their income from a single earner. However, in the next two ranges (covering $25,000 to $75,000) single-earner families comprise, respectively, only 19.4 percent and 18.7 percent of the totals. Below $25,000, the single-earner proportion begins to rise again.

| | PERCENTAGES | | | |
	No Earners	*One Earner*	*Two Earners*	*Three or More*
Over $75,000	0.8%	32.5%	35.3%	31.2%
$50,000–$75,000	1.9%	19.4%	37.1%	41.7%
$25,000–$50,000	1.6%	18.7%	52.0%	27.7%
$20,000–$25,000	3.5%	28.9%	54.5%	13.2%
$15,000–$20,000	5.6%	35.5%	49.7%	9.2%
$10,000–$15,000	16.5%	42.9%	35.4%	5.2%
$5,000–$10,000	35.6%	42.3%	19.7%	2.4%
Under $5,000	51.9%	34.9%	11.5%	1.7%
All families	12.9%	30.9%	41.5%	14.7%

Unfortunately, figures are not available on how much each family member contributes to the total. The Census counts a person as an "earner" even if that income is comparatively small. Thus the median income of individuals aged 15 to 19 comes to $1,679, or $32.29 a week. Still, the presence of such earnings would give a family an extra earner in the statistical tables.

[46]

MARRIED COUPLES

Altogether, 97.2 percent of all married couples fell into one of the following ten categories:

HUSBAND'S WORK EXPERIENCE	WIFE'S WORK EXPERIENCE	PERCENTAGE OF FAMILIES	MEDIAN FAMILY INCOME
Full-time year-round	Full-time year-round	19.6%	$32,187
Full-time year-round	Part-time year-round	5.5%	$29,075
Full-time year-round	Part-year	18.1%	$26,428
Part-year	Full-time year-round	3.5%	$24,010
Part-year	Part-year	5.3%	$18,508
Full-time year-round	None	22.9%	$26,976
Part-year	None	6.1%	$16,648
None	Full-time year-round	2.2%	$20,119
None	Part-year	1.6%	$13,939
None	None	12.4%	$11,903
All couples		97.2%	$24,374

[46]

WORKING COUPLES

Among married couples in which the husband had full-time year-round employment and his wife worked a lesser schedule, his median income was $18,526 and hers was $6,545.

With couples where both spouses were full-time year-round workers, his median income was $16,862 and hers was $10,199.

Among couples where both spouses did some work during the year, her earnings amounted to 26.9 percent of the family's income.

Where the husband worked year-round at a full-time job, and the wife worked part-time throughout the year, her earnings contributed 18.4 percent to the family's income. When both worked year-round at full-time jobs, her contribution came to 34.7 percent.

And when the husband worked only part of the year, while the wife had a full-time year-round job, her earnings comprised 44.4 percent of the family total.

[46]

WORKING WIVES

In 1979 the nation had 48,180,000 married couple families. The following was the employment status of the wives in those families at various income ranges.

(It should be noted that "full-time employment" means that *when* the wife worked, she worked at least 35 hours of work per week. However, she need *not* have worked the full year. Also, not all husbands in these families were themselves full-time workers.)

| | PERCENTAGES | | |
	Wife Employed Full-Time	Wife Employed Part-Time	Wife Not Employed at All
Over $75,000	28.0%	13.1%	58.9%
$50,000–$75,000	43.0%	13.9%	43.1%
$25,000–$50,000	46.4%	15.4%	38.2%
$20,000–$25,000	36.6%	15.9%	47.5%
$15,000–$20,000	31.6%	15.1%	53.3%
$10,000–$15,000	20.4%	12.6%	67.0%
$5,000–$10,000	11.1%	8.3%	80.6%
Under $5,000	8.2%	6.8%	85.0%
All couples	33.0%	13.8%	53.2%

[46]

RACE AND SEX

With married couples where both spouses worked full-time (but not necessarily for the whole year) the median income of black families was 90.9 percent of the figure for white families.

The following were the percentages of white and black women, aged 25 through 64, broken down by marital status, who held full-time year-round jobs in 1979. Median incomes are also given, along with the racial ratios.

| | PERCENTAGE WORKING | | MEDIAN INCOMES | | BLACK AS PERCENTAGE |
	White	Black	White	Black	OF WHITE
Married	31.0%	45.5%	$10,675	$10,263	96.1%
Separated	40.7%	35.6%	$11,278	$9,656	85.6%
Widowed	35.4%	24.6%	$11,682	$8,788	75.2%
Divorced	56.4%	50.7%	$11,939	$10,789	90.4%
Single	61.4%	43.2%	$12,344	$10,024	81.2%

Black *married* women are more likely to work than are their white counterparts. On the other hand, white *nonmarried* women are more apt to have employment. [46]

The 1980 Census asked families what their incomes had been during the previous year. According to provisional Census reports, for white families the median income in 1979 came to $20,840; for black families it was $12,618; and for families of Asian or Pacific Island origin the figure was $22,075.

Among white families, 17.5 percent made more than $35,000; 7.5 percent of black families were at that level; while 23.2 percent of Asian and Pacific Island families made $35,000 or more.

In terms of education, 17.2 percent of all white individuals aged 25 or over had completed four or more years of college. Among black Americans, 8.4 percent were at that educational level, and 32.5 percent of persons of Asian or Pacific Island origin had completed college.

[9]

EARNINGS OF CORPORATE EXECUTIVES

The following were the compensations—salaries plus bonuses—received by the chief executives of some of the country's largest corporations during 1981. These figures do not include stock options, deferred earnings, low-interest loans, or other fringe benefits.

More Than $1 Million. Union Oil Company ($1,541,000); International Telephone and Telegraph ($1,136,000); Revlon ($1,133,000); International Harvester ($1,034,000); United Technologies ($1,025,000); Mobil Oil ($1,022,000).

More Than $750,000. Exxon ($992,000); Sears, Roebuck ($986,000); Union Pacific ($954,000); Faberge ($928,000); American Telephone and Telegraph ($889,000); Philip Morris ($878,000); Bristol-Myers ($860,000); Shell Oil ($858,000); Columbia Broadcasting System ($855,000); Du Pont ($851,000); Gulf Oil ($845,000); General Electric ($825,000); Westinghouse ($808,000); Eastman Kodak ($806,000); U. S. Steel ($784,000); Atlantic-Richfield ($754,000); Boeing Aircraft ($751,000).

More Than $500,000. Monsanto Chemical ($748,000); American Broadcasting Company ($746,000); Xerox ($731,000); Anheuser-Busch ($721,000); J. P. Morgan ($686,000); Johnson & Johnson ($655,000); American Can ($653,000); International Business Machines ($646,000);

J. C. Penney ($635,000); General Mills ($630,000); Aluminum Corporation of America ($625,000); Radio Corporation of America ($621,000); Firestone ($609,000); Avon Products ($604,000); Kellogg ($600,000); Time, Inc. ($582,000); H. J. Heinz ($579,000); Procter & Gamble ($549,000); Burlington Industries ($548,000); Delta Airlines ($546,000); Texaco ($535,000); Bethlehem Steel ($525,000); McDonald's ($500,000).

Under $500,000. General Foods ($499,000); Quaker Oats ($499,000); General Motors ($475,000); Levi Strauss ($449,000); Ford Motor Company ($440,000); Corning Glass ($439,000); R. H. Macy ($434,000); Walt Disney Productions ($413,000); Holiday Inns ($391,000); American Airlines ($375,000); Chrysler ($362,000); Black & Decker ($358,000); Eastern Airlines ($341,000); Polaroid ($315,000); Pacific Gas & Electric ($293,000).

[128]

STATE PER CAPITA PERSONAL INCOME: 1980

1. Alaska	$12,790	26. Oregon	$9,317
2. Connecticut	11,720	27. New Hampshire	9,131
3. California	10,938	28. Oklahoma	9,116
4. New Jersey	10,924	29. Florida	8,996
5. Wyoming	10,898	30. Missouri	8,982
6. Nevada	10,727	31. Indiana	8,936
7. Illinois	10,521	32. Arizona	8,791
8. Maryland	10,460	33. North Dakota	8,747
9. Delaware	10,339	34. Montana	8,536
10. Washington	10,309	35. Louisiana	8,458
11. New York	10,260	36. Georgia	8,073
12. Massachusetts	10,125	37. Idaho	8,056
13. Hawaii	10,101	38. Maine	7,925
14. Colorado	10,025	39. New Mexico	7,841
15. Kansas	9,983	40. Vermont	7,827
16. Michigan	9,950	41. North Carolina	7,819
17. Minnesota	9,724	42. South Dakota	7,806
18. Texas	9,545	43. West Virginia	7,800
19. Ohio	9,462	44. Tennessee	7,720
20. Rhode Island	9,444	45. Utah	7,649
21. Pennsylvania	9,434	46. Kentucky	7,613
22. Virginia	9,392	47. Alabama	7,488
23. Nebraska	9,365	48. Arkansas	7,268
24. Iowa	9,358	49. South Carolina	7,266
25. Wisconsin	9,348	50. Mississippi	6,580

[173]

THE WEALTHIEST AND POOREST COUNTIES
IN EACH STATE BY PERSONAL PER CAPITA
INCOME IN 1979

	WEALTHIEST		POOREST	
Alabama	Jefferson	$8,823	Greene	$4,712
Alaska	Juneau	14,605	Wade Hampton	2,737
Arizona	Maricopa	9,322	Apache	4,671
Arkansas	Pulaski	8,856	Newton	3,837
California	Colusa	13,684	Trinity	5,952
Colorado	Phillips	13,242	Hinsdale	3,880
Connecticut	Fairfield	12,266	Windham	7,720
Delaware	New Castle	10,052	Kent	7,327
Florida	Palm Beach	10,520	Franklin	3,974
Georgia	DeKalb	11,027	Crawford	3,778
Hawaii	Honolulu	9,573	Hawaii	7,760
Idaho	Clark	9,972	Madison	4,669
Illinois	DuPage	12,080	Pope	4,471
Indiana	Bartholomew	9,786	Crawford	5,643
Iowa	Polk	10,165	Decatur	5,582
Kansas	Wichita	18,599	Elk	6,244
Kentucky	Franklin	9,537	Owsley	3,411
Louisiana	Lafayette	9,898	Madison	4,205
Maine	Cumberland	8,483	Aroostook	5,580
Maryland	Montgomery	13,541	Somerset	5,195
Massachusetts	Norfolk	10,304	Hampshire	7,198
Michigan	Oakland	12,058	Oscoda	4,408
Minnesota	Hennepin	11,253	Clearwater	4,334
Mississippi	Hinds	8,929	Carroll	4,134
Missouri	St. Louis	10,940	Ripley	3,899
Montana	Toole	10,794	Wibaux	3,265
Nebraska	Dundy	9,755	Loup	3,626
Nevada	Eureka	12,592	Esmeralda	6,171
New Hampshire	Hillsborough	8,859	Coos	6,692
New Jersey	Bergen	12,369	Gloucester	7,400
New Mexico	Los Alamos	12,464	Mora	3,844
New York	New York	13,589	Lewis	5,552
North Carolina	Mecklenburg	9,737	Hyde	3,677
North Dakota	Billings	9,550	Rolette	4,965
Ohio	Cuyahoga	10,515	Adams	5,213
Oklahoma	Cimarron	20,100	Adair	4,129
Oregon	Multnomah	10,962	Wheeler	6,452
Pennsylvania	Montgomery	11,975	Fulton	5,907
Rhode Island	Bristol	9,296	Newport	7,958
South Carolina	Beaufort	8,720	Clarendon	4,117
South Dakota	Minnehaha	8,929	Shannon	3,280

(continued)

(continued)

	WEALTHIEST		POOREST	
Tennessee	Davidson	9,572	Pickett	3,723
Texas	Loving	17,882	Starr	3,640
Utah	Salt Lake	8,204	San Juan	3,661
Vermont	Windsor	7,939	Orleans	5,966
Virginia	Arlington	16,027	Greensville	4,783
Washington	Lincoln	11,362	Pend Oreille	5,896
West Virginia	Hancock	9,964	Doddridge	4,607
Wisconsin	Ozaukee	10,396	Forrest	5,031
Wyoming	Natrona	12,842	Big Horn	6,684

[171]

THE 25 WEALTHIEST METROPOLITAN AREAS BY PERSONAL PER CAPITA INCOME IN 1979

1. Reno, Nevada — $12,317
2. Bridgeport, Connecticut — 12,266
3. Anchorage, Alaska — 12,200
4. San Francisco, California — 11,741
5. Midland, Texas — 11,712
6. Washington, D.C. — 11,313
7. San Jose, California — 11,064
8. Salinas, California — 10,838
9. Seattle, Washington — 10,788
10. Houston, Texas — 10,638
11. Los Angeles, California — 10,606
12. Anaheim, California — 10,547
13. West Palm Beach, Florida — 10,520
14. Newark, New Jersey — 10,500
15. Nassau, New York — 10,468
16. Chicago, Illinois — 10,455
17. Detroit, Michigan — 10,433
18. Sarasota, Florida — 10,425
19. Peoria, Illinois — 10,295
20. Ann Arbor, Michigan — 10,275
21. Las Vegas, Nevada — 10,175
22. Cleveland, Ohio — 10,167
23. Denver, Colorado — 10,133
24. Portland, Oregon — 10,067
25. Cedar Rapids, Iowa — 10,037

[171]

THE 25 POOREST METROPOLITAN AREAS (OUT OF 273) BY PERSONAL PER CAPITA INCOME IN 1979

249.	Monroe, Louisiana	$6,945
250.	Albany, Georgia	6,943
251.	Killeen, Texas	6,935
252.	Johnson City, Tennessee	6,878
253.	Pensacola, Florida	6,859
254.	Bryan, Texas	6,817
255.	Fort Smith, Arkansas	6,810
256.	Tuscaloosa, Alabama	6,767
257.	Columbus, Georgia	6,758
258.	Clarksville, Tennessee	6,678
259.	St. Cloud, Minnesota	6,620
260.	Bloomington, Indiana	6,571
261.	Panama City, Florida	6,487
262.	Fayetteville, North Carolina	6,448
263.	Biloxi, Mississippi	6,436
264.	Pascagoula, Mississippi	6,343
265.	Anniston, Alabama	6,251
266.	Alexandria, Louisiana	6,236
267.	El Paso, Texas	6,207
268.	Las Cruces, New Mexico	6,091
269.	Lawton, Oklahoma	6,089
270.	Brownsville, Texas	5,731
271.	Provo, Utah	5,721
272.	Laredo, Texas	5,106
273.	McAllen, Texas	5,024

[171]

EXPENDITURES

The Consumer Price Index. Using the price levels of 1967 as a baseline (100.0), the Consumer Price Index had ascended to 272.3 by 1981. Put another way, the purchasing power of a full dollar declined to 37 cents during this 14-year period. And while the median family income was

$22,390 in 1981, its buying power amounted to $8,223 by 1967 standards. Over those 14 years, real family income rose by a total of 3.1 percent.

	CONSUMER PRICE INDEX	DOLLAR'S REAL VALUE	MEDIAN FAMILY INCOME On Paper	In Reality
1967	100.0	$1.00	$7,974	$7,974
1968	104.2	.96	8,632	8,284
1969	109.8	.91	9,433	8,591
1970	116.3	.86	9,867	8,484
1971	121.3	.82	10,285	8,479
1972	125.3	.80	11,116	8,872
1973	133.1	.75	12,051	9,054
1974	147.7	.68	12,902	8,735
1975	161.2	.62	13,719	8,511
1976	170.5	.59	14,958	8,773
1977	181.5	.55	16,009	8,820
1978	195.4	.51	17,640	9,028
1979	217.7	.46	19,684	9,042
1980	247.0	.40	21,023	8,511
1981	272.3	.37	22,390	8,223

[43, 44, 162]

PRICES, PRODUCTS, AND SERVICES

The Consumer Price Index takes 1967 as its base year, with price levels for that year expressed as a quotient of 100.0. The CPI includes a list of items an average family is apt to purchase. To achieve a composite CPI, the Bureau of Labor Statistics factors in the current prices of various goods and services, and also weights those items to accord with a "typical" family budget, which looks something like this:

	PERCENTAGE
Food and beverages	12.6%
Home purchase costs	7.1%
Home financing, taxes, and insurance	8.3%
Other residential expenses	16.0%
Apparel plus cleaning and repairs	3.4%
Purchase of an automobile	2.5%
Motor fuel	4.1%
Other transportation costs	6.6%
Medical care	3.2%
Energy costs other than motor fuel	7.5%
All other services	28.7%
	100.0%

By November of 1981, the Consumer Price Index for all items weighted to this formula had risen to 280.7, signifying an inflation of 180.7 percent over the previous 14-year period. However, the prices of some goods and services rose at a greater rate than others, as shown on the table following.

NOVEMBER 1981 PRICE LEVELS (1967 = 100.0)

Fuel oil	706.8	Apples	248.0
Mortgage interest costs	666.8	Butter	248.0
Hospital room charges	515.4	Beauty parlor services	244.8
Piped gas	437.0	Canned hams	243.1
Gasoline	409.5	White bread	241.3
Fish and seafood	358.9	Bacon	238.1
Roasted coffee	341.0	Intracity public transit	235.6
Postage	337.5	Toilet goods	232.5
Airline fares	319.8	Cigarettes	228.9
Away-from-home lodgings	318.6	Wine	227.5
Oranges	314.0	Fresh whole milk	220.8
Physicians' services	311.3	Pork chops	217.0
Intercity bus fares	308.0	Residential rents	215.0
Water and sewer charges	306.1	Furniture and bedding	209.2
Automobile maintenance	302.8	Property taxes	208.0
Cola drinks (nondiet)	298.8	Tomatoes	206.9
Electricity	298.6	All footwear	205.4
Potatoes	286.3	Beer and ale	204.0
Chuck roast	282.6	New cars	195.3
Used cars	281.4	Eggs	194.7
ALL GOODS AND SERVICES	280.7	Bicycles	194.3
Taxi fares	275.6	Fresh whole chickens	190.9
Dental services	272.3	Automobile tires	189.7
Home purchases	270.2	Men's and boy's apparel	183.6
Soaps and detergents	269.7	Prescription drugs	179.6
Newspapers	267.1	Refrigerators and freezers	178.7
Ground beef	266.1	Women's and girls' apparel	160.6
Automobile insurance	265.4	Telephone service	155.6
Infants' apparel	264.9	Automobile registrations	149.0
Frankfurters	259.9	Whiskey	144.8
Intercity train fares	255.7	Television sets	104.8
Margarine	255.2		

[168]

THE COST OF FOOD

Between 1970 and 1980, while the overall Consumer Price Index increased by 112.4 percent, the average retail prices of these food products rose to the following amounts:

	1970	1980	PERCENTAGE INCREASE
1 lb. can of coffee	$.91	$2.82	209.9%
1 lb. margarine	.30	.73	143.3%
1 lb. sliced bacon	.95	1.71	80.0%
½ gallon ice cream	.85	1.92	125.9%
1 lb. butter	.87	1.97	126.4%
1 lb. frying chicken	.41	.76	85.4%
1 lb. onions	.16	.30	87.5%
1 lb. potatoes	.09	.22	144.4%
1 lb. chuck roast	.73	1.87	156.2%
1 lb. sirloin steak	1.35	2.93	117.0%
1 dozen large eggs	.61	1.00	63.9%

[74]

PRICE LEVELS IN VARIOUS METROPOLITAN AREAS

During January and February of 1982, the Consumer Price Index averaged 283.0 for "all urban consumers," a figure based on price levels in 85 major cities and their surrounding areas. This Index is generally the one used for the country as a whole.

However, price levels varied somewhat among principal urban areas:

ABOVE THE OVERALL URBAN INDEX		BELOW THE OVERALL URBAN INDEX	
San Diego	323.1	Baltimore	282.1
Minneapolis	306.0	Atlanta	279.8
Denver	305.4	Detroit	279.3
Houston	304.1	Pittsburgh	278.6
Seattle	295.9	St. Louis	278.4
San Francisco	295.8	Washington, D.C.	278.0
Dallas	293.6	Kansas City, Mo.	276.0
Milwaukee	291.3	Philadelphia	275.6
Portland, Ore.	288.4	Chicago	275.2
Cleveland	285.9	Boston	274.0
Los Angeles	285.7	New York	268.8
Cincinnati	285.7	Honolulu	262.2

[170]

In the fall of 1981, the Bureau of Labor Statistics computed the incomes necessary to raise a family of four in various sections of the country. A "lower level" budget averaged $15,323; an "intermediate" budget called for $25,407; and a "higher level" budget required $38,060. This is what it cost to maintain an "intermediate" budget in the metropolitan areas of the following cities:

Honolulu	$31,893	Chicago	$25,358
Anchorage	$31,890	Detroit	$25,208
New York	$29,540	Baltimore	$25,114
Boston	$29,213	Los Angeles	$25,025
Washington, D.C.	$27,352	Denver	$24,820
San Francisco	$27,082	San Diego	$24,776
Milwaukee	$26,875	Pittsburgh	$24,717
Philadelphia	$26,567	Kansas City	$24,528
Seattle	$25,881	St. Louis	$24,498
Minneapolis	$25,799	Houston	$23,601
Cleveland	$25,598	Atlanta	$23,273
Cincinnati	$25,475	Dallas	$22,678

[81]

PERSONAL CONSUMPTION

In 1979 "personal consumption expenditures" in the United States amounted to $1,510,898,000,000. This sum represents all purchases by individuals and households, but does not include tax payments or personal investments. Of course, not everyone spends money on every item on the list, so it is best to imagine that if all Americans lived in a single household, this is what their expenditures would be. The figures that follow show how much of every $10,000 in personal income was spent in each of the areas.

Food, Drink, and Tobacco: $2,193. This category included food purchased for eating at home ($1,314); food eaten out ($455); meals provided by employers ($31); and food grown and consumed on farms ($9).

Individuals and households also bought alcoholic beverages for drinking at home ($164) and to drink outside their homes ($93), and tobacco products ($127).

Clothing and Personal Care: $917. The principal items included: women's, girls', and infants' clothing ($357); men's and boys' clothing ($190); shoes for everyone ($107); jewelry and watches ($64); toilet articles and preparations ($90); barbershops, beauty parlors, and health clubs ($52); and cleaning and repairing of shoes and clothing ($37).

Housing: $2,912. Of this sum, $1,484 either went for rent or the annual costs of owning a home. Another $58 was spent on transient accommodations such as hotels and dormitories.

The remaining housing costs went for operating a residence. The chief items were: utilities ($475); furniture ($121); china, tableware and glassware ($52); household appliances, such as dishwashers, air conditioners, and sewing machines ($111); telephone charges ($166); and domestic service ($42).

Medical Expenses: $956. Within this sum were drugs and sundries ($105); physicians' fees ($240); dental bills ($81); charges by private hospitals ($397); and health insurance premiums paid individually or by employers ($73).

Transportation: $1,573. Most of this amount went for "user-operated travel," where the main items were: purchase of new cars ($327); purchase of used cars ($106); purchase of other motor vehicles ($88); tires, parts and accessories ($112); repairs, parking, tolls and washing ($219); insurance ($58); and oil and gasoline ($453).

In addition, local transportation took $35 out of each $10,000, of which $16 went for buses or subways, and another $16 for taxicabs. Intercity travel called for $66, of which $53 was for plane flights and $6 on buses.

Education and "Personal Business": $781. This category covered college tuitions ($59); fees to private schools ($51); and religious and welfare activities ($138).

Under the heading of "personal business" came such costs as: life insurance premiums ($99); legal services ($72); brokerage and bank charges ($65); and funeral expenses ($26).

Recreation: $687. The main items on this list included foreign travel ($31); books ($41); magazines and newspapers ($54); and also "flowers, seeds and potted plants" ($29). In addition, there were motion picture admissions ($17); theater, opera and dance ($8); and tickets to spectator sports ($14); plus the purchase of radios, television sets, records and musical instruments ($135); and repairs for those items ($22). Also included were the purchases of pleasure boats and airplanes, sports equipment, and "durable toys" ($104), along with "nondurable toys" and sports supplies ($85).

Expenses for clubs and fraternal organizations were also on the recreation list ($14), as were "commercial participant amusements" ($36) such as billiard parlors, bowling alleys, golf courses, and places for "dancing, riding, shooting, skating, and swimming." Finally, $12 of every $10,000 went for legal betting, or, more accurately, that sum represented total net losses after counting up one's winnings.

Analyzed another way, of each $10,000 the nation's households spend, $1,574 goes for "durable goods"; $3,809 for "nondurable" goods; and $4,615 on "services."

[112]

HEALTH CARE EXPENDITURES

During the 12-month period ending in March 1981, expenditures for health care totaled $255.8 billion, or 9.4 percent of the Gross National Product. (In 1960 the health portion was 5.2 percent, and by 1970 it had grown to 7.6 percent.)

Expenditures for this 1980–1981 period broke down as follows: hospital care (40.5 percent), physicians' services (18.8 percent), dentists' services (6.4 percent), drugs (7.7 percent), eye-glasses and appliances (2.1 percent).

Also included were: nursing home care (8.4 percent), government public health activities (2.9 percent), health-related research (2.2 percent), construction of medical facilities (2.5 percent); prepayments and administration (4.0 percent); and other services and materials (4.5 percent).

Individual Expenditures. During this period, health care expenditures averaged $975 for each American, or $3,900 for a family of 4.

In the $975 per capita figure, hospital charges averaged $448 and physicians' fees came to $207. And of this $975 spent on or by individuals, $589 came from private funds and $386 was provided by public programs.

[179]

HEALTH CARE PAYMENTS: 1960–1981

In 1960 private funds (including private insurance plans) accounted for 55.4 percent of the costs of hospital care. In the 12-month period ending March 1981, the private share was down to 45.9 percent. Of the remaining 54.1 percent provided by public payments, 41.4 percent came from federal programs and 12.7 percent from state or local governments.

In 1960 private funds provided 93.9 percent of payments to physicians, but by March of 1981 the private share had declined to 73.4 percent. Of the 26.6 percent from public sources, 20.5 percent came from federal agencies and 6.1 percent from state or local governments.

Third-Party Payments, During 1980, "third party" agencies—usually private insurance plans or governmental programs—paid for 90.9 percent of all hospital care costs and 62.7 percent of all physicians' bills. Two public programs, Medicare and Medicaid, paid for 27.8 percent of all personal health care costs incurred by individuals during the year. And in 1980 individuals and organizations paid $64.9 billion in premiums to private health insurance plans. This was somewhat less than the $70.9 billion the federal government paid for health care costs; but almost double the $33.3 billion states and localities paid for health services.

[176, 179]

HEALTH AND PENSION COVERAGE

In 1980 the Census surveyed Americans who had worked during the year to discover how many were covered by pension and health insurance plans paid for by their unions or employers.

- 36.6 percent had both private pension and insurance coverage.
- 17.1 percent had health coverage only.
- 5.5 percent had pension coverage only.
- 40.7 percent had neither kind of coverage.

It should be added that a considerably higher proportion of the women than the men did not have their own health coverage—55.0 percent as opposed to 39.3 percent. This is partly because many married women who work are covered by their husband's plans. With respect to pensions, the difference was somewhat smaller: 64.7 percent of the women were not covered, contrasted with 52.5 percent of the men. In this case, women are more apt to work part-time and are therefore less eligible for pension coverage.

[37]

THE COST OF AN AUTOMOBILE

In 1979 the Federal Highway Administration computed it would cost $21,717 to purchase a $6,650 compact car and drive it 100,000 miles during the coming ten years. Ownership and operation would thus average 21.7 cents a mile (in 1979-value dollars), assuming "suburban-based" driving conditions.

The $21,717 broke down as follows: oil and gasoline ($4,963); maintenance ($4,161); insurance ($2,283); tires and accessories ($642); parking and tolls ($768); garaging ($2,400); depreciation ($5,175); plus $1,326 for taxes on all of the above.

Year-by-year costs were calculated this way:

YEAR	MILES DRIVEN	OPERATING COSTS	OWNING COSTS	TOTAL COSTS
1979	14,500	$998	$1780	$2778
1980	13,000	985	1383	2368
1981	11,500	1031	1293	2324
1982	10,000	1008	1225	2233
1983	9,900	1060	1137	2197
1984	9,900	1297	1127	2424
1985	9,500	1428	1060	2488
1986	8,500	826	938	1764
1987	7,500	801	1056	1857
1988	5,700	458	826	1284
	100,000	$9,892	$11,825	$21,717

[120]

THE COST OF A CHILD

The Department of Agriculture has estimated that it will cost a total of $134,414 to raise an average child born in 1979 to his or her eighteenth birthday if the family lives in "the urban North Central region" of the country.

According to the study, the child's first-year expenses in 1979 came to $2,972. By the age of 6, the annual cost will be $5,060, assuming an annual inflation rate of 8 percent. At age 12, the child will require $9,378; and by 17 he or she will need $15,624 during the year.

Over the 18-year period, the costs of the food the child consumes at home will come to $32,915. Food away from home will total $3,730, and clothing will cost $12,129. (As before, all these accumulated expenses assume an 8 percent inflation each year.) Housing for the child will amount to $41,121; medical care, $6,703; and the child's share of family transportation costs, $20,355. Another $17,461 in expenses will bring the total to $134,414.

These calculations do not include the costs of college, which presumably come after the child's eighteenth birthday.

[110]

CHAPTER EIGHT

GOVERNMENT: TAXES AND SERVICES

In 1980 Americans paid $745.2 billion in taxes, a sum equal to 28.4 percent of that year's Gross National Product. Of this amount, 69.8 percent went to the federal government, 18.4 percent was paid to the states, and 11.8 percent was assessed by local governments.

Most of these funds were then handed back to people. For example, the federal tax receipts included Social Security contributions, which came to $160.7 billion in 1980, or 30.9 percent of all federal collections. However, $138.0 billion of that sum was paid in the same year to persons with pensions and other benefits under the Social Security program.

Statutes which mandate taxes and services contain elaborate tables specifying rates and benefits, but those tables do not show how much people actually pay or end up receiving. This chapter will provide much of that information. For instance, for the 434,041 individuals and families who declared incomes between $100,000 and $200,000 on their 1980 federal tax returns, the average tax payment came to 33.5 percent of their income. And for the 4,112 returns declaring incomes of $1 million or over, the typical tax bill totaled 48.5 percent.

By the same token, the average Social Security benefit for the 20,039,216 retired workers as of October of 1981 was $4,921 for the year. Where workers resided with a spouse, the couple received a further $2,259, for a total of $7,180. By the same token, the 3,843,000 families on public assistance—typically one parent plus two children—

received an average annual stipend of $3,453 as of the end of 1980. The law also dictates that child support payments be collected from fathers of children in public assistance programs. In 1980 the sums that were obtained added up to 4.4 percent of the public assistance budget.

TAXES

In 1980 the Internal Revenue Service received a total of 93,143,629 personal income tax returns.

Of these, 88,945,000 were checked for accuracy by computer, which found that 6,468,000 (or 7.3 percent) contained errors. Among the returns that had mistakes, 45.2 percent made overpayments averaging $203. The other 54.8 percent made underpayments averaging $315 per return. This means that errors in which taxpayers paid too much came to $590,832,000, whereas where they, paid too little totaled $1,119,633,000.

Altogether, 73,835,353 refunds were paid to filers of 1040 and 1040A forms. The overall sum returned was $44,753,862,000, with the average refund amounting to $606.

In 1980 a total of 25,300,000 returns (or 27.2 percent) designated payments to the Presidential Election Campaign Fund. The amount thus collected was $38,800,000, because double payments are permitted on joint returns.

[133]

Audits. In 1980 the Internal Revenue Service audited or examined 1,528,927 returns, or 1.9 percent of those submitted during 1979. Here are the results by income range, with the average additional taxes recommended:

INCOME RANGE	NUMBER EXAMINED	PERCENTAGE EXAMINED	AVERAGE ADDITIONAL TAX
Under $10,000	438,150	1.1%	$589
$10,000–15,000	255,975	2.0%	$438
$15,000–$50,000	725,465	2.7%	$540
Over $50,000	109,337	8.7%	$3,760
	1,528,927	1.9%	$767

[133]

Penalties and Credits. In all, 10,125,499 taxpayers were assessed penalty fees during 1980. The major reasons were: failure to file a return (4,938,220), insufficient payment of estimated taxes (3,914,428), bad checks (127,142), and fraud (8,145).

In 1980 $775,000,000 was claimed in child care credits on 3,700,000 returns, for an average of $209 per return. Another $478,000,000 was claimed on 4,800,000 returns for energy-conserving home improvements, averaging $99 per return.

The Internal Revenue Service computes that it spends $4.40 to collect each $1,000 in taxes.

[133]

Sources of Federal Taxes. In 1980 the Internal Revenue Service collected a net total of $465,871,222,000 from individuals, businesses, estates, and other sources.

Individuals' income taxes accounted for 52.1 percent of the total; corporate income taxes represented 13.9 percent; Social Security payments 26.2 percent; and excise, estates, and unemployment insurance payments represented most of the remaining 7.8 percent.

In 1960 the proportions were rather different. Individuals paid 49.0 percent and corporations 24.2 percent. Social Security came to 11.1 percent, and excise and other taxes came to 15.7 percent.

[133]

EXEMPTIONS AND DEDUCTIONS

The Office of Management and Budget calculated that federal tax payments by individuals in 1981 were $220,060,000,000 less than what they might have been, due to the fact that certain kinds of income are exempted from taxes or taxed at a partial rate.

Here are some of the sums in taxes that are "lost" because of various exemptions or deductions.

- Employers provide certain *benefits* which are not counted as income: contributions for medical insurance premiums and medical care ($14,165,000,000), payments of educational fees ($35,000,000), meals or lodging paid for by employers ($380,000,000), payments toward private pensions ($23,605,000,000), untaxed benefits and allowances to armed forces personnel ($1,585,000,000), employer payments for group life insurance ($1,855,000,000).

- *Interest income* that can be omitted for tax purposes: on life insurance savings ($4,080,000,000), from state and local bonds ($1,885,000,000), on industrial development and pollution control bonds ($460,000,000), state and local housing and hospital bonds ($790,000,000).

- *Interest payments* that can be deducted in computing personal taxes: mortgage interest paid on homes ($19,805,000,000), interest paid for consumer credit ($5,260,000,000).

- *Tax payments* that can be deducted: property taxes on homes ($8,915,000,000), other state and local tax payments ($18,405,000,000), special treatments for capital gains by individuals ($23,645,000,000).

- *Parental exemptions* for students aged 19 or over ($1,045,000,000), additional exemptions for the elderly ($2,260,000,000), credits for child and dependent care ($1,025,000,000).

- *Money not counted as income:* Social Security retirement benefits ($10,270,000,000), Workmen's Compensation benefits ($2,675,000,000), unemployment insurance benefits ($5,275,000,000), public assistance payments ($465,000,000), disability benefits ($2,115,000,000).

- *Also:* charitable contributions ($9,510,000,000), scholarship and fellowship income ($410,000,000), deducted medical expenses ($3,580,000,000), contributions to self-employment pension plans ($2,105,000,000), deducted casualty losses ($715,000,000), and special tax treatment for income earned abroad ($640,000,000).

[115]

FEDERAL INCOME TAXES

Each year the Internal Revenue Service releases information obtained from its income tax returns. Its most recent report deals with returns declaring 1980 income. More detailed statistics are available for 1978 and 1979.

The IRS simply recounts the information presented on its forms, without remarking on its accuracy or honesty. The base figure on the form is the sum taxpayers declare as their "adjusted gross income." Certain kinds of receipts can be omitted in arriving at this figure; however, in most cases they are relatively minor.

It should also be noted that the IRS statistics are derived from tax returns. Some of these represent the incomes of married couples and some individuals living alone, while other filers are single heads of households or even wives and husbands who choose to file separately.

- A total of 93,616,278 returns were received declaring income for 1980.* Together these returns listed adjusted gross incomes totaling $1,606,265,685,000, for an average income of $17,158 per return.

- Among the returns, 59,468,311 (or 63.5 percent) used the "zero bracket amount" method of computation, which meant they did not itemize deductions. Another 28,791,240 returns (or 30.8 percent) presented itemized deductions. (The IRS did not indicate the status of the remaining 5,356,727 returns.)

* This total is somewhat higher than the one cited earlier, as 472,649 additional returns came in between the issuance of the two reports.

- Altogether, 73,739,632 of the returns (or 78.8 percent) were required to pay some taxes. The total figure came to $248,400,602,000, averaging $3,369 per taxed return.

- Among the returns that paid no taxes, 903 had declared incomes between $100,000 and $200,000; 52 had incomes between $200,000 and $500,000; 6 fell between $500,000 and $1 million; and 10 declared incomes of $1 million or over.

- There were 4,112 returns for 1980 with declared incomes of $1 million or over. Their total adjusted gross income came to $8,368,749,000, giving this group an average annual income of $2,035,200. On average, its members paid $986,748 in taxes, which came to 48.5 percent of their income as a group.

- Of the $1,606,265,685,000 adjusted gross income total of all returns, $1,345,004,185,000 (or 83.7 percent) came from wages or salaries. The remaining $261,261,500,000 (or 16.3 percent) was received from other sources. These were the proportions of the incomes in various ranges which were from wages or salaries:

	PERCENTAGE		PERCENTAGE
Over $1 million	17.9%	$75,000–$100,000	64.9%
$500,000–$1 million	34.7%	$50,000–$75,000	73.6%
$200,000–$500,000	49.5%	$25,000–$50,000	87.2%
$100,000–$200,000	59.7%	$20,000–$25,000	88.6%

[175]

INCOME DECLARED AND TAXES PAID IN 1980

RANGES OF DECLARED ADJUSTED GROSS INCOMES	NUMBER OF RETURNS	PERCENTAGE OF RETURNS	PERCENTAGE OF NATIONWIDE AGI	PERCENTAGE PAID BY TAXPAYERS IN THIS RANGE	PERCENTAGE OF NATIONWIDE TAXES PAID
Over $1,000,000	4,112	0.004%	0.5%	48.4%	1.6%
$500,000–$1,000,000	12,105	0.01%	0.5%	45.2%	1.5%
$200,000–$500,000	97,232	0.1%	1.7%	40.5%	4.5%
$100,000–$200,000	434,041	0.5%	3.6%	33.4%	7.6%
$75,000–$100,000	524,031	0.6%	2.8%	27.5%	4.9%
$50,000–$75,000	2,009,790	2.1%	7.4%	22.8%	10.9%
$25,000–$50,000	17,724,448	18.9%	36.8%	16.3%	38.8%
$20,000–$25,000	9,127,402	9.8%	12.8%	13.0%	10.8%
$15,000–$20,000	11,083,032	11.8%	12.0%	11.8%	9.2%
$10,000–$15,000	14,278,662	15.3%	11.0%	9.6%	6.9%
$5,000–$10,000	18,369,635	19.6%	8.5%	5.7%	3.1%
Under $5,000	19,951,788	21.3%	2.4%	1.6%	0.2%
TOTAL	93,616,278	100.0%	100.0%	15.5%	100.0%

[175]

In 1979 the total amount of declared adjusted gross income came to an overall figure of $1,463,666,582,000. The principal sources of this income were:
- wages and salaries, $1,229,353,731,000 (or 84.0 percent);
- business and professional earnings, $55,828,874,000 (or 3.8 percent);
- pensions and annuities, $37,181,977,000 (or 2.5 percent);
- dividends, $33,078,347,000 (or 2.3 percent);
- interest, $73,217,952,000 (or 5.0 percent);
- sales of capital assets, $26,810,024,000 (or 1.8 percent);
- with the remainder (0.6 percent) coming from such sources as unemployment compensation, alimony, and sales of noncapital property.

[174]

SOURCES OF INCOME IN THREE RANGES: 1979

Figures for 1979 illustrate the differing sources of income in three different tax-return ranges.

	RETURNS WITH INCOMES OF:		
	$1,000,000 and Over	$50,000 to $100,000	$20,000 to $25,000
Number of returns	3,542	1,880,482	9,009,214
Average income	$2,194,491	$65,094	$22,358
	PERCENTAGES		
Wages and salaries	13.7%	67.2%	90.2%
Business or professions	7.2%	10.5%	2.6%
Partnerships	1.8%	3.8%	0.4%
Dividends	22.5%	5.1%	0.9%
Interest	6.4%	6.9%	3.4%
Royalties	2.0%	0.5%	—
Estates or trusts	2.0%	0.5%	—
Pensions or annuities	0.1%	1.4%	2.0%
Sales of assets	44.2%	3.5%	0.6%
Other sources	0.1%	0.6%	—
	100.0%	100.0%	100.0%

It is not possible to be precise about which of these sources are "earned" or "unearned." The problem is that with businesses, professions, and partnerships, an individual may work full-time, or have an ownership interest but not be a working member. So if those sources are omitted, it emerges that those in the $1 million and over range got 13.7 percent from wages and salaries versus 77.3 percent from unearned sources. In the $50,000 to $100,000 range, those respective proportions were 67.2 percent and 17.7 percent; while at $20,000 to $25,000, they were 90.3 percent and 7.0 percent.

[174]

FURTHER FINDINGS FROM 1979

A total of $213,754,094,000 in taxes were due in April of 1980, and $199,772,867,000 had been withheld from wages and salaries during 1979. However, of the withheld amount, $43,069,222,000 (or 21.6 percent) was refunded. In fact, of the returns filed for 1979, a total of 69,846,610 (or 75.4 percent) received refunds.

Altogether, 309,384 returns declared income from alimony, with an average of $4,473 per return. Within this group, 944 returns with total incomes of over $100,000 received alimony, and their payments averaged $33,537.

A total of 6,323,186 returns listed income as unemployment compensation, with an average of $1,129 from this source. Altogether, 2,290 returns with total incomes exceeding $100,000 received such compensation; their payments averaged exactly $1,300.

And 17,952,362 returns claimed medical and dental deductions, averaging $715 each. For those with incomes of over $100,000, the average claim was $1,222.

[174]

MARITAL STATUS OF TAXPAYERS IN 1978

Of the 89,771,551 returns, 44,483,348 (or 49.6 percent) were joint filings of married couples; 37,212,370 (or 41.5 percent) came from single individuals; 6,382,444 (or 7.1 percent) were from nonmarried or separated persons who headed households; 1,567,250 (or 1.7 percent) came from married persons filing separate returns; and the remaining 126,139 (or 0.1 percent) were from widows or widowers whose spouse died during the previous year.

Between 1965 and 1978, filings by married couples fell from 58.2 percent of the total to 49.6 percent.

RETURNS FROM OLDER PERSONS IN 1978

In 1978 a total of 8,370,125 income tax returns were filed by individuals aged 65 or over. Of these, less than half (46.6 percent) declared income from private pensions or annuities.

Altogether, 904,818 (or 7.2 percent) of persons 65 or older filing income tax returns had incomes of $25,000 or over.

$1,000,000 and over	729
$500,000 to $1,000,000	2,090
$100,000 to $500,000	64,630
$50,000 to $100,000	177,559
$25,000 to $50,000	659,810
	904,818

[107]

MILLION-DOLLAR INCOMES IN 1978

Among the 2,041 tax returns declaring incomes of $1,000,000 or over, 1,632 came from married couples, 293 from single individuals, 65 from nonmarried heads of families, 43 from married persons filing separate returns, and 8 from widows or widowers whose spouse had died during the previous year.

Of these 2,041 returns, 729 (or 35.7 percent) were from persons aged 65 or over, or married couples where at least one of the spouses was over 65.

[107]

WHERE MILLIONAIRES LIVED IN 1978

Of the 2,041 persons declaring incomes of $1,000,000 or over, the largest number lived in California (352), followed by New York (316), Texas (233), Florida (125), and Illinois (113).

In terms of the proportion of $1,000,000 returns for every 1,000,000 returns filed, Delaware came first with 23 returns, or 94.0 per million filed. Nevada's 26 came to 76.1 per million, and the District of Columbia's 21 amounted to 65.4 per million. New York and Texas were next, at 45.3 and 43.6 respectively. Connecticut, with 50 returns of $1,000,000, had a rate of 37.6. California and Florida followed, with 36.3 and 34.1.

Of the 194,787 returns from abroad, 9 declared $1,000,000 incomes, for a rate of 46.2.

[107]

STATE AND LOCAL TAXES

State Tax Collections. In 1980 the 50 states collected a grand total of $136,913,324,000 in taxes and other assessments. Across the country as a whole this averaged out to $623.91 per resident. (This figure does *not* include taxes at the local level.)

The states that collected the most money were: Alaska ($3,541 per capita), Hawaii ($1,091), Delaware ($886), Wyoming ($863), and California ($853).

The states that collected the least were: New Hampshire ($302 per capita), South Dakota ($393), Missouri and Tennessee (both $430), and Ohio ($444).

[54]

SOURCES OF STATE TAXES

Taken together, state revenue collections came from the following sources in 1980:

PERCENTAGE SALES AND EXCISE TAXES		PERCENTAGE LICENSE FEES		PERCENTAGE OTHER TAXES	
General sales	31.5%	Motor vehicles	3.6%	Individual income taxes	27.1%
Motor fuels	7.1%	Corporations	1.0%	Corporate income taxes	9.7%
Tobacco	2.7%	Vehicle operators	0.3%	Severance taxes	3.0%
Public utilities	2.3%	Hunting and		Property taxes	2.1%
Insurance	2.3%	fishing	0.3%	Death and gift taxes	1.5%
Alcoholic beverages	1.8%			Other revenues	3.7%
	47.7%		5.2%		47.1%

[54]

STATE INCOME TAXES

The states with the highest proportions of their revenues coming from personal income taxes were: Oregon (59.6 percent), Massachusetts (47.4 percent), Delaware (45.7 percent), New York (45.4 percent), and Wisconsin (42.5 percent).

The states with the smallest part of their revenues from personal income taxes were: Tennessee (1.6 percent), New Hampshire (3.9 percent), New Mexico (5.1 percent), Connecticut (5.5 percent), and Alaska (7.0 percent).

And six states have no income tax at all: Florida, Nevada, South Dakota, Texas, Washington, and Wyoming.

[54]

LOCAL TAXES

The states tend to vary with respect to their localities' share of combined state and local tax revenues. For the country as a whole, the share of local governments averages 39.2 percent.

The states where local taxes account for the highest proportions are: New Hampshire (58.8 percent), New Jersey (52.4 percent), New York (51.9 percent), Nebraska (47.3 percent), and Massachusetts (46.7 percent).

The states where local taxes comprise the smallest shares are: New Mexico (17.9 percent), Delaware (18.4 percent), Hawaii (19.8 percent), Kentucky (20.2 percent), and West Virginia (20.8 percent).

[54]

CITY PER CAPITA TAXES

In 1979 the Census published figures on the per capita tax levels in the nation's 46 largest cities:

Washington, D.C.	$1,280	Houston	$203
New York	841	Los Angeles	200
Boston	708	New Orleans	200
San Francisco	416	Portland	193
Philadelphia	413	Tulsa	185
Nashville	391	Cleveland	182
Baltimore	380	Oakland	178
Newark	379	Omaha	172
St. Louis	356	Fort Worth	165
Denver	350	Austin	165
Cincinnati	273	Indianapolis	160
Detroit	268	Jacksonville	157
Atlanta	237	Milwaukee	155
Dallas	237	Columbus	155
Chicago	234	Phoenix	154
Honolulu	231	San Jose	154
Buffalo	224	Toledo	151
Seattle	223	Long Beach	151
Miami	222	Memphis	146
Oklahoma City	222	Kansas City	138
Minneapolis	215	San Diego	120
Louisville	204	El Paso	102
Pittsburgh	203	San Antonio	88

[58]

Taxes by Size of Cities. In 1979 city taxes averaged $207.58 per resident.

Cities of a million or more averaged $496 in taxes per capita; 500,000 to a million, $292; 300,000 to 500,000, $226; 200,000 to 300,000, $223.

Then: 100,000 to 200,000, $202; 50,000 to 100,000, $186; and less than 50,000, $116.

[58]

SERVICES

"TRANSFER PAYMENTS"

In 1979 the federal government administered a total of $204,923,000 in "transfer payments." This sum consists of money taken from some people in the form of taxes, channeled through the government, and given to other individuals as part of public programs. (In fact, many people both pay taxes *and* receive transfer payments.)

Out of every $1,000 in transfer payments, $501 went for Social Security pensions and disability benefits: $143 paid the medical bills of retired persons, $122 went for military pensions and other veterans' benefits, $63 covered the pensions of retired federal employees, and $50 was for workers' injury compensation and unemployment benefits.

Another $31 paid for food stamps, $26 consisted of direct federal payments to low-income individuals, $21 provided pensions for retired railroad workers, $8 went to former miners suffering from black lung disease, and the remaining $35 consisted chiefly of educational assistance and foster care payments.

In all, $858 of each $1,000 in transfer payments consisted of pensions for retired persons or payments to the disabled.

[112]

SOCIAL WELFARE EXPENDITURES: 1970–1979

Between 1970 and 1979 the costs of welfare programs at all levels of government rose from $145,856,000,000 to $428,333,000,000, an increase of 193.7 percent over the 9-year period. If an adjustment is made for inflation, the 9-year rise works out to 103.7 percent. (Full figures for 1980 are not yet available.)

In per capita terms, the program's costs for each American came to $701 in 1970 and $1,912 in 1979. This reflected a 172.8 percent increase, or one of 55.4 percent if adjusted for inflation.

Ratios to Other Budgets. In 1970 social welfare costs consumed 15.2 percent of the Gross National Product, 40.1 percent of the federal government's budget, and 48.2 percent of outlays at all governmental levels. By 1979 those respective ratios had risen to 18.5 percent, 55.0 percent, and 56.8 percent.

In 1970 federal funds paid for 53.0 percent of all social welfare costs. In 1979 they contributed 61.7 percent.

The following table page shows the rise in costs of major welfare programs, with their growth rates adjusted for inflation, plus the federal share as of 1979.

[155]

GROWTH OF GOVERNMENT SOCIAL WELFARE PROGRAMS: 1970–1979 (IN 000,000's)

	1970	1979	PERCENTAGE GROWTH Actual	Adjusted	PERCENTAGE FEDERAL SHARE: 1979
Social Security: old-age, disability, survivors	$29,686	$102,596	245.6%	131.1%	100.0%
Medicare	$ 7,149	$ 29,155	307.8%	164.3%	100.0%
Public employees retirement	$ 8,659	$ 33,774	290.0%	154.8%	67.3%
Unemployment insurance	$ 3,820	$ 11,313	196.2%	104.8%	21.7%
Workers' compensation	$ 2,950	$ 11,109	276.6%	147.7%	21.0%
Public assistance (including welfare allowances)	$ 9,221	$ 17,299	87.6%	46.8%	53.1%
Public assistance medical services (including Medicaid)	$ 5,213	$ 23,401	348.9%	186.3%	51.8%
Food stamps	$ 577	$ 6,478	1022.7%	546.0%	100.0%
Other health-care programs	$ 5,313	$ 11,628	118.9%	63.5%	53.5%
Medical research	$ 1,635	$ 4,225	158.4%	84.6%	90.0%
Veterans compensation	$ 5,394	$ 9,898	83.5%	44.6%	100.0%
Other veterans services	$ 3,684	$ 10,557	186.6%	99.6%	92.0%
Elementary and secondary education	$38,632	$ 77,280	100.0%	53.4%	8.0%
Higher education	$ 9,907	$ 24,111	143.4%	76.6%	18.7%
Housing programs	$ 701	$ 6,226	788.2%	420.8%	93.2%
Child nutrition (including school lunches)	$ 896	$ 3,939	339.6%	181.3%	85.7%
All other programs	$12,419	$ 45,344	265.1%	141.5%	60.8%
TOTAL	$145,856	$428,333	193.7%	103.7%	61.7%

[155]

WHO RECEIVES PUBLIC SERVICES?

The number of persons receiving public services can be identified in two different ways. One set of figures comes from an annual Census Bureau survey, which actually asks people what benefits they receive. The most recent Census studies were conducted in 1980 and 1981.

The other source of statistics is from the agencies themselves, whose most recent reports range from 1977 to 1982. These figures are not strictly comparable with those from the Census studies, because the agencies count individual beneficiaries whereas the Census focuses on total households. Due to this discrepancy the two sets of figures will be treated separately.

FOOD STAMPS

Of the total of 82,368,000 households covered in the 1981 Census study, 6,769,000 (or 8.2 percent) received food stamps at some time during the year.

Within this group, 62.6 percent of the households were white and 35.1 percent were black, with the remainder of other races. In addition, 40.7 percent were households headed by women; and 17.3 percent consisted of individuals aged 65 or older.

The 1980 study found that 48.3 percent of the households receiving food stamps contained persons who had worked at some point during the year, and among all the households receiving stamps, the average value of that benefit was $812.00.

SCHOOL LUNCHES

Of the 34,329,000 households in 1981 that had children under the age of 18, 5,532,000 (or 16.1 percent) received free or reduced-price school lunches. Among this group, 62.0 percent of the recipient families were white and 34.1 percent were black.

The 1980 study found that 52.7 percent of the school lunch households had both parents present. And of all the households in the school lunch program, the median income was $9,191; with 21.8 percent of the families having incomes of $15,000 or over.

SUBSIDIZED HOUSING

Of the 26,487,000 households that resided in rental premises in 1981, 2,777,000 (or 10.5 percent) lived in publicly owned or subsidized housing.

Within this group, 58.0 percent where white; 34.4 percent included persons aged 65 or over; and 37.1 percent were families headed by women.

MEDICARE

Medicare is mainly a program for older citizens, although it also covers younger persons who have been deemed "disabled" by the Social Security Administration. In 1981 a total of 19,788,000 (or 24.0 percent) of the nation's households had one or more persons eligible for Medicare. Of these households, 88.9 percent were white and 9.9 percent were black.

The 1980 study of Medicare recipients found that their median household income came to $8,584, with 25.7 percent having incomes of $15,000 or over.

And among the individuals using Medicare in 1980, a total of 57.8 percent were women, but only 37.7 percent of them were still living with a husband. Of the men using Medicare, 72.7 percent were living with a wife.

MEDICAID

Medicaid assistance is intended for low-income households, regardless of the age of the recipients. Of the nation's households in 1981, altogether 8,287,000 (or 10.1 percent) used Medicaid services.

Among this group, 67.1 percent were white, 36.7 percent were families headed by women, and 30.3 percent had one or more persons aged 65 or over. While most individuals aged 65 or over are also eligible for Medicare, it offers only partial coverage of charges. As a result, a considerable number of people find they must use Medicaid to make up the difference.

The 1980 Census study showed that the median household income of Medicaid recipients was $5,990, with 17.8 percent having incomes of $15,000 or over.

And of all those using Medicaid in 1980, 61.1 percent were women, 18.1 percent were persons of both sexes over 65, and 33.7 percent were youngsters aged 14 or under.

[37, 45]

DISTRIBUTION OF GOVERNMENTAL BENEFITS

The Census Bureau found that 34.3 percent of the nation's households received benefits under one or more of the programs that were analyzed. The recipients were distributed among the following categories.

	PERCENTAGE
Medicare only	50.9%
Medicare and Medicaid	8.3%
School lunches only	7.4%
Medicaid only	4.5%
Food stamps and Medicaid	4.3%
Food stamps, school lunches, and Medicaid	3.9%

(continued)

(continued)

	PERCENTAGE
Food stamps only	3.4%
Food stamps, Medicare, and Medicaid	2.5%
Food stamps and school lunches	2.0%
Public or subsidized housing only	1.9%
Housing and Medicare	1.9%
All other combinations	9.0%
	100.0%

[37]

MEDICAL SERVICES FINANCED BY GOVERNMENT

MEDICARE

During 1980 persons aged 65 and older received a total of 131,109,000 bills for physicians' and hospital services, for which Medicare made reimbursements to the patients totaling $26,926,400,000.

Of these bills, 9,534,000 were charges for in-patient hospital treatment, which came to an average of $2,888 for a 9.9 day stay. Medicare reimbursed 69.7 percent of these costs, which meant a typical patient still had to pay $875.

Medicare patients also received 13,033,000 surgeons' bills, which averaged $271. Of these fees, 78.5 percent were reimbursed, so the average patient still had an outlay of $58.

Patients also incurred 92,011,000 medical bills from regular physicians averaging $56. Of these charges 77.3 percent, or all but $13, was reimbursed.

Finally, they had 16,531,000 bills for out-patient hospital visits, for which Medicare made an average reimbursement of $61.

[156]

MEDICAID

In 1978 a total of 22,196,000 different low-income persons received 62,309,000 separate medical services under Medicaid programs, for which the government made payments of $17,966,000,000, an average of $809 per person.

The people provided for by Medicaid included: members of families with low or no earnings (4,699,000 adults and 9,493,000 children), older people with additional medical bills not paid for by Medicare (3,374,000), disabled individuals (2,634,000) and persons who are blind (86,000).

Services paid for by Medicaid included: visits to physicians (15,329,000), prescription drugs (14,736,000), out-patient hospital services (8,288,000), laboratory and X-ray tests (5,574,000), dental treatments (4,336,000), in-patient stays at hospitals (3,732,000), family planning services, including sterilizations and abortions (1,302,000), and time spent in nursing homes (615,000).

[177]

VETERANS ADMINISTRATION

During 1980 the Veterans Administration operated 172 hospitals and 158 other facilities having a total of 194,331 employees.

Altogether, 1,275,446 in-patients were treated in the hospitals, for an average stay of 28.0 days, and at an average cost of $4,312 per stay.

In addition, Veterans Administration facilities performed 238,904 surgical procedures and handled 17,971,407 out-patient visits. They conducted 5,707,389 X rays, dispensed 36,687,165 prescriptions, and carried out 214,818,805 laboratory tests.

The VA also ran 92 nursing homes, with an average of 12,750 patients in residence. The average cost per patient came to $17,169, and the average patient stay was 3.11 years.

[130]

AMERICANS IN RETIREMENT

While it is not possible to state precisely how many Americans are "retired," we can chart changes in the ratio between younger and older Americans. In 1950 there were 144 persons aged 65 or over for every 1,000 in the 21-to-64 age group. By 1970 that ration had risen to 193 per 1,000. And according to the 1980 Census, there were 205 Americans 65 or over for every 1,000 in the 21-to-64 cohort.

Between 1960 and 1980, the number of Americans receiving Social Security retirement benefits rose from 14,157,138 to 30,936,668, an increase of 118.5 percent.

Between 1960 and the end of 1979, the number of retired Federal Civil Servants receiving Civil Service retirement benefits grew from 515,265 to 1,640,205, a rise of 218.3 percent.

From 1960 to 1980, the number of former military personnel receiving military retirement benefits rose from 256,007 to 1,330,150, a growth of 419.6 percent.

And over the same period, the number of persons receiving disability pensions under Social Security increased from 687,451 to 4,682,172, a rise of 581.1 percent.

[114, 138, 153, 160]

SOCIAL SECURITY RECIPIENTS

As of August of 1981, a total of 35,711,312 persons were receiving Social Security benefits. The recipients were:

	NUMBER	PERCENTAGE
Retired men workers	10,635,308	29.6%
Retired women workers	9,292,693	26.0%
Disabled former workers	2,814,150	7.9%
Widows and widowers	5,012,271	14.0%
Spouses of retired or disabled workers	3,460,528	9.7%
Children	4,482,373	12.6%
All others	13,989	0.1%
TOTAL	35,711,312	100.0%

[159]

COVERAGE

As of 1977—the most recent year for these figures—of the 106,100,000 individuals who had employment subject to Social Security deductions, 15,700,000 (or 14.8 percent) reached the maximum level of earnings for which deductions are made. (Among the women workers, only 2.5 percent attained that level.)

Of these 106,100,000 persons subject to Social Security, 68,500,000 (or 64.6 percent) were employed throughout the year, 7,600,000 (or 7.1 percent) were self-employed, and the remaining 30,000,000 (or 28.3 percent) worked less than a full year.

Among the 42,680,000 women who worked, 36.7 percent did so less than a full year. Of those who did work throughout the year, 30.5 percent earned less than $4,800. Moreover, of the full-year women workers, only 3.8 percent made the maximum income subjected to Social Security deductions.

[160]

SOCIAL SECURITY BENEFITS: NEWLY RETIRED PERSONS

In 1981 the typical man who retired from work that year received $5595 as his annual Social Security benefit. The typical woman who retired received $3629.

Here were the first-year benefits received by men and women workers who retired between 1960 and 1980. The actual dollar figures are given, plus the value of those amounts in 1981 purchasing power.

| | MEN | | WOMEN | |
	Actual Benefit	1981 Dollar Equivalent	Actual Benefit	1981 Dollar Equivalent
1960	$1104	$3389	$ 759	$2330
1965	1249	3599	918	2645
1970	1642	3845	1244	2913
1975	2876	4858	2078	3510
1980	5097	5619	3311	3650

Between 1960 and 1980 men's benefits rose by 65.8 percent in constant-value dollars. Women's benefits increased by 56.7 percent.

[157]

SOCIAL SECURITY BENEFITS: ALL RETIRED PERSONS

In 1981 the average Social Security benefit for all retired men came to $4880. The average sum for women was $3403, or 69.7 percent of the men's amount.

The following were the average annual benefits received by all retired men and women on the Social Security rolls in various years between 1960 and 1980. The actual dollar amounts are given, plus the value of those figures in 1981 purchasing power.

| | MEN | | WOMEN | |
	Actual Benefit	1981 Dollar Equivalent	Actual Benefit	1981 Dollar Equivalent
1960	$ 973	$2987	$ 691	$2121
1965	1107	3190	802	2311
1970	1550	3629	1143	2676
1975	2622	4429	1935	3269
1980	4285	4724	3008	3316

Between 1960 and 1980 men's benefits rose by 58.2 percent. Women's benefits increased by 56.3 percent.

[157]

SIZE OF PENSIONS

The most recent analysis of the size of Social Security pensions focuses on benefits awarded in January of 1979. Since then the payments have increased, as they rise with the Cost of Living Index. Even so, pensions are based on how much workers made when they were employed. This means that older retired workers, who had jobs when wages and deductions were lower, receive smaller pensions than those who retired more recently.

	PERCENTAGES			
Pension Amount	Retired Men Workers	Retired Women Workers	Married Couples	Widows or Widowers
$8,400 and over	—	—	3.6%	—
$7,200 to $8,400	—	—	6.5%	—
$6,000 to $7,200	—	—	21.6%	0.2%
$4,800 to $6,000	10.4%	3.5%	33.6%	1.3%
$3,600 to $4,800	39.8%	20.0%	16.4%	21.3%
$2,400 to $3,600	29.0%	33.2%	11.7%	48.7%
Under $2,400	20.7%	43.3%	6.6%	28.5%
	100.0%	100.0%	100.0%	100.0%
Average pension	$3,079	$2,764	$5,250	$2,924
Highest possible	$5,876	$5,876	$8,815	$7,832

If both spouses worked, they each received their own retirement checks. If only one worked, they received a joint check as a married couple. And in that case, if the retired worker dies, the spouse then gets a check as a widow or widower.

[160]

CONTRIBUTIONS COMPARED WITH BENEFITS

Individuals who entered employment in 1937 and continued working until 1981, and who made the maximum level of Social Security payments during those 44 years, would have contributed a total of $14,765.69 into the system. Their employers would have paid in an identical amount, bringing the full contribution to $29,531.38.

If those individuals retired in June of 1981, their annual Social Security pensions would have begun at $9,034.80.

[160]

SOCIAL SECURITY AND INCOME TAXES

The following were typical amounts paid by both "average earners" and "maximum earners" in Social Security and income taxes over the past forty years. (An "average earner" had wages at the national average. A "maximum earner" had reached the top level from which Social Security taxes are deducted.)

The final column shows where Social Security tax rates compare to those of income taxes.

		SOCIAL SECURITY		INCOME TAXES		
Average Earners	Income	Annual Payment	Percentage of Income	Annual Taxes	Percentage of Income	Social Security as Percentage of Taxes
1940	$ 1,195	$ 12	1.0%	—	0.0%	—
1950	2,544	38	1.5%	$ 185	7.3%	20.5%
1960	4,007	120	3.0%	485	12.1%	24.7%
1970	6,186	297	4.8%	695	11.2%	42.7%
1980	12,455	763	6.1%	1,148	9.2%	66.5%
Maximum Earners						
1940	3,000	30	1.0%	19	0.6%	157.9%
1950	3,000	45	1.5%	265	8.8%	17.0%
1960	4,800	144	3.0%	629	13.1%	22.9%
1970	7,800	374	4.8%	985	12.6%	38.0%
1980	25,900	1,588	6.1%	4,316	16.7%	36.8%

[156]

RECIPIENTS AMONG THE STATES

As of 1979 a total of 92.5 percent of all persons aged 65 or over were receiving Social Security benefits. The range ran from New Hampshire, where 99.1 percent were covered, to Louisiana, where the comparable figure was 87.2 percent.

After New Hampshire, the states with the most beneficiaries were: Maine (98.3 percent), Vermont (97.3 percent), Michigan (96.7 percent), and Delaware and Wisconsin (both 96.3 percent).

Following Louisiana, the states with the lowest proportions were: Florida (89.2 percent), Mississippi (89.4 percent), Maryland (89.8 percent), and Georgia and Alabama (both 90.1 percent).

[156]

RETIRED WOMEN: 1960–1981

Between 1960 and June of 1981, the number of women receiving Social Security checks rose from 6,732,773 to 17,103,439, an increase of 154.0 percent.

In 1960 a total of 42.3 percent of the women received benefits based on their own earnings as workers. By 1981 that proportion had increased to 53.9 percent.

In 1960 altogether 34.8 percent of the women received benefits as wives of retired workers. By 1981 that proportion had declined to 20.2 percent.

And in 1960 a total of 22.9 percent of the women received benefits as the widows of retired workers. By 1981 that proportion had grown to 25.9 percent, largely because more women were outliving their husbands for longer periods of time.

[156, 160]

WOMEN: WORKERS AND WIDOWS

In 1978 a total of 8,430,000 women received Social Security payments based on their own earnings as workers. However, of this group, 2,163,011 (or 25.7 percent) would have received larger checks had they never worked at all and simply received benefits as the wives or widows of retired working husbands.

What Social Security does, therefore, is raise the payments of these 836,004 wives and 1,322,897 widows to match those received by their nonworking counterparts. The arrangement is called "dual entitlement."

There are also 45,479 men eligible for "dual entitlement" because their earnings records as workers bring them smaller Social Security pensions than they would receive as the husbands or widowers of retired working women.

[160]

CHILDREN

In September of 1981, a total of 3,265,276 children under the age of 18 were receiving Social Security benefits. There were also 759,414 students between the ages of 18 and 21 receiving funds. An additional 459,470 persons over 18 "with childhood disabilities" received Social Security payments as well.

These 4,484,160 individuals qualified for Social Security payments as follows: 632,057 were children of retired workers; another 2,560,769 were sons or daughters of deceased workers; and a further 1,291,334 had parents who were disabled workers.

[159]

RECIPIENTS BY RACE

In 1978—the most recent year for figures—the average white male worker who had retired received an annual Social Security pension of $3,556. The typical white woman worker's pension was $2,804, or 78.9 percent of the men's amount.

Pensions for black men averaged $2,900, or 81.6 percent of the figure for white men. Black women workers averaged $2,244, which was 77.4 percent of the amount for black men, and 80.0 percent of the figure for white women.

[160]

EARLY RETIREMENT

As of September 1981, over half—57.1 percent—of the men who were receiving Social Security pensions had retired before they reached the age of 65. As a result, they got a lower level of benefits, averaging $4,720 per year as against the $5,723 for those who worked until 65.

Even more women workers—69.7 percent—retired early and received reduced benefits: $3,693 per year for choosing to retire before 65, as against $4,703 for waiting until that age.

[159]

RECIPIENTS LIVING ABROAD

At the end of 1979, a total of 311,665 Social Security checks were being sent to retired workers or their survivors living outside the United States. The largest numbers went to Mexico (53,852) and Canada (47,388), while the rest of Latin America and the Caribbean countries accounted for 14,693 checks.

Outside the Western Hemisphere, Italy led in the number of checks received (with 42,199), followed by the Philippines (34,587). Then came Greece (17,051) and West Germany (16,639), plus the United Kingdom (12,703), followed by Israel (6,789), Ireland (6,721), Spain (6,342), Portugal (5,957), Norway (5,251), Yugoslavia (4,609), France (4,510), Sweden (4,070), Japan (3,819), and Poland (3,412).

In all, 1,211 checks went to Africa, of which 516 were to the Cape Verde Islands. Among the others on the list were: Switzerland (2,564), Australia (1,417), Finland (1,010), Malta (654), Hungary (370), New Zealand (289), Turkey (214), Thailand (194), India (186), Macao (120), and Luxembourg (103).

Payments are not sent to Albania, Cuba, East Germany, North Korea, or the Soviet Union because, the Social Security Administration states, "There was no reasonable assurance that the payee would actu-ally receive the check and be able to negotiate it."

[160]

AID TO FAMILIES

The Aid to Families with Dependent Children (AFDC) program pro-vides payments to parents who have no other source of income, so they can support their children at a subsistence level. In most of these house-holds, the mother is the only parent; and she receives the payment on behalf of the children.

In 1960 a total of 803,000 American households received AFDC pay-ments; the children in them represented 3.0 percent of all youngsters under the age of 18.

By the end of 1980, the AFDC total had grown to 3,842,534 families, consisting of 7,599,376 children and the 3,501,773 parents who cared for them. This worked out to 1.98 children per AFDC household; together they comprised 12.2 percent of all American children under the age of 18.

[156]

AID PAYMENTS

As of December of 1980, the typical monthly AFDC payment came to $288.77 for a household having one parent and an average of 1.9 children.

The states providing the largest stipends were: California ($431.00 per month), Rhode Island ($405.59), Alaska ($392.15), Michigan ($390.20), and Hawaii ($385.71).

The states with the lowest averages were: Mississippi ($87.89 per month), Texas ($108.29), Alabama ($110.17), Tennessee ($112.93), and South Carolina ($115.98).

[158]

RECIPIENT FAMILIES

In June of 1980, the Social Security Administration released a study of individuals being assisted by the Aid to Families with Dependent Chil-dren program. At the time of the study, 3,523,294 families with 7,835,803 children were being aided.

The typical family receiving aid had 2.2 children. Altogether, 40.3 percent of the families had only 1 child; 27.3 percent had 2; 16.1 percent had 3; 8.2 percent had 4; and the remaining 8.1 percent had 5 or more.

Race. In terms of race, 52.6 percent of the members of the households were white, 43.0 percent were black, 1.1 percent were American Indian, 0.4 percent were Asian, and for the other 2.9 percent race was not recorded.

In addition to the racial figures, the study showed that 443,242, or 12.6 percent, of the recipient families were of Hispanic origin (most of these were also in the "white" category). They broke down as Puerto Ricans (204,061), Mexican Americans (180,202), Cubans (4,476), and other Spanish origins (54,503).

Heads of Recipient Households. In all, 360,220 families (or 10.2 percent) had a father or adoptive father living with the household. However, only 4.9 percent of those fathers were employed full-time, and 3.3 percent were working part-time. (The rest, for the most part, were unemployed or incapacitated.)

Families containing persons who are employed can be aided by the AFDC program if their earnings fall below a certain level. Thus 8.4 percent of the mothers had full-time jobs, and another 5.4 percent worked part-time.

Altogether, 21.0 percent of the families had a man as "head" of the household. Here were the various people heading assisted households:

MALE HEADS	Percentage	FEMALE HEADS	Percentage
Father	8.8%	Mother or step-	
Stepfather	4.3%	mother	69.8%
Grandfather	5.7%	Grandmother	7.2%
Other male relative	1.2%	Other female relative	1.5%
Male nonrelative	1.0%	Female nonrelative	0.5%
	21.0%		78.9%

Mothers' Age and Education. The ages of the mothers in aided families distributed as follows: under 20, 8.1 percent; in their twenties, 44.5 percent; in their thirties, 26.6 percent; 40 or over, 15.2 percent; and the last 5.6 percent, unknown.

Of the mothers whose education was recorded, 33.8 percent had completed high school; 5.0 percent had attended college; and another 0.7 percent had graduated from college.

Fathers. The fathers of the 7,835,803 children in the program fell in the following categories: 21.4 percent were divorced from the children's mothers, 25.5 percent were separated, and 33.8 percent had never been married to the mother.

Among the remaining fathers, 2.6 percent were deceased, 5.0 percent were in the household but unemployed, another 5.9 percent were incapacitated, 0.2 percent were in the armed forces, and the status of 5.6 percent was not known.

ESTABLISHING PATERNITY

In 3,163,830 cases, attempts were made to "establish the paternity" of children in the program. In 2,244,451 instances (or 70.9 percent) the father was identified; and in 919,379 (or 29.1 percent) he wasn't.

In 4,186,548 cases, efforts were made to "locate the absent parent" of children in the program, and in 2,181,183 instances (or 52.1 percent) he or she was located; in 2,005,365 (or 47.9 percent) he or she wasn't.

Enforcing Support. In 2,751,254 cases, attempts were made to "enforce support obligations" on the part of parents. In 1,172,433 instances (or 42.6 percent) these efforts were at least partially successful; and in 1,578,821 (or 57.4 percent) the efforts had no result.

In 1,003,816 cases an absent parent was under "court order or other obligation" to provide child support, and of these, 340,165 (or 33.9 percent) made at least partial payments; 663,651 (or 66.1 percent) did not.

[100]

Collecting from Fathers. The Department of Health and Human Services is mandated by Congress to collect child support payments from the fathers of children in public assistance programs.

In August 1980 a total of $47,219,282 in such payments was collected, which came to 4.4 percent of the $1,075,515,289 budget for public assistance.

The states that collected the largest percentages from fathers were: Utah (11.4 percent), Idaho (9.6 percent), Oregon (8.6 percent), Iowa (7.9 percent), and Wisconsin (7.6 percent).

The states collecting the smallest percentages were: Mississippi (0.7 percent), Georgia (1.2 percent), Oklahoma and Illinois (both 1.8 percent), and Virginia (1.9 percent).

[99]

HOW MANY MOTHERS ARE ON WELFARE?

The Aid to Families with Dependent Children program (AFDC) provides living allowances to households containing children but where the adults cannot work, or prefer not to do so, or have jobs with very low wages. As of December 1980, a total of 3,842,534 families with

7,599,376 children were being supported under this program, which is usually referred to as welfare.

A study by the Social Security Administration, published in 1980, found that 69.8 percent of all AFDC families were headed by the children's mother. Applying that percentage to the figure of 3,842,534 AFDC households, it would appear that 2,682,089 mothers headed welfare families.

At the same time, provisional findings from the 1980 Census reported that in the country as a whole, there were 5,029,954 mothers living alone with their children in their care. If, as just noted, 2,682,089 of these mothers were on welfare, it follows that 2,347,865 were not, with the respective percentages being 53.3 percent and 46.7 percent.

Not All Recipients Are Mothers. However, the proportion of AFDC families headed by mothers varies from state to state. In New Hampshire, for example, 92.7 percent of these families have mothers as their heads, whereas in Alabama only 42.1 percent do. The reason for differences such as these is that the welfare recipient is often a person other than the children's mother. In West Virginia, for instance, 28.3 percent of the recipients are fathers, as are 24.7 percent in Vermont. And in Georgia, 19.6 percent of the checks go to children's grandmothers, as do 19.0 percent in South Carolina and 17.8 percent in Texas. Allowing for these variations, the states can be ranked according to how many of their single mothers are on the welfare rolls. ("Single" in this case means that the mother may be divorced, widowed, never married, or married but living apart from her husband.)

HOW MANY SINGLE MOTHERS ARE ON WELFARE?
U.S.A. = 53.3%

Hawaii	90.8%	Connecticut	57.3%
Pennsylvania	80.3%	Alaska	55.8%
Massachusetts	79.4%	Maryland	54.8%
New Jersey	78.4%	Ohio	54.2%
Michigan	78.3%	Washington	53.8%
Wisconsin	74.1%	Missouri	50.6%
Maine	71.7%	Delaware	50.0%
Rhode Island	66.6%	New Hampshire	46.2%
California	66.0%	New Mexico	46.1%
Iowa	64.6%	West Virginia	45.5%
Minnesota	64.4%	Kansas	44.8%
New York	64.2%	Nebraska	44.3%
Illinois	59.9%	South Dakota	44.1%
Vermont	58.7%	Kentucky	42.0%

(continued)

(continued)

North Dakota	41.8%	Tennessee	33.8%
Louisiana	40.4%	Virginia	32.7%
Oregon	39.2%	Montana	31.4%
Idaho	38.9%	Alabama	30.9%
Mississippi	38.4%	North Carolina	30.1%
South Carolina	37.6%	Wyoming	27.5%
Arkansas	36.5%	Georgia	27.3%
Oklahoma	35.6%	Florida	27.2%
Colorado	35.0%	Arizona	26.4%
Indiana	34.5%	Texas	20.2%
Utah	34.0%	Nevada	18.2%

[9, 100, 159]

COSTS OF MEDICAL CARE

During 1979 children and their parents and other eligible persons received a total of $17,938,000,000 in public assistance payments.

Payments to "vendors" providing medical care under public assistance programs—hospitals, nursing homes, physicians, dentists, and pharmacists—totaled $23,401,000,000. Thus for every dollar going directly to public assistance recipients, the health care industry received another $1.30.

[160]

CHAPTER NINE

GOVERNMENT: PERSONNEL AND POLITICS

As of October of 1980, a total of 18,092,302 Americans were on one or another of the nation's public payrolls. Of these government workers, 2,726,625 (or 15.1 percent) were federal civilian employees; another 2,050,627 (or 11.3 percent) were on active military duty; while 3,753,106 (or 20.7 percent) were at the state level, with the remaining 9,561,944 (or 52.9 percent) employed by a variety of localities.

Statistics on government employment tend to be mercurial because they depend on the dates when the counts were made. When there are differences in the figures for a given year, it is usually because they were compiled in different months or express an annual average.

Government employment covers a wide range of occupations and activities. The Postal Service had a January 1981 payroll of 655,748 persons, while the Arms Control and Disarmament Agency got by with a staff of 191. The Veterans Administration employed 235,480 persons, whereas the Battle Monuments Commission had 383. The Congress had 40,898 people working for it, and the Supreme Court of the United States made do with 377.

The military had 148,773 women in its services, of whom 8.2 percent were officers. Looked at another way, it had 689,965 persons of sergeant or equivalent rank, of whom 4.3 percent were women. The federal civilian payroll contained 126 actuaries, 132 autopsy assistants, 45 podiatrists, and 24 fish hatchery managers.

Federal salaries also change every year, according to a statutory pay scale, so the figures given here will soon be out-of-date. However, as of 1982, the top military and civilian salaries were given a ceiling. While a small percentage increase is allowed each year, it still means that officials in the several highest grades were all getting the same pay.

This chapter includes three principal sections. The first provides figures on civilian employment at the federal, state, and local levels, the second contains information on current military personnel, and the third presents statistics on recent voting and elections.

CIVILIAN EMPLOYEES

As of October of 1980, a total of 16,041,675 civilians were on various public payrolls:

	NUMBER	PERCENTAGE
Federal	2,726,625	17.0%
State	3,753,106	23.4%
Local	9,561,944	59.6%
	16,041,675	100.0%

Local employment broke down as follows: school districts (4,269,998), municipalities (2,560,516), counties (1,852,744), special districts (484,456), and townships (394,230).

[55]

TOTAL GOVERNMENT EMPLOYMENT: 1952 AND 1980

Between 1952 and 1980, total government employment rose from 6,708,000 to 16,266,000, an increase of 142.5 percent.

However:

- Employment at the Federal level only went from 2,574,000 to 2,821,000, for a rise of 9.6 percent.

- Employment at the state and local levels rose from 4,134,000 to 13,445,000, and increase of 225.2 percent.

- In 1952 persons employed by the Federal government comprised 38.4 percent of the total public payroll. In 1980 the Federal share had declined to 17.3 percent.

- In 1952 there were 163 Federal employees for every 10,000 people in the country. In 1980 that ratio had decreased to 125 per 10,000.

- Between 1952 and 1980, state and local employees went from 262 per 10,000 population to 594 per 10,000 residents.

[115]

PUBLIC AND PRIVATE EMPLOYMENT

Measured another way, between 1952 and 1980, the number of persons on public payrolls rose from 13.5 percent of all employed Americans to 17.9 percent.

However, during this period the proportion holding federal jobs fell from 5.0 percent of all workers to 3.2 percent.

In contrast, state and local government employees rose from 8.6 percent of the nation's work force to 14.8 percent.

[167]

STATE AND LOCAL GOVERNMENTS

The Census Bureau collects figures on state and local governments twice during each decade, and the most recent published information is for 1977. (The next survey is scheduled for 1982, but its reports will not be available until late in 1984.)

Altogether, there were 79,862 governmental units at the local level, including Counties (3,042), Municipalities (18,862), Townships (16,822), School Districts (15,174), and Special Districts (25,962).

In the 25 years between 1952 and 1977, 7 counties disappeared, 2,084 municipalities were created, 52,172 school districts went out of existence, and 13,643 special districts were created.

[53]

STATE EMPLOYEES

The states with the largest numbers of employees were: California (309,872), New York (230,938), Texas (200,496), Michigan (161,323), and Illinois (154,954).

The states with the smallest numbers were: Wyoming (11,146), Nevada (14,571), South Dakota (16,435), North Dakota (17,089), and Delaware (17,396).

In the nation as a whole, there were 137 state employees for every 10,000 persons in the population. The states with the highest ratios of state employees were: Alaska (416 per 10,000), Hawaii (378), Delaware (262), New Mexico (259), and Vermont (215).

The states with the lowest payroll ratios were: California (105 state employees per 10,000 residents), Florida, Ohio, and Pennsylvania (all 107 per 10,000), and Illinois (108 per 10,000).

[55]

PUBLIC AND PRIVATE EMPLOYMENT IN THE STATES

In addition to computing public employees per 10,000 persons in the population, they can be measured against each 1,000 people in the private work force. For the country as a whole, there were 174 individuals in state or local jobs for every 1,000 persons in private employment.

The states with the highest proportions of their work force in state or local positions were: Alaska (285 per 1,000 in private occupations), North Dakota (263 per 1,000), New Mexico (256), Montana (252), and Mississippi (247).

The states with the lowest proportions were: Connecticut (127 per 1,000 private employees), Nevada (133 per 1,000), Pennsylvania (143), Rhode Island (145), and New Hampshire (148).

[167]

CITY AND COUNTY EMPLOYEES

In 1980 city governments had a total of 2,560,578 persons on their payrolls. However, 489,411 of these were only part-time workers, so the full-time equivalent figure came to 2,116,399.

County governments, calculated in the same way, had a full-time equivalent work-force of 1,651,048.

Here is how city and county workers were distributed by function:

| | PERCENTAGE | |
	City Employees	County Employees
Education*	15.7%	21.2%
Police and corrections	17.7%	11.8%
Fire protection	8.8%	1.1%
Health and hospitals	7.7%	19.6%
Welfare	1.9%	9.5%
Sanitation	7.6%	1.2%
Highways and streets	5.6%	7.3%
Parks and recreation	4.8%	1.9%
Utilities and water	6.6%	0.4%
Libraries	1.6%	1.0%
Transit	3.1%	0.3%
Housing	2.0%	0.2%
General administration	8.3%	15.3%
Other functions	8.6%	9.2%
	100.0%	100.0%

[56, 57]

*Does not include employees of school districts.

Local Government Employees. The average number of local government employees for the country as a whole is 351 for every 10,000 residents. The states with the highest ratios are: Wyoming (450 per 10,000), New York (416), Georgia and Nevada (both 410), and Alaska (387).

The states with the lowest ratios of local employees are: Hawaii (125 per 10,000), Delaware and Kentucky (both 265), Vermont (267), and Utah (287).

[55]

STATE AND LOCAL EMPLOYEES: POLICE, LIBRARIANS, PROFESSORS

When state and local employees are taken together in the following three fields, these are the states with the highest and lowest proportions per 10,000 residents:

HIGHEST RATIOS		LOWEST RATIOS	
State and Local Police Officers (U.S. = 20.6)			
Nevada	34.6	Iowa	14.9
New Jersey	29.5	Kentucky	14.9
New York	27.8	Vermont	14.9
Illinois	26.9	North Dakota	15.1
Massachusetts	26.2	Mississippi	15.5
Librarians (U.S. = 2.9)			
Washington	5.4	Hawaii	0.1
New Jersey	4.8	Mississippi	0.6
Maryland	5.1	North Carolina	0.8
Nevada	4.5	North Dakota	0.9
Indiana	4.2	Vermont	1.0
Public College Faculties (U.S. = 19.1)			
Wisconsin	34.5	Pennsylvania	8.8
Colorado	33.5	Maine	9.9
Alaska	32.6	Massachusetts	10.2
Arizona	30.8	New Jersey	12.7
Oregon	30.5	Florida	13.5

[55]

FEDERAL EMPLOYMENT

As of January of 1981, the federal agencies with the largest number of civilian employees were: Defense (972,990), Postal Service (655,748), Veterans Administration (235,480), Health and Human Services

(159,945), Treasury (131,637), Agriculture (122,899), Interior (79,546), Transportation (71,641), and Justice (56,867).

The other Cabinet departments were: Commerce (47,010 employees), Labor (23,544), State (23,521), Energy (21,692), Housing and Urban Development (16,726), and Education (7,538).

Among the smallest federal agencies were: the American Battle Monuments Commission (383 employees), National Endowment for the Arts (358), Federal Maritime Commission (335), National Endowment for the Humanities (317), Commission on Civil Rights (292), Farm Credit Administration (267), Arms Control and Disarmament Agency (191), Selective Service System (116), Postal Rate Commission (71), National Mediation Board (63), U. S. Maritime Board (53), and the Presidential Commission on Ethical Problems (26).

The Congress had 40,898 employees, of whom 7,873 worked for the Senate and 12,986 for the House of Representatives. The remaining 20,039 were employed conjointly, of which the largest sections were the General Accounting Office (5,434), the Library of Congress (5,321), and the U.S. Government Printing Office (6,552).

The Executive Office of the President had 1,783 employees, of which the largest sections were the Office of Management and Budget (615) and the White House office (346, of whom one was the President).

The Supreme Court of the United States had a payroll of 337 persons, and the rest of the federal judiciary had 14,811 employees, including 516 district judges and 132 members of the Courts of Appeals.

[117]

POSITIONS AND PAY SCALES

The United States Civil Service has 18 "General Schedule" grades for its white-collar employees. As of October 1980, these were the number of persons at various levels, plus the average salary for those in each of the grades.

GRADE	AVERAGE SALARY	CIVIL SERVANTS
GS-18	$50,113	
GS-17	$50,113	1,372
GS-16	$49,819	
GS-15	$46,670	
GS-14	$39,549	85,076
GS-13	$33,532	
GS-12	$27,981	264,834

(continued)

Note: Under current statutes, Civil Service salaries are not allowed to exceed a specified ceiling. As a result, everyone in grades GS-17 and GS-18 has reached that point and now receives the same salary.

(continued)

GRADE	AVERAGE SALARY	CIVIL SERVANTS
GS-11	$23,153	150,942
GS-10	$21,246	
GS-9	$19,034	164,664
GS-8	$17,875	
GS-7	$15,667	156,430
GS-6	$14,410	
GS-5	$12,716	273,067
GS-4	$11,148	166,036
GS-3	$ 9,545	86,448
GS-2	$ 8,285	23,327
GS-1	$ 7,310	2,744

[76]

CIVIL SERVICE OCCUPATIONS

The following were some of the occupations on the federal payroll as of October 1979, along with the number of people holding them and their average salaries at that time:

126	Actuaries	$31,785
24	Alcohol tax technicians	18,431
367	Archivists	26,127
132	Autopsy assistants	12,706
172	Biomedical engineers	25,539
119	Cemetery administrators	20,854
47	Ceramic engineers	34,708
18	Cryptographers	25,250
251	Curators	27,645
42	Deportation and exclusion examiners	45,616
773	Entomologists	31,103
289	Exhibits specialists	20,280
24	Fish hatchery managers	24,144
239	Geneticists	33,268
191	Interpreters	18,323
658	Landscape architects	27,240
695	Law clerks	19,826
301	Manual arts therapists	20,225
706	Messengers	9,312
51	Music specialists	21,493
778	Oceanographers	28,956
72	Optometrists	27,919
45	Podiatrists	35,161
44	Sanitarians	23,034
26	Theater specialists	18,441

[118]

When classified by race and sex, the major groups on the "general schedule" payroll of the federal civil service are: white men (49.0 percent); white women (32.3 percent); black women (8.8 percent); and black men (4.6 percent). The remaining 5.3 percent are Orientals, American Indians, and Hispanic Americans of whatever race.

Thus for every 100 white men on the payroll, there are 66 white women, whereas for every 100 black men there are 191 black women.

The groups rank as follows along the payscale:

	PERCENTAGE			
	White Men	White Women	Black Men	Black Women
GS 16–18	0.9%	0.05%	0.3%	0.02%
GS 14–15	11.8%	0.9%	4.3%	0.4%
GS 12–13	32.1%	4.7%	15.1%	3.4%
GS 9–11	30.8%	17.4%	22.2%	13.3%
GS 5–8	18.6%	43.7%	35.5%	44.9%
GS 1–4	5.9%	33.3%	22.6%	37.9%
	100.0%	100.0%	100.0%	100.0%

If white men and black men are compared, it is clear that white men predominate in the middle and upper levels, while black men cluster toward the bottom. Thus 58.1 percent of the black men are ranked as GS 1–8, whereas that is so of only 24.5 percent of the white men.

White women do better than black women, but only by a moderate margin. Thus while 5.7 percent of the white women are at GS 12 or higher, so are 3.8 percent of black women. In contrast, 44.8 percent of white men are in those grades, over double the 19.7 percent for black men.

It follows that black women fare more favorably when compared with black men than white women do when compared with white men. Among black civil servants, the proportion of women who are in Grades 12–15 works out to 19.6 percent of the men in those positions. Among their white colleagues, the women's representation at that rank is only 12.8 percent of that for the men.

[138]

SITES OF FEDERAL EMPLOYMENT

The 2,852,328 civilians employed by the federal government at the beginning of 1979 held jobs in the following locations:

- 129,183 (or 4.5 percent) were outside the United States.
- 208,051 (or 7.3 percent) had offices within the District of Columbia.
- 133,520 (or 4.7 percent) were in adjacent counties of Maryland or Virginia.
- 2,381, 574 (or 83.5 percent) were located in the rest of the United States.

The states with the largest numbers of federal employees were: California (290,052), New York (166,194), Texas (148,022), Virginia (144,075), Maryland (130,370), and Pennsylvania (128,018).

The states with the fewest were: Vermont (4,424), Delaware (4,990), Wyoming (6,398), North Dakota (8,316), and Nevada (9,218).

[138]

Union Membership. Among federal civilian employees in the following agencies, these proportions belong to labor unions: Postal Service, 87.1 percent; Treasury, 82.5 percent; Veterans Administration, 70.4 percent; the Air Force, 67.9 percent; the Navy, 64.1 percent; Health, Education and Welfare (since reorganized), 61.1 percent; the Army, 56.0 percent.

[138]

SEXUAL HARASSMENT IN THE CIVIL SERVICE

In 1981 the government's Merit System Protection Board released its report on "Sexual Harassment in the Federal Workplace." According to its survey of civil servants, 42 percent of all women in governmental employment had experienced sexual harassment, as had 15 percent of the men.

Among the women, 95 percent said they had been sexually harassed by men with whom they worked; 3 percent said they were bothered by women; and 2 percent said both men and women had given them trouble.

The experience of the men was somewhat different: 22 percent said they received sexual overtures from other male employees, but 72 percent said their harassment came from women. (The remaining 6 percent had been annoyed by both men and women.)

Of the women, 37 percent suffered sexual harassment from supervisors, with the other 63 percent of their annoyances from coworkers or subordinates. With men, only 14 percent were sexually harassed by supervisers, while 86 percent of their trouble came from subordinates and coworkers.

From Rape to Leering. The study defined harassment as ranging from "actual or attempted rape" and "pressure for sexual behaviors" to instances of "leaning over, cornering, or pinching" and "sexually suggestive looks." The report did not detail the extent to which men and women were subjected to each of these problems.

Harassing Departments. The report said that women were most likely to be sexually victimized in the Department of Labor (where 56 percent of all women employees had been harassed), followed by Transportation (55 percent of all women), Justice (53 percent), Housing and Urban Development (47 percent), and the Air Force and Veterans' Administration (both 46 percent).

Men were most apt to experience sexual annoyance in Health and Human Services and the Veterans' Administration (both 22 percent), followed by Justice, Housing and Urban Development, and the General Services Administration (all 16 percent).

The study estimated that the costs of sexual harassment came to $188,700,000 in 1981, of which $5,000,000 was due to time lost because of "emotional stress."

[119]

RETIREMENT AND PENSIONS

As of October 1979, a total of 1,640,205 persons were receiving federal civilian pensions.

Of these, 1,212,904 were retired civil servants, for a ratio of 425 for every 1,000 currently employed. Their average annual pension came to $10,937.

There were also 427,301 survivors of retired civil servants, whose pensions averaged $4,078 per year.

[138]

POSTAL SERVICE

Between 1900 and 1980, the number of post offices in the United States declined from 76,688 to 30,326. In 1900 there was one post office for every 991 persons; in 1980 there was one for every 7,469.

A total of 106,311,062,000 items went through the mails in 1980. Of these, 60,276,119,000 were First Class letters, 10,220,274,000 were Second Class periodicals or "controlled circulation publications," 30,380,886,000 were Third Class circulars, and 633,395,000 were Fourth Class parcels.

Additional items included 304,789,000 Mailgrams and Priority and Express letters, 963,780,000 letters and parcels sent overseas,

511,869,000 pieces which used the government's franking privilege, 27,840,000 items sent "free for the blind," and 2,992,110,000 items in other categories.

In per capita terms, the typical person received 266 letters, 45 periodicals, 134 circulars, and 3 parcels during the year.

In 1974 the average postal employee processed 127,977 pieces of mail throughout the year. By 1980 that figure had increased to 156,528.

[129]

MILITARY PERSONNEL

As of September 30, 1980, the American military establishment consisted of 5,348,093 persons, as follows: 2,050,627 men and women on active duty, 2,169,485 members of the Reserve and National Guard, 93,295 persons in officer training while at college, and 1,034,686 civilian employees.

If the 2,826,559 dependents of active duty personnel are added in, the total rises to 8,174,652.

[114]

ACTIVE DUTY

Of the 2,050,627 persons on active duty, 777,036 (or 37.9 percent) were in the Army, 557,969 (or 27.2 percent) were in the Air Force, 527,153 (or 25.7 percent) were in the Navy, and 188,469 (or 9.2 percent) were in the Marine Corps.

Officers and Enlisted Personnel. Among the 2,050,627 active duty personnel, there were 175 officers for every 1,000 enlisted men and women; however, that ratio varied among the services. In the Marines, there were 107 officers per 1,000 enlisted persons; in the Navy, the ratio was 137 per 1,000. The Army had 146 officers for each 1,000 enlisted persons, and the Air Force had 214 officers for every 1,000 enlisted men and women.

Military and Civilian Personnel. The Army had 511 civilian employees for each 1,000 of active duty personnel. The Navy and Marine Corps had 438 civilians for every 1,000 persons on military duty, and the Air Force ratio was 442 per 1,000. (These figures do not count the 77,674 civilians who work directly for the Department of Defense.)

[114]

STATIONED IN THE STATES

Altogether 2,231,783 Department of Defense personnel are located in the 50 states; 1,359,942 military on active duty and 871,841 civilian employees.

The states having the largest share of these persons are: California (317,834), Texas (196,101), Virginia (182,344), Georgia (108,265), North Carolina (98,213), and Florida (95,348).

The states with the smallest numbers are: Vermont (509), Iowa (1,830), West Virginia (2,083), Oregon (4,123), Wisconsin (4,288), and Minnesota (4,694).

A total of 22,954 persons—10,982 military and 11,972 civilians—work inside the Pentagon, which is located in Virginia.

[114]

STATIONS: HOME, ABROAD, AND AFLOAT

Of military personnel on active duty, 1,266,125 (or 61.7 percent) are stationed in the continental United States, 429,375 (or 20.9 percent) are stationed abroad, 210,780 (or 10.3 percent) are on shipboard and afloat, 63,128 (or 3.1 percent) are in Alaska or Hawaii, and 13,409 (or 0.7 percent) are in United States territories, ranging from 9,053 on Guam to 7 on Wake Island. The remaining 68,009 (or 3.3 percent) were "in transit" on September 30, 1980.

Of the 429,375 stationed abroad, 300,287 (or 69.9 percent) were in the fourteen NATO countries: West Germany (244,320), United Kingdom (24,312), Italy (11,903), Turkey (5,269), Greece (4,445), Iceland (2,868), Netherlands (2,630), Belgium (2,114), Portugal (1,367), Norway (645), Greenland (287), France (77), Denmark (44), and Luxembourg (6).

Other contingents were in: Japan and Okinawa (46,004), South Korea (38,780), the Philippines (13,387), Panama (9,146), Spain (8,974), Cuba (2,150), Bermuda (1,350), Saudi Arabia (502), Egypt (495), Israel (97), and Antarctica (76).

The military also had 68 persons in the Soviet Union, consisting of 20 embassy attachés and 48 Marine Corps guards.

[114]

EDUCATION

Altogether, 95.3 percent of commissioned officers were college graduates, ranging from 97.2 percent in the Army to 83.7 percent in the Marine Corps.

Of enlisted personnel, 1.5 percent had graduated from college, ranging from 2.1 percent in the Air Force to 0.5 percent in the Marines.

Of these enlisted men and women, 88.8 percent were at least high school graduates, ranging from 97.7 percent in the Air Force to 83.9 percent in the Navy.

AGE

Of all male active duty personnel, 14.9 percent were under 20, 37.5 percent were between 20 and 24, 18.6 percent were 25 to 29, 23.0 percent were in their thirties, 5.7 percent were in their forties, and 0.3 percent were 50 and over.

The median age of all men on active duty was 26.3 years. (Comparable data are not given for women.)

[114]

RANK AND SEX

The 2,050,627 men and women on active duty hold the following ranks, or their naval equivalents. The first percentage column shows each rank's percentage of the total military strength, the second the percentage of positions in the rank held by women.

	TOTAL	PERCENTAGE OF TOTAL FORCE	WOMEN	PERCENTAGE HELD BY WOMEN
Generals	1,111	0.05%	7	0.6%
Colonels	13,938	0.7%	235	1.7%
Lt. Colonels	32,833	1.6%	831	2.5%
Majors	49,194	2.4%	2,172	4.4%
Captains	85,778	4.2%	7,681	9.0%
Lieutenants	77,148	3.8%	10,381	13.5%
Officers	260,002	12.7%	21,307	8.2%
Warrant Officers	17,620	0.9%	159	0.9%
Sergeants	689,965	33.7%	29,412	4.3%
Corporals	396,280	19.3%	41,489	10.5%
Privates	673,448	32.8%	77,872	11.6%
Enlisted personnel	1,759,693	85.8%	148,773	8.5%
Cadets	13,312	0.6%	1,179	8.9%
Total	2,050,627	100.0%	171,418	8.4%

[114]

WOMEN PERSONNEL

Altogether, women comprise 8.4 percent of the military personnel on active duty. However, their proportion varies considerably by rank and branch of service.

	PERCENTAGE OF WOMEN
Air Force Academy cadets	11.4%
Air Force enlisted personnel	11.3%
Army enlisted personnel	9.1%
Air Force officers	8.7%
West Point cadets	8.6%
Army officers	7.7%
Navy officers	7.7%
Annapolis cadets	6.6%
Navy enlisted personnel	6.5%
Marine enlisted personnel	3.7%
Marine officers	2.7%

[114]

RACIAL REPRESENTATION

In 1980, among armed services personnel aged 17 to 24, 74.8 percent were white, 22.0 percent were black, and 3.2 percent were of other races.

In 1966 the racial representation was 91.1 percent white, 8.1 percent black, and 0.8 percent of other races.

[39]

DEPENDENTS OF MILITARY PERSONNEL

Personnel on active duty had 2,826,559 dependents, 1,089,826 spouses, 1,601,374 children, and 135,359 parents or other dependents.

The Department of Defense computes the average number of dependents per 100 men on active duty. These ratios are as follows: 266 dependents for every 100 Army officers, 196 per 100 Navy officers, and 192 per 100 Marine officers. In addition, there are 172 per 100 Army enlisted men; 156 per 100 Air Force enlisted men; 100 per 100 Navy enlisted men; and 74 per 100 male Marines. (Comparable figures are not available for women.)

RETIRED PERSONNEL

There are 1,306,232 retired military personnel receiving pensions or disability benefits, or 637 such persons for every 1,000 individuals on active duty.

[114]

WARTIME SERVICE

A total of 35,311,557 men and women served in the armed forces during the four major conflicts of this century:

	SERVICE PERSONNEL	BATTLE DEATHS	DEATHS PER 10,000
World War I	4,734,991	53,402	113
World War II	16,112,566	291,557	181
Korea	5,720,000	33,629	59
Vietnam	8,744,000	47,239	54
TOTAL	35,311,557	425,827	121

In World War I the proportion of service personnel who were drafted came to 59.4 percent. In World War II the figure was 61.3 percent; for Korea and Vietnam, the proportions were 27.1 percent and 20.0 percent, respectively.

[114]

VETERANS

As of September 1980, a total of 30,118,000 persons were veterans of military service. Of these, 26,065,000 served during periods of hostilities. There were 521,000 veterans of World War I and 12,422,000 survivors of World War II. An additional 5,826,000 served during the Korean conflict, and 9,015,000 did service in the Vietnam era. (There were also 147 living Spanish-American War veterans).

Within these totals are 1,167,000 veterans who served in both World War II and Korea, and 552,000 who experienced both Korea and Vietnam.

In addition to these who did active duty, 3,050,000 individuals served between Korea and Vietnam; another 1,003,000 completed their service since the withdrawal from Vietnam.

[130]

Women Veterans. In 1980 there were 713,000 women veterans, including nurses, comprising 2.4 percent of former service personnel. Among them were 8,000 veterans of World War I and 286,000 from World War II, constituting 1.5 percent and 2.3 percent of the survivors of those wars. And 74,000 and 193,000 women served in the Korean and Vietnam conflicts, for 1.3 percent and 2.1 percent of the veterans of those respective periods.

A further 56,000 women were in the service between Korea and Vietnam, followed by 96,000 who served after Vietnam, amounting to 1.8 percent and 9.6 percent of the veterans from these respective periods.

[130]

Disabled Veterans. As of September 1980, a total of 2,273,589 veterans were receiving financial compensation for disabilities incurred while in the service.

Of these, 27,720 had served in World War I, 1,193,196 in World War II, 235,654 in Korea, 553,326 in Vietnam, and 261,685 did their service during peacetime periods.

The total cost of this compensation came to $6,068,113,000, an average annual sum of $2,669 per disabled veteran.

[130]

POLITICS

ELECTED OFFICIALS

In 1977 the country had a total of 80,449 popularly elected officials. Of these, 537 were at the federal level: the President, the Vice-President, 100 Senators, and 435 members of the House of Representatives.

The 50 state governments had a total of 15,294 elected officials, for an average of 305.9 per state. (Not all of these were elected on a statewide basis. Most elected judges, for example, came from constituencies covering only a section of the state.)

At the local level, the nation's counties had 62,922 elected officials, an average of 20.7 per county. Municipalities had 134,017 and townships 118,966, an average of 7.1 in each case. School districts had 87,062 elected officials, mainly board members who averaged 5.7 per district; special districts elected 72,377 officials, an average of 2.8 each.

[53]

The states with the largest numbers of elected officials at all levels were: Illinois (40,457), Pennsylvania (28,903), Texas (24,728), New York (24,076), and Ohio (19,890).

Those with the fewest were: Hawaii (172), Delaware (996), Rhode Island (1,103), Nevada (1,138), and Alaska (1,362).

Ranked by elected officials per 10,000 population, the states with the most were: North Dakota (283.2 elected officials per 10,000 residents), Vermont (155.1), South Dakota (134.9), Nebraska (102.0), and Kansas (74.8).

States electing the fewest officials per capita were: Hawaii (2.0 per 10,000), Maryland (5.3), Florida (5.9), Virginia (6.1), and North Carolina (9.7).

[53]

VOTER TURNOUT

Every so often the Census asks a nationwide sample of people whether they voted in the last election, and then provides information on those who said they voted.

However, there is a problem with this kind of survey. A considerable number of people said they voted when in fact they hadn't. In the study of the 1980 election, those who claimed to have been at the polls exceeded the actual turnout by 7.6 percent. So the figures that follow should be taken with a few grains of salt: they are all several percentage points higher than what actually occurred.

A total of 59.2 percent of those questioned said they had voted in the 1980 Presidential election. For men the figure was 59.1 percent; while for women it was slightly higher, at 59.4 percent.

Race and Age. A total of 60.9 percent of white citizens claimed to have voted, with both men and women responding at that level. For blacks the figure was 50.5 percent, with men at 47.5 percent and women at 52.8 percent. Among citizens of Spanish origin, the reported turnout was 29.9 percent: 29.2 percent for the men and 30.4 percent for the women.

With respect to age, reported voting rose from ages 18 through 64 after which a decline set in:

AGE	PERCENTAGE
18 and 19	34.2%
20–24	42.2%
25–29	51.2%
30–34	58.1%
35–44	64.4%
45–54	67.5%
55–64	71.3%
65–74	69.3%
75 and over	57.7%
Median age	44.5

Marital and Social Status. Married men and women reported voting at a level of 65.6 percent. Among those who were widowed or divorced, 53.1 percent said they had voted, as did 46.4 percent of those who were still single. Separated persons were less apt to participate, with only 40.6 percent reporting they had voted. Of those in the widowed and divorced group, 54.3 percent of the women said they voted, whereas only 49.8 percent of the men said they had.

As might be expected, voting correlated with social status. Of persons with 4 or more years of college, 79.9 percent said they had voted. So did 73.8 percent of those having family incomes of $25,000 or over.

Among those who failed to finish high school, turnout came to 44.1 percent. And for individuals with family incomes under $10,000, 45.9 percent said they had cast ballots.

White-collar workers outvoted blue-collar workers by 70.9 percent to 48.0 percent. Persons with jobs were more likely to go to the polls, with 61.8 percent claiming to vote, compared with 41.2 percent of those who were unemployed. And homeowners were more apt than renters to take part in the election, by a margin of 68.3 percent to 44.6 percent.

Turnout Among the States. In the 1980 election, 30 states had reported turnouts higher than the nationwide figure of 59.2 percent. The remaining twenty states were below that proportion. The table on the following page lists percentages.

PERCENTAGES OF RESIDENTS WHO SAID THAT THEY HAD VOTED IN THE 1980 ELECTION

ABOVE THE NATIONAL AVERAGE		BELOW THE NATIONAL AVERAGE	
Wisconsin	74.5%	New Mexico	58.8%
South Dakota	74.5%	Maryland	58.6%
Minnesota	73.3%	West Virginia	58.4%
Utah	72.2%	Arkansas	57.2%
North Dakota	71.9%	Kentucky	56.9%
Idaho	70.1%	Alaska	56.8%
Maine	68.2%	Tennessee	56.7%
New Hampshire	68.2%	Alabama	56.4%
Iowa	67.7%	Hawaii	55.9%
Connecticut	67.6%	Florida	55.5%
Montana	67.6%	Virginia	55.2%
Mississippi	67.3%	Pennsylvania	54.9%
Missouri	67.3%	New York	54.8%
Illinois	66.4%	California	53.8%
Oregon	65.9%	Arizona	53.5%
Massachusetts	65.6%	Georgia	53.5%
Rhode Island	64.7%	North Carolina	52.2%
Michigan	64.1%	South Carolina	51.4%
Louisiana	63.9%	Texas	51.1%
Kansas	63.6%	Nevada	49.3%
Colorado	63.4%		
Nebraska	63.3%		
Indiana	61.6%		
Vermont	61.3%		
Washington	61.2%		
Ohio	60.7%		
Delaware	60.4%		
New Jersey	59.6%		
Oklahoma	59.4%		
Wyoming	59.4%		

[33]

PRESIDENTIAL PERCENTAGES

In the 16 Presidential elections from 1920 through 1980, none of the winning candidates received more than 61.1 percent of the popular vote:

	CANDIDATE	PERCENTAGE OF POPULAR VOTE	PARTY
1964	Lyndon Johnson	61.1%	Democratic
1936	F. D. Roosevelt	60.8%	Democratic
1972	Richard Nixon	60.7%	Republican

(continued)

(continued)

	CANDIDATE	PERCENTAGE OF POPULAR VOTE	PARTY
1920	Warren Harding	60.4%	Republican
1928	Herbert Hoover	58.1%	Republican
1932	F. D. Roosevelt	57.4%	Democratic
1956	D. D. Eisenhower	57.4%	Republican
1952	D. D. Eisenhower	55.1%	Republican
1940	F. D. Roosevelt	54.7%	Democratic
1924	Calvin Coolidge	54.0%	Republican
1944	F. D. Roosevelt	53.4%	Democratic
1980	Ronald Reagan	50.7%	Republican
1976	Jimmy Carter	50.1%	Democratic
1960	John Kennedy	49.7%	Democratic
1948	Harry Truman	49.6%	Democratic
1968	Richard Nixon	43.4%	Republican

[113]

THIRD-PARTY CANDIDATES

In 11 of the 16 Presidential elections between 1920 and 1980, the two major candidates together received at least 97.1 percent of the popular vote.

In 1968 third parties attained 13.9 percent of the vote, and in 1924 they achieved 17.2 percent.

In 1948 and 1920, third-party candidates received 5.3 percent and 5.5 percent respectively. In the 1980 election, John Anderson got 6.6 percent of the votes and other candidates got 1.7 percent, for a total of 8.3 percent.

[113]

PRESIDENTIAL VOTING IN 1980

In the 1980 Presidential election, Ronald Reagan received 50.7 percent of the popular vote; Jimmy Carter got 41.0 percent; and John Anderson's portion came to 6.6 percent.

The states voting most strongly for Ronald Reagan were Utah (72.8 percent of its popular vote), Idaho (66.4 percent), Nebraska (65.6 percent), North Dakota (64.2 percent), and Wyoming (62.6 percent).

Jimmy Carter's strongest supporters were Georgia (55.8 percent), West Virginia (49.8 percent), Tennessee (48.4 percent), South Carolina (48.2 percent), and Mississippi (48.1 percent).

John Anderson got his strongest support in Massachusetts (15.2 percent), Vermont (14.9 percent), Rhode Island (14.4 percent), New Hampshire (12.9 percent), and Connecticut (12.2 percent).

[113]

CAMPAIGN FUND CONTRIBUTIONS

Each income tax return asks the persons submitting the form if they want one dollar from what they pay to go into a Presidential Election Campaign Fund (such a payment does not increase their taxes).

In 1978 there were 38,914,181 tax returns from married couples on which taxes had to be paid. Of these, there were 617,708 where only one of the spouses checked for the contribution, and 12,668,229 where both did. Thus out of the 77,828,362 persons represented by these returns, 25,954,166, or 33.3 percent, requested the contribution.

Of the 30,706,564 returns filed by one person on which taxes had to be paid, 9,744,520, or 31.7 percent, checked "yes" for the contribution.

In all, out of the $108,534,926 that would have gone to the Fund if everyone had agreed, only $35,698,686, or 32.9 percent, was actually contributed.

[107]

CHAPTER TEN

CRIME AND PUNISHMENT

Statistics on the incidence of crime call for careful scrutiny; for instance, many crimes go undiscovered or are not reported to the police. For this reason, the Census conducts a survey every year in which a sample of Americans are asked whether they were victims of a crime during the preceding year; and, if so, whether anyone reported it to the authorities. However, the survey tends to leave defining the offense up to each individual. (As, for example, whether it was a burglary or a robbery. Or if a threatening situation was in fact an "attempted rape.") As a result, the responses are apt to be subjective. Moreover, the Census reports take several years to process. Even so, these estimates of "victimization" are the most comprehensive coverage currently available.

In addition, the Federal Bureau of Investigation collects figures from law enforcement agencies on local crimes which were reported or which they discovered on their own. This information comes chiefly from sheriffs and police departments, and is summarized in the FBI's annual "Uniform Crime Reports." However, these statistics, while detailed and precise, cover only crimes that came to the notice of authorities, and local law enforcement agencies can also differ in their interpretation of what constitutes a burglary or a larceny or an attempted rape. In addition there are difficulties in comparing these official figures with the responses in the Census surveys. For example, the FBI's statistics on robberies and motor vehicle thefts include those reported by businesses, whereas the Census only interviews members of households.

The FBI also publishes statistics on "crimes cleared by arrests." A crime is considered to have been "cleared" when a "law enforcement agency has identified the offender, has sufficient evidence to charge him, and actually takes him into custody." Here, too, some cautions are in order. First, some crimes are not cleared in the same year they happen, so the offense and apprehension may appear in different annual statistics. Second, an arrest may not lead to a conviction, or even an indictment. In fact, in some cases the arrested individual may not have committed the crime, or any crime at all. Third, the arrest of one suspect can end up clearing several crimes, or the clearing of a single crime may involve the arrest of several persons. So there are really no exact statistics on how many crimes have been "solved"; records of arrests are the best estimates we have.

MURDERS

Among the murders committed in 1980, the following weapons or causes were cited: firearms (13,650), "cutting or stabbing instruments" (4,212), "hands, fists, feet, etc." (1,265), "blunt objects" (1,094), strangulation (401), arson (291), asphyxiation (104), explosives (21), poisoning (17), and narcotics (12).

VICTIM-MURDERER RELATIONSHIP

In 49.1 percent of the murders, the murderer was not known to the victim, or their relationship was not reported. Here are the relationships in the other 50.9 percent (the victim is listed first):

RELATED	PERCENTAGE OF MURDERS	NOT RELATED	PERCENTAGE OF MURDERS
Wife–husband	4.7%	Girlfriend–boyfriend	1.8%
Husband–wife	3.6%	Boyfriend–girlfriend	1.3%
Father–child	0.8%	Other friends	3.4%
Mother–child	0.6%	Neighbors	1.4%
Son–parent	1.2%	Acquaintances	26.9%
Daughter–parent	0.9%		34.8%
Brother–sibling	1.1%		
Sister–sibling	0.2%		
Other family	3.0%		
	16.1%		

[103]

RACE

In cases where the victim and the murderer were known to be either black or white, the following patterns prevailed:

PERCENTAGES

	Murderer		
Victim	*White*	*Black*	*TOTAL*
White	45.5%	5.4%	50.9%
Black	2.1%	47.0%	49.1%
TOTAL	47.6%	52.4%	100.0%

SEX

And where the sex of both the victim and the murderer were known, the following patterns prevailed:

PERCENTAGES

	Murderer		
Victim	*Male*	*Female*	*TOTAL*
Male	63.0%	13.7%	76.7%
Female	21.2%	2.1%	23.3%
TOTAL	84.2%	15.8%	100.0%

[103]

AGE OF VICTIM

The following were the ages of murder victims in 1980:

UNDER 30	PERCENTAGE MURDER VICTIMS	30 AND OVER	PERCENTAGE MURDER VICTIMS
Under 1 year	1.0%	30–34	13.2%
1–4	1.5%	35–39	9.2%
5–9	0.7%	40–44	6.9%
10–14	1.0%	45–49	5.5%
15–19	9.0%	50–54	4.9%
20–24	17.6%	55–59	3.7%
25–29	17.1%	60–64	2.8%
	47.9%	Over 65	5.9%
			52.1%

THE EXPERIENCE OF CRIME: ROBBERY AND RAPE

Information about crime, from the victims' descriptions, is compiled by the Census Bureau on an annual basis. Its most recent report covers 1979. The following were its findings for two specific crimes: robbery and rape.

ROBBERY

- In 34.1 percent of the robberies, the persons victimized also said they incurred a physical injury.

- Altogether, 80.6 percent of the robberies were perpetrated by persons not previously known to the victim. However, the other 19.4 percent were committed by someone the victim knew in one way or another.

- In 34.8 percent of the crimes a knife was used, and in 32.6 percent a firearm was present. In the other 32.5 percent there was another weapon, or no weapon at all, or the victim was not sure.

- Where the value of the loss was known, it was put at more than $250 in 18.4 percent of the cases; between $50 and $250 in 39.3 percent; between $10 and $50 in 29.4 percent; and at less than $10 in 12.8 percent.

- A total of 62.9 percent of the robberies took place in the street, a park, or some other outdoor location. Another 13.3 percent occurred in a school or another nonresidential building. An additional 11.4 percent were in the victims' homes. And the other 12.4 percent were in other or unspecified places.

- Only 51.7 percent of the men who were victims said they reported the crime to the police. Among the women, however, 63.2 percent said they had.

- In terms of incidence, 73 white men were robbed during the year out of every 10,000 white men in the population. For black men, the rate was 209 victims per 10,000 black men. Among white women the rate was 38 per 10,000. For black women it was 56 per 10,000.

- In robberies where the victims and the perpetrators were reported as black or white, both were of the same race in 66.3 percent of the cases: in 49.4 percent, whites robbed whites, and in 16.9 percent blacks robbed blacks. In the 33.7 percent where the races interacted, the division was 32.3 percent blacks robbing whites, and in 1.4 percent whites robbing blacks.

[94]

RAPE

Of the 192,000 women who told the Census survey they had been victims of rape, 68,000 (or 35.4 percent) said the act had been "completed" and 124,000 (or 64.6 percent) said the crime had been "attempted." Unfortunately, the Census report does not separate the "completed" and "attempted" crimes in most of its statistical breakdowns.

- In 60.7 percent of the rapes, the offender was a stranger. In the other 39.3 percent, he was known to the victim to some extent.

- In 44.3 percent of the cases the perpetrator carried a knife; in 34.1 percent he had a gun; and in the other 21.7 percent he was not armed or the victim was not sure.

- In terms of incidence, 18 white women were rape victims for every 10,000 white women in the population. For black women, the rate was 26 victims per 10,000 black women.

- The rate for married women was 6 per 10,000 married women; for women who had not been married it was 38 per 10,000; and for divorced or separated women, it was 58 per 10,000.

- Where the victim was white, in 42.4 percent of the cases the offender was someone with whom she was acquainted. However, among black victims, only 19.9 percent of the perpetrators were persons they had known.

- Where the victim was single, 43.6 percent of the offenders were persons known to them. With married women, that proportion was 30.0 percent. And among the divorced or separated women, it was 37.1 percent.

- Altogether, 31.1 percent of the crimes occurred in the victims' homes. Another 35.9 percent were in an outdoor location; and 5.6 percent were in a nonresidential building. The other 27.4 percent were in other or unspecified places.

- In cases where both the victim and the offender were either black or white, both were of the same race in 77.4 percent of the cases; in 63.7 percent both were white, and in 13.7 percent both were black. In the other 22.6 percent where two races were involved, a black man raped a white woman in 19.2 percent of the assaults, while in 3.4 percent a white man raped a black woman, or such an attempt was made.

- In 50.5 percent of the cases, the victim said she reported the offense to the police. This was done in 52.6 percent of the cases where the offender was a stranger, and 45.6 percent where he was not.

- Where the crime was not reported, the following reasons were given: the victim considered it a "private or personal matter" (34.2 percent); she felt "nothing could be done" or there was "lack of proof" (15.8 percent); she was worried over "fear of reprisal" (15.7 percent); she felt it was "not important enought" (14.1 percent); she said the offense was "reported to someone else" (12.2 percent); or she believed the "police would not want to be bothered" (9.0 percent).

[94]

LARCENY THEFTS

During 1980 a total of 7,112,657 cases of "larceny theft" were reported to law enforcement agencies. These offenses differ from *robberies* because they do not involve confronting the victim with force or the threat of force, and they differ from *burglaries* as they do not involve breaking into or entering a home or business premises.

The following were the major categories of reported "larceny thefts" in 1980: accessories stolen from motor vehicles (19.1 percent), items taken from inside motor vehicles (17.3 percent), articles taken from buildings (16.7 percent), shoplifting (10.9 percent), stealing bicycles (10.0 percent), purse-snatching (1.5 percent), pickpocketing (1.2 percent), stealing from coin-operated machines (0.8 percent), all others (22.5 percent).

[103]

RECOVERY OF STOLEN PROPERTY

Only 25.5 percent of reported stolen property is eventually recovered.

Measured in terms of the value of the stolen items, the following were the recovery percentages: locally stolen motor vehicles (55.5 percent), livestock (19.7 percent), office equipment (11.6 percent), firearms (10.8 percent), furs and clothing (10.2 percent), notes and currency (8.0 percent), household goods (7.6 percent), televisions, stereos, and radios (6.0 percent), and jewelry and precious metals (5.7 percent).

[103]

ARRESTS

In 1980 law enforcement agencies made a total of 9,686,940 arrests for crimes committed in 1980 or earlier years. These were the major categories:

Driving while intoxicated (1,303,933), larceny theft (1,123,823), general drunkenness (1,049,614), disorderly conduct (724,404), drug offenses (533,010), burglary (479,639), general assaults (456,887), commercial liquor violations (427,829), aggravated assault (258,721), fraud (261,787), and vandalism (233,857).

Also: carrying or possessing weapons (157,157), robbery (139,476), motor vehicle theft (129,783), receiving or possessing stolen property (115,514), prostitution and commercialized vice (85,815), forgery and counterfeiting (72,643), general sex offenses (63,453), "offenses against family and children" (49,991), gambling (46,697), and vagrancy (29,348).

And, finally: rape (29,341), murder (18,745), arson (18,459), and embezzlement (7,885).

[103]

ARRESTS OF PERSONS RANKED BY RACE
PERCENTAGE

	White	Black	Other
Commercial liquor violations	96.3%	2.2%	1.5%
Driving while intoxicated	96.2%	2.5%	1.3%
General drunkenness	93.1%	4.6%	2.3%
Vandalism	86.4%	12.5%	1.1%
Drug violations	85.4%	13.7%	0.9%
Arson	84.4%	14.7%	0.9%
Vagrancy	79.3%	19.6%	1.1%
Embezzlement	78.5%	20.8%	0.7%
Forgery and counterfeiting	78.3%	20.5%	1.2%
Disorderly conduct	75.2%	23.9%	0.9%
General sex offenses	73.3%	25.6%	1.1%
Motor vehicle theft	73.2%	24.6%	2.2%
Burglary	72.9%	25.7%	1.4%
Offenses against family and children	72.8%	24.6%	2.6%
Fraud	72.6%	25.8%	1.6%
Receiving or possessing stolen property	72.2%	26.7%	1.1%
Carrying or possessing weapons	71.1%	27.4%	1.5%
General larceny thefts	70.3%	27.6%	2.1%
General assualts	66.3%	32.1%	1.6%
Aggravated assault	63.4%	35.2%	1.4%
Murder and nonnegligent manslaughter	54.4%	44.1%	1.5%
Prostitution and commercialized vise	45.1%	53.1%	1.8%
Rape	43.2%	55.3%	1.5%
Robbery	33.4%	65.5%	1.1%
Gambling offenses	21.4%	76.1%	2.5%
All arrests	76.7%	21.7%	1.6%

[103]

PERSONS UNDER 18

Persons under the age of 18 accounted for these percentages of those arrested for the following crimes: vandalism (49.4 percent), motor vehicle thefts (45.3 percent), burglaries (44.9 percent), robberies (30.1 percent), drug violations (18.9 percent), rapes (14.8 percent), assaults (14.7 percent), murders (9.3 percent), and drunk driving (2.3 percent).

[103]

The following were the numbers of crimes known to official agencies in 1970 and 1980. "Murder" includes cases of nonnegligent manslaughter; and "auto theft" includes all motor vehicles. It should be stressed that these are the numbers of reported (or discovered) crimes only, and do not include offenses where the police were not notified. At the same time, rise in the figures for rapes stems in some measure from the increased willingness of victims to report that offense. Also given are the incidence of each crime per 100,000 population, plus the rise in those rates during the decade.

| | REPORTED OFFENSES | | RATE PER 100,000 | | *Percentage* |
	1970	*1980*	*1970*	*1980*	*Rise In Rate*
Murder	15,810	23,044	7.8	10.2	Up 30.8%
Rape	37,270	82,088	18.3	36.4	Up 98.9%
Robbery	348,380	548,809	171.5	243.5	Up 42.0%
Assault	349,940	654,957	162.4	290.6	Up 78.9%
Burglary	2,169,300	3,795,193	1,067.7	1,668.2	Up 56.2%
Auto theft	921,400	1,114,651	453.5	494.6	Up 9.1%

[103, 105]

TWO SETS OF FIGURES: THE CENSUS AND FBI

The most recent study of criminal "victimization" was conducted by the Census in 1979. It reports the number of offenses people say happened to them that year, and whether they notified the police that the crime had occurred.

	NUMBER OF CLAIMED INCIDENTS	NUMBER CLAIMED REPORTED TO AUTHORITIES	PERCENTAGE REPORTED
Rapes and attempted rapes	192,000	97,000	50.5%
Robberies	1,116,000	619,000	55.5%
Aggravated assaults	1,769,000	907,000	51.3%
Residential burglaries	17,315,000	5,850,000	33.8%
Motor vehicle thefts or attempted thefts	1,393,000	950,000	68.2%

The Census' statistics can then be compared with the FBI's figures for 1979, showing the total number of crimes that local law enforcement agencies say were reported to them. The FBI totals are lower than not only the total number of incidents people said happened to them, but also the number they claimed they had reported to the police or other agencies.

	FBI TOTAL OF REPORTS RECEIVED BY POLICE	POLICE REPORTS AS PERCENTAGE OF CLAIMED INCIDENTS IN CENSUS STUDY	POLICE REPORTS AS PERCENTAGE OF CLAIMED REPORTS IN CENSUS STUDY
Rapes and attempted rapes	76,000	39.6%	78.4%
Robberies	467,000	41.8%	75.4%
Aggravated assaults	614,000	34.7%	67.7%
Residential burglaries	2,112,000	12.2%	36.1%
Motor vehicle thefts or attempted thefts	1,097,000	78.8%	115.5%

Note: The FBI's figures for robberies and motor vehicle thefts include those reported by businesses.

[94, 104]

CRIME CLEARANCE RATES: 1970 VS. 1980

In 1980 a total of 12,689 law enforcement agencies covering 91.8 percent of the population reported on how many of the crimes committed in their areas had been "cleared" due to the arrest of a suspect. (These figures do not indicate whether the suspect was convicted or acquitted, or if the charges were dismissed.)

Comparable figures on "cleared" offenses are also given for 1970. However, it should be noted that these clearances represent the activities of only 4,068 agencies covering 50.4 percent of the population.

	1970	1980	PERCENTAGE *Decrease in Clearance Rate 1970–1980*
Murder and nonnegligent manslaughter	86.5%	72.3%	16.4%
Aggravated assault	64.9%	58.7%	9.6%
Forcible rape	56.4%	48.8%	13.5%
Robbery	29.1%	23.8%	18.2%
Larceny thefts	18.4%	18.1%	1.6%
Motor vehicle thefts	16.9%	14.3%	15.4%
Burglary	19.4%	14.2%	26.8%

[103, 105]

MAJOR CRIME RATES PER 100,000 POPULATION: BY STATE (1980)

MURDER AND NONNEGLIGENT MANSLAUGHTER		FORCIBLE RAPE		ROBBERY	
1. Nevada	20.0	Nevada	67.2	New York	641.3
2. Texas	16.9	Alaska	62.5	Nevada	460.6
3. Louisiana	15.7	California	58.2	Maryland	392.7
4. Florida	14.5	Florida	56.9	California	384.2
5. Mississippi	14.5	Washington	52.7	Florida	355.5
6. California	14.3	Colorado	52.5	New Jersey	303.7
7. Georgia	13.8	Texas	47.3	Michigan	244.0
8. Alabama	13.2	Michigan	46.6	Massachusetts	235.5
9. New Mexico	13.1	Arizona	45.2	Ohio	223.7
10. New York	12.7	Louisiana	44.5	Missouri	223.6
11. South Carolina	11.4	Georgia	44.3	Connecticut	218.0
12. Missouri	11.1	New Mexico	43.3	Illinois	217.0
13. Tennessee	10.8	Oregon	41.5	Texas	208.5
14. North Carolina	10.6	Maryland	40.1	Georgia	197.6
15. Illinois	10.6	South Carolina	37.5	Louisiana	197.0
16. Arizona	10.3	Tennessee	37.4	Arizona	193.6
17. Michigan	10.2	Oklahoma	36.1	Hawaii	190.2
18. Oklahoma	10.0	Hawaii	34.7	Tennessee	180.6
19. Alaska	9.7	Ohio	34.3	Pennsylvania	177.9
20. Maryland	9.5	Indiana	33.1	Colorado	160.1
21. Arkansas	9.2	Missouri	32.6	Oregon	152.4
22. Indiana	8.9	Kansas	31.5	Indiana	141.4
23. Kentucky	8.8	New York	30.9	Delaware	137.0
24. Hawaii	8.7	New Jersey	30.7	Washington	135.1
25. Virginia	8.6	Alabama	30.0	Alabama	132.1
26. Ohio	8.1	Vermont	29.1	New Mexico	127.9
27. West Virginia	7.1	Wyoming	28.6	Virginia	120.1
28. Delaware	6.9	Utah	27.7	Rhode Island	118.6
29. Colorado	6.9	Virginia	27.4	South Carolina	118.1
30. New Jersey	6.9	Massachusetts	27.3	Kansas	113.1
31. Kansas	6.9	Illinois	26.9	Oklahoma	104.9
32. Pennsylvania	6.8	Arkansas	26.7	Minnesota	99.1
33. Wyoming	6.2	Mississippi	24.6	Kentucky	95.2
34. Washington	5.5	Delaware	24.2	Alaska	90.0
35. Oregon	5.1	Minnesota	23.2	North Carolina	82.3
36. Connecticut	4.7	Nebraska	23.2	Nebraska	82.2
37. Rhode Island	4.4	Pennsylvania	23.0	Mississippi	81.0
38. Nebraska	4.4	North Carolina	22.7	Arkansas	80.9
39. Massachusetts	4.1	Idaho	22.4	Utah	80.2
40. Montana	4.0	Connecticut	21.6	Wisconsin	70.7
41. Utah	3.8	Montana	21.0	Iowa	54.9

(continued)

(continued)

MURDER AND NONNEGLIGENT MANSLAUGHTER		FORCIBLE RAPE		ROBBERY	
42. Idaho	3.1	Kentucky	19.2	West Virginia	48.5
43. Wisconsin	2.9	New Hampshire	17.3	Idaho	46.8
44. Maine	2.8	Rhode Island	17.1	Wyoming	44.4
45. Minnesota	2.6	West Virginia	15.8	New Hampshire	42.0
46. New Hampshire	2.5	Wisconsin	14.9	Vermont	38.9
47. Vermont	2.2	Iowa	14.3	Montana	34.0
48. Iowa	2.2	Maine	12.9	Maine	30.8
49. North Dakota	1.2	South Dakota	12.5	South Dakota	20.1
50. South Dakota	0.7	North Dakota	9.5	North Dakota	7.7

[103]

MURDER, RAPE, AND ROBBERY RATES PER 100,000 POPULATION IN THE 25 LARGEST CITIES (1980)

MURDER		RAPE		ROBBERY	
1. St. Louis	49.9	Denver	143.9	New York	1429.2
2. Cleveland	46.3	Dallas	124.5	Washington, D.C.	1400.6
3. Detroit	45.7	Cleveland	122.8	Boston	1337.8
4. New Orleans	39.1	Memphis	122.2	St. Louis	1317.2
5. Houston	39.1	San Francisco	112.6	Baltimore	1277.2
6. Dallas	35.4	Detroit	109.7	Cleveland	1187.8
7. Los Angeles	34.2	New Orleans	105.4	Detroit	1121.6
8. Washington D.C.	31.5	Seattle	104.1	San Francisco	1116.5
9. Chicago	28.9	Los Angeles	95.3	Los Angeles	868.3
10. Baltimore	27.5	Houston	88.8	New Orleans	833.1
11. Philadelphia	25.9	St. Louis	87.0	Houston	670.8
12. New York	25.8	Boston	86.0	Philadelphia	647.3
13. Memphis	23.6	Columbus	81.8	Memphis	596.3
14. San Antonio	20.8	Jacksonville	76.3	Columbus	573.2
15. Denver	20.2	San Jose	76.3	Dallas	553.6
16. Boston	16.3	Baltimore	71.4	Chicago	544.5
17. San Francisco	16.3	Washington D.C.	69.1	Denver	483.5
18. Columbus	15.5	Phoenix	62.7	Seattle	458.0
19. Indianapolis	15.3	Indianapolis	58.7	Phoenix	392.9
20. Phoenix	13.3	Philadelphia	55.7	San Diego	341.3
21. Jacksonville	12.9	New York	52.7	Indianapolis	313.8
22. Seattle	12.8	San Antonio	45.9	Jacksonville	300.5
23. San Diego	11.8	Chicago	44.5	Milwaukee	283.3
24. Milwaukee	11.7	San Diego	41.4	San Jose	272.9
25. San Jose	9.9	Milwaukee	33.6	San Antonio	221.0

[103]

LAW ENFORCEMENT

Federal Bureau of Investigation. During 1980 arrests by the Federal Bureau of Investigation led to convictions in the following areas: 597 for organized crime, 1,502 for bank robberies, 1,235 for general property crimes, and "nearly 3,200 convictions" for white-collar crimes, which are defined as "illegal acts that use deceit and concealment rather than the use or threat of physical force or violence."

Convictions were also obtained in 13 cases of obstructing justice; 93 for civil rights violations; 49 for cases of extortion and 65 kidnappings; plus 86 for assaulting or killing federal officers or officials; 23 for "crime aboard aircraft," which includes skyjacking; and 1,005 for offenses in federal penitentiaries, military installations, and on Indian reservations.

[134]

FBI Personnel. At the end of 1980 the Federal Bureau of Investigation had 7,844 Special Agents, of whom 328 (or 4.2 percent) were women, and 543 (or 6.9 percent) were members of minority groups.

[134]

STATE AND LOCAL LAW ENFORCEMENT PERSONNEL

In 1978 the country had a total of 581,957 state and local law enforcement officers, making a ratio of 2.7 for every 1,000 persons in the country as a whole.

The states with the highest ratios were: New York (4.0 per 1,000); New Jersey and Nevada (both 3.6); Alaska (3.5); and Louisiana (3.3).

The lowest ratios were in North Dakota, Minnesota, and West Virginia (all 1.8 per 1,000), followed by South Dakota, Iowa, and Arkansas (all 1.9 per 1,000).

[93]

Here are the sizes of the police forces in the nation's 25 largest cities; the number of police officers per 10,000 population; and the proportion of each force that is composed of women:

	SIZE OF POLICE FORCE	POLICE PER 10,000	PERCENTAGE WOMEN
New York	22,590	32.2	3.1%
Chicago	12,392	41.7	3.9%
Los Angeles	6,587	22.3	2.7%
Philadelphia	7,454	44.4	3.3%
Houston	3,070	19.7	6.4%
Detroit	4,166	34.9	7.4%
Dallas	1,990	22.1	7.2%
San Diego	1,380	15.9	9.5%
Baltimore	3,171	40.4	4.3%
San Antonio	1,137	14.5	0.2%
Phoenix	1,622	20.8	3.1%
Indianapolis	969	13.9	8.9%
San Francisco	1,738	25.8	7.9%
Memphis	1,210	18.8	6.0%
Washington, D.C.	3,652	57.3	8.7%
Milwaukee	2,039	32.2	4.1%
San Jose	796	12.5	3.1%
Cleveland	1,877	32.8	7.2%
Boston	2,108	37.5	3.8%
Columbus	968	17.2	6.2%
New Orleans	1,397	25.1	4.8%
Jacksonville	951	17.6	2.2%
Seattle	1,036	21.1	6.1%
Denver	1,393	28.5	6.5%
St. Louis	1,950	43.5	3.4%

[103]

POLICE KILLED ON DUTY

A total of 1,238 law enforcement officers were killed in the line of duty between 1971 and 1981:

1971	129	1977	93
1972	116	1978	93
1973	134	1979	106
1974	132	1980	104
1975	129	1981	91
1976	111		

[103]

In 1979 the Federal Bureau of Investigation received 6,145,659 new fingerprint cards, bringing its collection to 172,253,444.

The major sources of these cards were: applicants for federal civilian positions (300,900), persons inducted into the armed services (466,319), employees of companies with military contracts (273,830), and law enforcement agencies (2,839,000). In 1980 a total of 88,198 cards were also received from companies in the securities industry.

And in 1980 a total of 400,665 fingerprint cards were removed as a result of "court-ordered expungements and purge requests from criminal justice agencies."

[134]

PRISONS AND PRISONERS

As of June of 1981, a total of 349,118 persons were incarcerated in state and federal prisons, serving sentences of longer than one year. This figure represented a 16.4 percent increase over the prison population of 1977, which was 300,024.

Of the inmates, 323,385 (or 92.6 percent) were in state institutions and 25,733 (the remaining 7.4 percent) were in federal prisons.

And of the total prison population, 334,462 inmates were men (95.8 percent) and 14,656 were women (4.2 percent).

State Prisoners. The states with the largest numbers of inmates were: Texas (30,954), California (26,792), New York (24,167), Florida (21,579), and North Carolina (16,095).

The states with the fewest prisoners were: North Dakota (295), New Hampshire (360), Wyoming (504), Vermont (512), and South Dakota (648).

[95]

Additional information is available for the beginning of 1979, when the total state prison population came to 276,799.

Sex and Race. The states with the largest number of women prisoners were: California (1147), Texas (1005), Florida (837), Michigan (621), New York (554), and Georgia (551).

With respect to race, the state prisons had 140,370 white inmates and 131,978 who were black, or a ratio of 106 whites for every 100 blacks.

In 18 of the 50 states, black inmates were in the majority. The states with the highest ratios of black prisoners were: Maryland (317 black inmates for every 100 whites), Louisiana (255), Mississippi (201), New Jersey (160), Georgia (151), and Michigan (147).

Escapes and Deaths. During the year 6,052 prisoners escaped from state prisons and 5,540 were returned to custody. Of those who escaped, 382 were women, of whom 367 were returned.

Altogether, 579 prisoners died while in state institutions, of whom 562 were men and 17 were women.

Of this total, 256 died from illness or old age; 77 by suicide or self-inflicted injuries; 73 at the hands of other inmates; and 173 from causes that were "not known."

[91]

PRISONERS PER 100,000 POPULATION (JUNE, 1981)*

1.	North Carolina	256	26. California	107
2.	South Carolina	247	27. Wyoming	107
3.	Nevada	241	28. Montana	105
4.	Georgia	238	29. Kentucky	103
5.	Louisiana	220	30. New Mexico	100
6.	Texas	218	31. Illinois	97
7.	Florida	217	32. Idaho	96
8.	Delaware	201	33. South Dakota	91
9.	Maryland	199	34. Colorado	91
10.	Arizona	175	35. Connecticut	89
11.	Alabama	173	36. Iowa	88
12.	Oklahoma	168	37. Wisconsin	87
13.	Tennessee	168	38. New Jersey	86
14.	Virginia	164	39. Vermont	77
15.	Alaska	155	40. Utah	73
16.	Mississippi	150	41. Hawaii	72
17.	Michigan	150	42. Pennsylvania	71
18.	Arkansas	138	43. Nebraska	69
19.	New York	137	44. Rhode Island	69
20.	Ohio	134	45. West Virginia	67
21.	Indiana	131	46. Maine	62
22.	Washington	118	47. Massachusetts	60
23.	Oregon	117	48. Minnesota	51
24.	Missouri	114	49. North Dakota	45
25.	Kansas	113	50. New Hampshire	39

*Inmates of state prisons serving sentences of longer than one year.

[95]

At the end of 1980, Federal prisons housed a total of 24,268 inmates. The Bureau of Prisons had 10,391 authorized positions on its payroll, or one for every 2.3 inmates. Its appropriation was $333,244,000, which came to $13,732 per inmate.

Inmates of federal prisons were there for the following offenses:

	PERCENTAGE
Narcotics offenses	25.1%
Robbery	24.1%
Larceny and theft	9.3%
Counterfeiting and forgery	5.0%
Immigration offenses	4.6%
Fraud and embezzlement	4.4%
Firearms offenses	3.8%
Motor vehicle theft	3.2%
Securities offenses	0.7%
Liquor offenses	0.1%
Other offenses	19.7%
	100.0%

[132, 134]

DEATH SENTENCES

At the end of 1981, a total of 838 persons in 29 states were under sentence of execution. Among the other 21 states, 14 had no death penalty in force, and the 7 that did had no inmates on Death Row. There was one execution in 1981, in Indiana.

The states with the most inmates on Death Row were Florida (161); Texas (144); Georgia (91); California (83); Illinois (41); Arizona (38); and Oklahoma (36).

Those on Death Row. Information on the characteristics of those awaiting execution is available for 1980, when there were 714 prisoners, of whom 706 were men and 8 were women. Altogether, 428 (or 59.9 percent) were white; 282 (or 39.5 percent were black); and 2 were Asians and 2 American Indians. All but one had been convicted of murder. (The exception was a white man under sentence for rape in Florida.)

Among the 714, 11 (or 1.5 percent) were under the age of 20, 369 (or 51.7 percent) were in their twenties, 242 (or 33.9 percent) were in their thirties, and 92 (or 12.9 percent) were 40 or older. Altogether, 43 (or 6.0 percent) had attended college.

Of the 563 for whom records were available, 357 (or 63.4 percent) had had prior felony convictions before committing the crime that got them the death sentence. The other 206 (or 36.6 percent) had had no previous felony convictions.

[96]

EXECUTIONS: 1930–1980

Between 1930 and the end of 1980, a total of 3,862 persons were executed in the United States. Of these:

- 3,829 (or 99.1 percent) were executed by the states, and 33 (or 0.9 percent) by the federal government.

- 3,668 (or 95.0 percent) were executed between 1930 and 1959; another 191 (or 4.9 percent) between 1960 and 1969; with 3 (or 0.1 percent) from 1970 to 1980.

- 1,754 (or 45.4 percent) were white, 2,066 (or 53.5 percent) were black, and the remaining 42 (or 1.1 percent) were of other races. In addition, 32 were women, of whom 20 were white and 12 were black.

- 3,337 (or 86.4 percent) were executed for murder and 455 (or 11.8 percent) for rape. Among the remaining 70 (or 1.8 percent), 25 were executed for armed robbery, 20 for kidnapping, 6 for sabotage, and 2 for espionage.

- Of the executions for murder, the rates for the races were almost equal: 1,667 for whites and 1,630 for blacks. However, whereas 405 blacks were executed for rape, only 48 whites were.

[96]

LOCAL JAILS

In 1978 the Department of Justice conducted a survey of the 158,394 persons confined in local jails. Of these individuals:

- 66,936 (or 42.3 percent) were awaiting trial, 12,359 (or 7.8 percent) had been convicted and were awaiting sentence, and 79,052 (49.9 percent) had been sentenced and were either serving their time in the local jail or awaiting transfer to a state institution.

- 148,839 (or 94.0 percent) were men, and 9,555 (or 6.0 percent) were women.

- 89,418 (or 56.5 percent) were white, and 65,104 (or 41.1 percent) were black, with the other 3,873 (or 2.4 percent) of other races.

- Black women and women of other races outnumbered white women inmates by 4,889 to 4,666.

- 71,370 (or 45.1 percent) were 24 or younger, 51,856 (or 32.7 percent) were 25 to 34, 24,941 (or 15.7 percent) were 35 to 54, and the remaining 3,460 (or 2.2 percent) were 55 or older. The median age was 25.3 (Information on age was not available for 6,767 prisoners.)

- 33,648 (or 21.2 percent) were married, 36,913 (or 23.3 percent) were separated or divorced, 85,128 (or 53.7 percent) had never been married, and the rest were widowed or did not report their status.

- 96,265 (or 60.8 percent) had not completed high school, 46,738 (or 29.5 percent) had high school diplomas, and 15,205 (or 9.6 percent) had one or more years of college.

- 70,574 (or 44.6 percent) had had full-time jobs at the time of their arrest, 18,953 (or 12.0 percent) had had part-time jobs, and 68,101 (or 43.0 percent) had not been employed.

- 104,405 of the jail inmates had used marijuana, 48,698 had used amphetamines, 46,917 barbiturates, 45,970 cocaine, 41,260 heroin, and 33,298 LSD.

[92]

CHAPTER ELEVEN

EDUCATION

Statistics on education should be examined in relation to the country's changing age profile. Due to the low birth rate in recent years, the number of Americans engaged in formal education has declined. Between 1970 and 1980 total enrollments dropped from 58,532,000 to 54,030,000, a decrease of 7.7 percent.

Elementary school attendance, the largest educational segment, fell from 33,950,000 to 27,449,000, a drop of 19.1 percent. High school enrollments began the decade at 14,715,000, rose to a height of 15,753,000 in 1977, and then fell back to 14,556,000 by 1980. Full-time college undergraduate attendance expanded from 5,208,000 to 6,315,000, a rise of 21.3 percent. However, in 1981 college figures were at about their 1980 level, signaling the end of the expansion.

Two areas of increase during the decade were at the ends of the educational spectrum. Full-time graduate school enrollments grew from 555,000 to 832,000, an increase of 49.9 percent. And youngsters in nursery school and kindergarten went from 4,279,000 to 5,163,000, a rise of 20.7 percent, even though the number of children of that age declined by 12.3 percent from 1970 to 1980.

Sources of Statistics. Figures for education come chiefly from two sources: the Bureau of the Census and the National Center for Education Statistics. The NCES works with information from local school districts, state education offices, and individual colleges and universities. Unfortunately, statistics for elementary and high schools take a long time to collect, and by the time they appear four or five years may have gone by. Figures for colleges and universities come in more rapidly, and the most recent will be used here.

The Census gets its information by interviewing a cross-section of young people concerning their educational status. By and large, its findings are similar to those of the NCES. For example, colleges and universities informed the NCES that they had 7,097,000 students in full-time attendance in the fall of 1980; the Census count taken at that time came up with 7,147,000. Both sources will be drawn on because they illuminate different aspects of the education scene.

NURSERY SCHOOL TO HIGH SCHOOL

NURSERY SCHOOL AND KINDERGARTEN

Between 1966 and 1980, the proportion of children aged 3 to 5 who attended nursery school or kindergarten increased from 29.4 percent to 52.5 percent. (It should also be noted that during this period, the number of children in this age range dropped from 12,486,000 to 9,284,000, a decline of 25.6 percent)

Of the children attending nursery schools in 1980, a total of 68.3 percent were enrolled in schools conducted under private auspices. In all, 73.8 percent of the white youngsters were in such private schools. In contrast, only 38.8 percent of the black children at the nursery level were enrolled in private schools.

[39]

ELEMENTARY AND HIGH SCHOOL ENROLLMENTS AND ETHNIC ORIGIN

Between 1970 and 1980, white students declined from 84.3 percent of elementary school enrollments to 82.0 percent. In the same period, black students rose from 14.3 percent to 15.5 percent.

At the high school level, white pupil enrollment fell from 86.5 percent to 82.8 percent, while black enrollments rose from 12.5 percent to 15.1 percent. From 1970 to 1980, the number of white high school students decreased from 12,723,000 to 12,056,000, a decline of 5.2 percent. At the same time, the figure for black students rose from 1,834,000 to 2,200,000, for an increase of 20.0 percent.

Statistics on students of Spanish origin have only been compiled since 1972. These pupils can be either black or white, although most choose the latter category. In the 8-year period from 1972 to 1980, enrollments of these students rose by 25.8 percent in the elementary grades and by 25.7 percent at the high school level. Students of Spanish origin went from 5.8 percent of the elementary total in 1972, to 8.7 percent in 1980. In the high schools, the Spanish origin proportion rose from 5.5 percent to 7.2 percent during this period.

[27]

EXPENDITURE PER PUPIL IN 1978–1979 AND CHANGES IN ENROLLMENT FROM 1970–1971 TO 1979–1980

PER PUPIL EXPENDITURE		PERCENTAGE ENROLLMENT CHANGE	
U.S.A.	$2,210	U.S.A.	− 9.4%
1. Alaska	$4,522	Arizona	+15.7%
2. New York	$3,180	Nevada	+15.6%
3. New Jersey	$2,818	Idaho	+11.5%
4. Wyoming	$2,759	Alaska	+11.3%
5. Michigan	$2,682	Wyoming	+10.3%
6. Massachusetts	$2,629	Utah	+ 9.5%
7. Washington	$2,575	New Hampshire	+ 7.5%
8. Delaware	$2,570	Florida	+ 5.6%
9. Maryland	$2,550	Texas	+ 1.2%
10. Pennsylvania	$2,524	Colorado	+ 0.2%
11. Colorado	$2,517	New Mexico	− 1.8%
12. Oregon	$2,487	Georgia	− 1.9%
13. Rhode Island	$2,450	South Carolina	− 2.0%
14. Wisconsin	$2,400	Arkansas	− 2.2%
15. Illinois	$2,399	Oregon	− 2.7%
16. Minnesota	$2,368	West Virginia	− 3.0%
17. Hawaii	$2,276	North Carolina	− 3.5%
18. Iowa	$2,264	Tennessee	− 3.8%
19. Connecticut	$2,231	Virginia	− 4.4%
20. Montana	$2,215	Vermont	− 4.9%
21. Nebraska	$2,198	Louisiana	− 5.0%
22. California	$2,173	Kentucky	− 5.8%
23. Kansas	$2,137	Alabama	− 6.3%
24. Nevada	$2,124	Washinton	− 6.5%
25. Utah	$2,114	Hawaii	− 6.6%
26. Texas	$2,073	Maine	− 6.9%
27. Arizona	$2,046	Oklahoma	− 7.0%
28. North Dakota	$1,977	Mississippi	− 9.7%

(continued)

(continued)

	PER PUPIL EXPENDITURE		PERCENTAGE ENROLLMENT CHANGE	
29.	Vermont	$1,976	Montana	−10.7%
30.	New Mexico	$1,942	Massachusetts	−11.3%
31.	Oklahoma	$1,941	Indiana	−11.9%
32.	Ohio	$1,917	California	−12.6%
33.	West Virginia	$1,905	Nebraska	−12.8%
34.	Virginia	$1,870	New Jersey	−13.1%
35.	New Hampshire	$1,860	Illinois	−13.3%
36.	Indiana	$1,859	Wisconsin	−13.7%
37.	Missouri	$1,856	Connecticut	−14.4%
38.	Florida	$1,847	New York	−14.6%
39.	Louisiana	$1,771	Michigan	−14.7%
40.	Idaho	$1,739	Maryland	−15.1%
41.	Maine	$1,731	Minnesota	−15.5%
42.	North Carolina	$1,712	Missouri	−16.0%
43.	Alabama	$1,700	Ohio	−16.5%
44.	South Dakota	$1,699	Pennsylvania	−16.5%
45.	South Carolina	$1,692	Iowa	−17.0%
46.	Georgia	$1,683	Kansas	−17.4%
47.	Kentucky	$1,643	Rhode Island	−18.1%
48.	Mississippi	$1,610	South Dakota	−19.3%
49.	Tennessee	$1,548	North Dakota	−19.7%
50.	Arkansas	$1,493	Delaware	−21.8%

[90]

PUPIL-TEACHER RATIOS

In 1954 the pupil-teacher ratio in elementary and high schools was 27.6 to 1. By 1964 it was down to 25.1 to 1; and in 1974 average classroom size was 20.8 pupils for each teacher.

In 1979 the ratio had fallen still further, to an average of 19.1 students under the supervision of each teacher.

[85]

STUDENTS AT GRADE-LEVEL

Of all children enrolled in school, 95.6 percent were in the appropriate grades for their age. Thus an 8-year-old was expected to be in either second or third grade, and a 16-year-old student should have reached the second or third year of high school.

At the age of 8, 95.2 percent of all boys and 97.2 percent of all girls were in the grades associated with their age. However, by the age of 16, the figures had fallen to 86.9 percent and 91.2 percent.

Among 16-year-olds, the breakdowns by race and sex were: white females, 92.6 percent at grade level; white males, 88.7 percent; black females, 84.4 percent; black males, 77.1 percent.

For 16-year-olds of Hispanic origin, 77.2 percent of the young women and 73.3 percent of the young men were in the grades expected for their age.

[23]

ATTRITION: FIFTH GRADE THROUGH FRESHMAN YEAR OF COLLEGE

Of the pupils who entered fifth grade in the fall of 1971, no less than 97.6 percent were still enrolled by the beginning of tenth grade. However, only 87.4 percent showed up to start eleventh grade, and 79.4 percent were present to begin their last year of high school.

Of those who started as fifth-graders, 74.3 percent actually graduated from high school, and 45.1 percent entered college as freshmen for the 1979–1980 academic year.

A quarter century earlier, of children who began fifth grade in 1946, a total of 77.5 percent made it to tenth grade, 64.1 percent to eleventh, and 58.3 percent to the senior year of high school. The proportion graduating from high school was 55.3 percent, and 28.3 percent went to college for the start of the 1954–1955 academic year.

[85]

PUBLIC AND PRIVATE SCHOOLS

Figures for 1979 and 1980 show that of Americans being educated from nursery school through graduate school, 87.7 percent are in public institutions and 12.3 percent in schools under private control.

The following are the proportions in private schools at various educational levels: nursery schools, 68.3 percent; kindergarten, 15.8 percent; grades 1 through 6, 11.5 percent; grades 7 and 8, 10.2 percent; high school, 7.4 percent.

After high school: the first 2 years of college, 18.6 percent of students are in private institutions; the second 2 college years, 25.2 percent; and at the graduate level, 31.6 percent.

[27, 39]

In the 1978–1979 academic year there were 87,006 public schools in the United States. Of these, 53,192 were elementary schools; 12,020 were junior high or middle schools; 16,639 were high schools; and another 5,155 were combinations or not classified by grades.

- Among the 53,192 elementary schools: 8,116 went from preprimary through the fifth grade, 25,618 preprimary through the sixth grade, 7,229 through the eighth grade, and the remaining 12,229 used other variations.

- Among the 12,020 junior high or middle schools, 2,888 had grades 6 through 8; 2,132 grades 7 and 8; 3,790 grades 7 through 9; and the remaining 3,210 had other combinations.

- Among the 16,639 high schools, 4,045 had grades 7 through 12; 7,584 grades 9 through 12; 2,813 grades 10, 11, and 12; and the remaining 2,197 used other combinations.

[90]

Private School Enrollments. In the 1978–1979 academic year, a total of 5,084,297 students were enrolled in 19,663 private schools throughout the country. Of these, 4,337,567 (or 85.3 percent) attended 15,719 schools under religious sponsorship. The other 746,730 (or 14.7 percent) were in 3,944 schools that did not have religious affiliations.

	ENROLLMENTS	SCHOOLS	STUDENTS PER TEACHER
Roman Catholic	3,269,761	9,849	22.8
Lutheran	217,406	1,485	21.3
Baptist	204,144	858	17.5
Seventh-Day Adventist	148,157	1,106	14.4
Jewish	101,758	406	13.2
Episcopal	76,452	314	12.4
Calvinist	47,269	166	20.6
Friends	14,611	50	10.6
Presbyterian	12,823	60	14.9
Methodist	11,187	60	15.2
Eastern Orthodox	2,682	14	15.8
Other affiliations	231,317	1,351	15.8
Nonreligious	746,730	3,944	11.8

[90]

Private High Schools. Between 1971 and 1979, enrollments in the nation's public high schools went from 13,886,000 to 13,756,000, a decline of just under 1 percent.

However, during this period enrollments in religious and secular private high schools increased from 1,340,000 to 1,545,000, for a growth of 15.3 percent.

Back in 1955 the private share of high school enrollments stood at 11.0 percent; by 1971 their proportion had fallen to 8.8 percent. So the 1979 share of 10.1 percent represents something of a comeback for nonpublic high schools.

[85]

COLLEGE PREPARATORY PROGRAMS

In the spring of 1980, a total 38.2 percent of all high school seniors were enrolled in college preparatory programs. Altogether, 38.5 percent of the men and 37.9 percent of the women were enrolled in such programs.

In terms of ethnic background, 39.3 percent of white students were in college preparatory programs, compared with 32.4 percent of black students. And 26.2 percent of Hispanic students were on a college preparatory track, as were 51.8 percent of Asian-origin students.

Subjects Offered. Among the nation's high schools, 97 percent had courses in geometry and second-year algebra; and 93 percent offered chemistry and 89 percent gave physics. However, only 76 percent offered trigonometry and 47 percent calculus. And so far as languages are concerned, 45 percent gave third-year Spanish; 39 percent three years of French; and 20 percent a third-year course in German.

Among all tenth, eleventh, and twelfth grade students, 44.8 percent were taking college preparatory mathematics, 23.7 percent were taking a foreign language, and 19.8 percent were enrolled in physics or chemistry.

If students in private schools are counted separately, 63.4 percent were taking mathematics, 44.2 percent a foreign language, and 28.5 percent physics or chemistry.

[90]

SUSPENSIONS AND EXPULSIONS: RACIAL RATIOS

Among the students in public elementary and high schools in the fall semester of 1978, there were 213 black pupils for every 1,000 whites.

Of the students who were suspended during that semester, there were 453 black pupils for every 1,000 whites. Of those who were expelled, there were 415 black students for every 1,000 whites.

[90]

Here is how students who live at home travel to school:

	PERCENTAGES			
	Grades 1–6	*Grades 7–8*	*High School*	*College*
Walk	36.2%	30.9%	21.4%	6.1%
School bus	43.7%	48.7%	38.3%	0.8%
Car	17.1%	14.3%	30.9%	80.0%
Bicycle	1.8%	2.7%	1.4%	1.1%
Public transportation	1.2%	3.5%	8.0%	12.0%
	100.0%	100.0%	100.0%	100.0%
Median distance (in miles)	1.4	2.4	3.0	9.3

[24]

COLLEGES AND UNIVERSITIES

During the ten academic years running from 1972–1973 through 1981–1982, the number of colleges and universities in the United States grew from 2,936 to 3,253, an increase of 10.8 percent.

The number of private institutions went from 1,529 to 1,755, a rise of 14.8 percent. For public institutions, the increase was from 1,407 to 1,498, up only 6.5 percent. Looked at another way, whereas in 1972–1973 the public proportion had been 47.9 percent of America's colleges and universities, by 1981–1982 the public share had declined to 46.0 percent.

During this decade the number of 2-year institutions grew from 1,114 to 1,275, an increase of 14.5 percent. Institutions with 4-year programs (including those with graduate schools) went from 1,822 to 1,978, a rise of 8.6 percent. Stated a different way, between 1972–1973 and 1981–1982, 4-year institutions declined from 62.1 percent of the total to 60.8 percent.

The 1,755 private institutions in 1981–1982 included 168 that were run on a profit-making basis; 814 conducted under independent auspices; and 773 with religious affiliations, of which 506 were Protestant, 228 Roman Catholic, 24 Jewish, and 14 with other sponsorships.

Sexual Status. Figures on the sexual status of colleges and universities are available for 1970 and 1980. In 1970 a total of 84.2 percent of all institutions were coeducational; 6.8 percent admitted only men; and 9.0 percent admitted only women. In 1980 the respective percentages were: 92.8 percent coeducational, 3.6 percent men only, and another 3.6 percent women only.

Of the 228 single-sex colleges remaining in 1980—there had been 402 in 1970—all but two were privately controlled.

[85, 89]

COLLEGE AND UNIVERSITY ENROLLMENTS

During the academic decade that ran from 1972–1973 to 1981–1982, total full-time enrollments in colleges and universities rose from 6,312,000 to 7,209,825, an increase of 14.2 percent.

In 1981–1982, full-time enrollments in public institutions came to 5,286,204, or 73.3 percent of the total. Private institutions had 1,923,621 full-time students, or 26.7 percent of the total.

As there were 1,498 public colleges and universities, this meant they had an average full-time enrollment of 3,529 students. And the 1,755 private institutions averaged 1,096 full-time students.

Sex and Students. Among the full-time students, 3,720,365 (or 51.6 percent) were men and 3,489,460 (or 48.4 percent) were women. In 1972–1973, men accounted for 58.8 percent of all full-time enrollments and women 41.2 percent. This means that the men's proportion declined by 12.2 percent during the decade, whereas the women's share rose by 17.5 percent.

Among full-time enrollments in 1981–1982, a total of 5,372,204 (or 74.5 percent) were in colleges and universities with 4-year programs. The remaining 1,837,621 (or 25.5 percent) were in 2-year institutions.

Part-Time Students. There were also 5,112,644 students enrolled on a part-time basis. Of these, 2,221,784 (or 43.5 percent) were men and 2,890,860 (or 56.5 percent) were women.

So of the 12,322,469 full-time and part-time students in 1981–1982, the 5,942,149 men made up 48.2 percent of the total and the 6,380,320 women comprised 51.8 percent.

Figures for 1970 and 1980 also show that the proportion of young men aged 20 and 21 who were enrolled in school fell from 42.7 percent to 32.6 percent during that decade. In that period, the proportion of women pursuing education at that age rose from 23.6 percent to 29.5 percent.

[27, 88]

In the 1979–1980 academic year, a total of 1,271,686 degrees were awarded by American colleges and universities. Of this number, 939,436, or 73.9 percent, were at the bachelors' level. Another 299,492, or 23.6 percent, were masters' degrees. And 32,758, or 2.6 percent, were doctorates.

Of the bachelors' degrees, 67.0 percent were granted by public institutions and 33.0 percent by private colleges. Of the masters' degrees, 62.9 percent were from public institutions, and 37.1 percent from private universities. And with the doctorates, public institutions awarded 63.1 percent and private institutions 36.9 percent.

Women accounted for 49.2 percent of the bachelors' degrees; 49.5 percent of those at the masters' level; and 29.5 percent of the doctorates. Among the masters' degrees received by women, 49.2 percent were in education, as were 36.5 percent of women's doctorates. And of the doctorates in psychology, 41.7 percent were granted to women.

[87]

UNDERGRADUATE DEGREES AWARDED: 1970 AND 1980

In 1980 a total of 939,436 persons received bachelors' degrees from American colleges and universities. This constituted an 18.6 percent rise from the 792,316 graduates in the class of 1970.

The following are the numbers of individuals receiving degrees in various undergraduate fields. ("Health professions" includes nursing programs and "Letters" includes English, literature, philosophy, and religious studies.)

EXPANDING FIELDS	1970	1980	PERCENTAGE CHANGE
Computer science	1,544	11,114	+619.8%
Health professions	21,109	64,046	+203.4%
Agriculture	9,144	23,036	+151.9%
Architecture	3,902	9,109	+133.4%
Home economics	10,217	18,613	+ 82.2%
Business	105,180	189,197	+ 79.9%
Engineering	44,479	69,170	+ 55.5%
Biological sciences	37,389	47,434	+ 26.9%
Psychology	33,606	42,550	+ 26.6%
CONTRACTING FIELDS			
Music and art	46,473	40,951	− 11.9%
Education	165,453	121,202	− 26.7%

(continued)

(continued)

CONTRACTING FIELDS	1970	1980	PERCENTAGE CHANGE
Social sciences	154,013	105,021	− 31.8%
Letters	75,297	40,754	− 45.9%
Foreign languages	21,109	11,314	− 46.4%
Mathematics	27,442	11,480	− 58.2%

[87, 89]

UNDERGRADUATE DEGREES AWARDED TO WOMEN

During the 1971–1972 academic year, women received 43.7 percent of all the bachelors' degrees that were awarded. Eight years later, in 1979–1980, degrees awarded to women came to 49.2 percent of the total, which meant the women's share rose by 12.6 percent.

The proportion of degrees going to women also changed in various fields. In these areas, the women's share increased:

	PERCENTAGE		
	1971–1972	1979–1980	Percentage Change
Engineering	1.0%	9.3%	+830.0%
Agriculture	5.5%	29.1%	+429.1%
Business	9.7%	33.7%	+247.4%
Architecture	12.0%	27.6%	+130.0%
Computer science	13.6%	30.3%	+122.8%
Physical sciences	15.1%	23.8%	+ 57.6%
Psychology	46.4%	70.4%	+ 51.7%
Biological sciences	29.6%	42.3%	+ 42.9%
Social sciences	36.3%	43.7%	+ 20.4%

In other areas, the women's percentage declined or remained relatively stable:

Letters	60.1%	59.4%	− 1.2%
Home economics	96.5%	95.4%	− 1.1%
Education	74.1%	73.9%	− 0.3%
Foreign languages	75.1%	75.7%	+ 0.8%
Music and art	59.5%	63.2%	+ 6.2%

[83, 87]

Between 1970 and 1980, the number of degrees conferred in dentistry rose from 3,718 to 5,321, for an increase of 43.1 percent. The number of medical degrees went up from 8,314 to 15,046, a rise of 81.0 percent.

In 1980 a total of 35,855 law degrees were awarded, compared with 14,916 in 1970, for an increase of 140.4 percent. And in 1980 a total of 55,499 persons received the Master of Business Administration degree, as against 21,325 in 1970, a rise of 160.3 percent.

[87, 89]

Professional Degrees Awarded to Women. During the 8-year period from 1971–1972 to 1979–1980, the proportions of professional degrees granted to women underwent the following changes:

Law, 7.2 percent in 1971–1972 to 30.2 percent in 1979–1980; medicine, 9.0 percent to 23.4 percent; optometry, 2.2 percent to 15.7 percent; theology, 1.9 percent to 14.4 percent; dentistry, 1.2 percent to 13.5 percent; and veterinary medicine, 9.4 percent to 32.8 percent.

[83, 89]

DOCTORAL DEGREES

During the 1979–1980 academic year, a total of 30,982 doctoral degrees were awarded by American universities. The following were the principal areas of study, with information on the persons receiving the degrees:

		PERCENTAGE WOMEN	PERCENTAGE FOREIGN STUDENTS	MEDIAN AGE AT AWARD	AVERAGE YEARS B.A. TO PH.D.
TOTAL	30,982	30.3%	16.4%	32.3	9.3
Education	7,576	44.5%	8.5%	37.0	13.1
Social sciences	6,253	34.6%	12.0%	31.6	8.7
Life sciences	5,325	25.2%	18.0%	30.0	7.3
Arts and humanities	3,863	39.6%	9.2%	33.4	10.6
Physical sciences	3,151	12.3%	22.1%	29.1	6.8
Engineering	2,479	3.6%	47.8%	30.3	7.6
Mathematics	745	12.8%	28.0%	29.3	7.0
Computer science	218	9.6%	26.4%	29.5	7.4

[102]

FACULTY MEMBERS: RANK AND SEX

During the academic year ending in June 1981, American colleges and universities had a total of 359,880 full-time faculty members.

Of these, 102,183 (or 28.4 percent) were full professors; 94,046 (or 26.1 percent) were associate professors; 92,880 (or 25.8 percent) were assistant professors; 34,581 (or 9.6 percent) were lecturers or instructors; and the remaining 36,190 of the teachers (or 10.1 percent) had no academic rank.

Of the faculty total, 25.5 percent were women. However, they comprised only 10.1 percent of the full professors; 20.3 percent of the associate professors; 34.7 percent of the assistant professors; over half—51.7 percent—of the lecturers and instructors; and 35.0 percent of those without an academic rank.

Women's representation among academic ranks was roughly similar in public and private institutions. At public 4-year colleges and universities, women accounted for 9.0 percent of the full professors and 51.3 percent of the lecturers and instructors. At private colleges and universities the percentages were 10.0 percent and 50.6 percent.

[86]

IN-STATE AND OUT-OF-STATE ENROLLMENTS OF FULL-TIME STUDENTS

The colleges and universities in the following states had the largest numbers of out-of-state students in full-time attendance in the fall of 1979: California (36,839), Massachusetts (31,296), New York (29,961), Pennsylvania (24,787), and Texas (22,919).

Student "Deficits" and "Surpluses." These states had the largest student "deficits," computed as the number of their residents who went out-of-state for their educations minus the out-of-state persons who came to enroll in the state: New Jersey (33,263), New York (22,278), Illinois (14,927), Connecticut (10,722), and Maryland (7,332).

And these states had the largest student "surpluses," which meant that more out-of-state students arrived compared with in-state students going elsewhere: Massachusetts (10,388), North Carolina (7,349), Texas (7,226), Tennessee (6,296), and Utah (6,050).

There were 77,327 full-time foreign students in American colleges and universities, amounting to 3.1 percent of all full-time enrollments. (These students are included in all the "out-of-state" totals.) The states with the largest numbers of foreign students were: California (15,512), Texas (6,602), New York (5,820), Florida (3,893), and Michigan (3,184).

Leaving or Staying at Home. The states where the largest proportions of their student populations went elsewhere for their educations were: Alaska (56.5 percent), Nevada (46.8 percent), Connecticut (45.7 percent), New Jersey (39.0 percent), and Vermont (38.1 percent).

The states where the largest proportions of their full-time students stay at home were: Texas (93.2 percent), California (92.3 percent), North Carolina (91.7 percent), Mississippi (91.4 percent), and Oklahoma (90.2 percent).

[84]

COLLEGE STUDENTS AND OUT-OF-STATE ATTENDANCE

	NUMBER OF RESIDENTS WHO ARE FULL-TIME COLLEGE STUDENTS	PERCENTAGE ATTENDING OUT-OF-STATE COLLEGES		NUMBER OF RESIDENTS WHO ARE FULL-TIME COLLEGE STUDENTS	PERCENTAGE ATTENDING OUT-OF-STATE COLLEGES
California	274,940	7.7%	South Carolina	34,337	12.0%
New York	250,250	18.8%	Oregon	31,809	14.2%
Texas	138,476	6.8%	Colorado	31,128	20.4%
Illinois	128,691	21.4%	Mississippi	30,580	8.6%
Pennsylvania	111,076	21.7%	Kentucky	28,410	14.4%
Ohio	99,318	17.3%	Kansas	28,229	16.4%
New Jersey	98,636	39.0%	Arizona	27,889	15.4%
Michigan	95,256	11.5%	Arkansas	19,138	15.6%
Massachusetts	82,775	22.0%	Nebraska	18,973	17.2%
Florida	79,963	20.9%	Utah	15,141	10.9%
North Carolina	69,963	8.3%	West Virginia	12,856	19.1%
Wisconsin	58,968	13.4%	New Mexico	11,976	30.0%
Virginia	55,084	21.9%	Rhode Island	11,812	29.6%
Minnesota	46,489	22.0%	Hawaii	11,205	26.8%
Missouri	46,075	18.4%	Maine	10,571	31.1%
Maryland	44,234	31.3%	North Dakota	9,972	21.3%
Washington	42,756	14.0%	New Hampshire	9,555	36.7%
Indiana	41,859	17.8%	Idaho	9,535	29.3%
Georgia	41,757	17.6%	Montana	9,052	25.2%
Connecticut	40,407	45.7%	South Dakota	8,343	23.8%
Tennessee	37,996	14.3%	Delaware	7,241	35.5%
Iowa	37,815	17.6%	Vermont	5,554	38.1%
Alabama	37,323	11.2%	Wyoming	5,046	29.7%
Oklahoma	35,773	9.8%	Nevada	4,673	46.8%
Louisiana	34,998	10.9%	Alaska	3,793	56.5%
District of Columbia	6,360	47.4%	U. S. A.	2,472,848	17.8%

[8

CHARACTERISTICS OF COLLEGE STUDENTS

Older Students. Between 1972 and 1980, the proportion of people enrolled in college aged 25 or older rose from 27.9 percent of the total to 34.3 percent. (Figures for years prior to 1972 are not available.)

Married Students. Of all full-time college students, 10.0 percent are married. Of these, 58.0 percent are husbands and 42.0 percent are wives.

Of part-time students, 44.9 percent are married. Of those, 47.9 percent are husbands and 52.1 percent are wives.

[27]

Part-Time and Full-Time Students. Among students in their first year of college, 28.2 percent are attending part-time. In their second and third years, 24.2 percent are on a part-time basis. By the fourth year, part-time students are down to 20.3 percent.

However, in the first year of graduate study, 57.6 percent were part-time students; in the second and successive years the figure was down to 48.8 percent.

Graduate Students. Between 1970 and 1980, the number of women who were full-time graduate students increased from 123,000 to 332,000, a rise of 169.9 percent. In that period, men's full-time graduate enrollments went from 432,000 to 500,000, up only 15.7 percent.

[27]

ENROLLMENTS OF BLACK STUDENTS

In 1965 black students accounted for 4.8 percent of all college enrollments. By 1970 their proportion was up to 7.0 percent; and in 1980, it had reached 9.9 percent.

Put another way, between 1965 and 1980, while white enrollments rose by 66.9 percent, black registrations increased by 267.5 percent.

Among black students, women made up 56.6 percent of all those enrolled in 1980.

Among black young men aged 20 and 21, a total of 64.7 percent had graduated from high school. Of black young women of those ages, 74.4 percent had.

If a black young man finishes high school, he is more apt to go to college than a black woman high school graduate. But because fewer of the men actually finish high school, there are more black women in college than black men.

[27]

WHERE COLLEGE STUDENTS LIVE

The most recent report by the Census Bureau, for October 1978, showed that among full-time college students, 56.3 percent lived at home, 29.6 percent lived on campus, and the remaining 14.1 percent resided away from home but not on their college campus.

[24]

COLLEGE STUDENTS' PARENTS

In October 1979 the Census Bureau conducted a study of 4,816,000 college students aged 18 to 24 who were still financially dependent on their parents.

Of this group, 24.2 percent came from families with annual incomes of under $15,000, 29.5 percent had families in the $15,000 to $25,000 range, and 46.3 percent's families made over $25,000.

In fact, incomes in the last group must have been considerably more than $25,000, because the median income of all the students' families was $23,845.

Parents' Education. Among the students enrolled full-time at college, 35.3 percent had parents who completed college; 16.6 percent's parents attended but did not finish; 31.7 percent had parents who graduated from high school; and the remaining 16.3 percent had parents who never finished high school.

[27]

FAMILIES WITH CHILDREN IN COLLEGE

Of the 3,436,000 families with one or more children who are full-time college students, 45.8 percent have incomes of $25,000 or over; 29.0 percent made between $15,000 and $25,000; and 25.2 percent earn less than $15,000.

Daughters and Sons. Looked at another way, of the children in families with annual incomes of $25,000 or over, 53.5 percent were enrolled in college. Of those where the family made $15,000 or under, 33.3 percent were enrolled.

Of the higher-income families, 56.5 percent of their daughters were at college, compared with 51.2 percent of their sons. At the lower income level, the imbalance was somewhat smaller, with the sons at 34.4 percent and daughters at 32.4 percent.

Of the full-time college students whose families had incomes of $25,000 or over, 53.9 percent were men and 46.1 were women. In the $15,000 to $25,000 range, however, the ratio is 47.7 percent men to 52.3 percent women. And at under $15,000, only 46.4 percent are men and 53.6 percent are women.

[27]

Sex, Income, and Private Education. Of the students from families with incomes of $25,000 or over, 25.3 percent of the men were at private colleges, compared with 29.4 percent of the women.

However, where their families had incomes of $15,000 or under, 30.5 percent of the men were at private colleges, as opposed to 24.2 percent of the women.

[27]

EDUCATIONAL ATTAINMENT

Men and Women. Among the 3,918,000 young men in the country aged 20 to 21, a total of 18.0 percent did not graduate from high school. Of the 82.0 percent who did, 30.4 percent were in college and 51.6 percent were not.

Among the 4,182,000 young women 20 and 21, those who failed to finish high school numbered 15.6 percent. Of the 84.4 percent who did, 27.8 percent were in college and 56.6 percent were not.

In actual numbers, however, there were 1,162,000 of the women in college, compared with 1,191,000 of the men, a difference of only 2.5 percent.

[25]

Educational Activity: 1960–1980. In 1960, of all persons aged 18 to 21, a total of 38.4 percent were enrolled in some kind of educational pursuit. By 1970 that proportion had grown to 47.7 percent. However, by 1980 the percentage of 18- to 21-year-olds in school had dropped to 38.7 percent.

[39]

PERSONS WHO HAVE COMPLETED FOUR YEARS OF HIGH SCHOOL AND COLLEGE

		PERCENTAGE COMPLETED HIGH SCHOOL USA = 66.3%		PERCENTAGE COMPLETED COLLEGE USA = 16.3%	
1.	Alaska	82.8%	Colorado	23.0%
2.	Utah	80.3%	Alaska	22.4%
3.	Colorado	78.1%	Connecticut	21.2%
4.	Wyoming	77.8%	Hawaii	20.4%
5.	Washington	77.0%	Utah	20.3%
6.	Nevada	75.5%	Massachusetts	20.0%
7.	Montana	75.4%	California	19.8%
8.	Oregon	74.7%	Maryland	19.8%
9.	Nebraska	73.8%	Vermont	19.5%
10.	California	73.6%	Virginia	19.2%
11.	Hawaii	73.4%	Washington	18.8%
12.	Idaho	72.8%	New York	18.7%
13.	Massachusetts	72.7%	New Jersey	18.6%
14.	Minnesota	72.4%	New Hampshire	18.4%
15.	Kansas	72.3%	Montana	17.3%
16.	Arizona	72.3%	New Mexico	17.3%
17.	New Hampshire	72.0%	Wyoming	17.2%
18.	Iowa	71.2%	Oregon	17.2%
19.	Connecticut	70.5%	Arizona	16.8%
20.	Vermont	70.5%	Minnesota	16.7%
21.	Wisconsin	70.0%	Delaware	16.3%
22.	Maine	68.5%	Idaho	16.1%
23.	South Dakota	68.5%	Nebraska	16.1%
24.	Michigan	68.2%	Texas	16.0%
25.	New Mexico	68.2%	Kansas	15.7%
26.	New Jersey	67.8%	Oklahoma	15.7%
27.	Delaware	67.8%	Rhode Island	15.3%
28.	Ohio	67.4%	Georgia	15.3%
29.	Florida	67.2%	Michigan	15.2%
30.	Maryland	66.7%	North Dakota	15.2%
31.	Oklahoma	66.7%	Nevada	15.1%
32.	North Dakota	66.5%	Wisconsin	14.9%
33.	New York	66.2%	Ohio	14.8%
34.	Indiana	65.9%	Florida	14.7%
35.	Illinois	65.0%	Illinois	14.5%
36.	Pennsylvania	64.5%	South Dakota	14.2%
37.	Missouri	63.7%	South Carolina	14.2%
38.	Virginia	62.5%	Iowa	14.1%
39.	Texas	61.4%	Maine	14.0%
40.	Rhode Island	60.7%	Missouri	14.0%

(continued)

(continued)

PERCENTAGE COMPLETED HIGH SCHOOL USA = 66.3%		PERCENTAGE COMPLETED COLLEGE USA = 16.3%	
41. Louisiana	58.0%	Louisiana	13.4%
42. Alabama	56.7%	North Carolina	13.4%
43. West Virginia	56.6%	Pennsylvania	13.3%
44. Georgia	56.5%	Mississippi	13.0%
45. Tennessee	55.4%	Alabama	12.6%
46. North Carolina	55.3%	Indiana	12.4%
47. Mississippi	55.1%	Tennessee	11.9%
48. Arkansas	54.9%	Kentucky	11.0%
49. South Carolina	54.0%	West Virginia	10.5%
50. Kentucky	51.9%	Arkansas	9.7%

[9]

Note: These percentages apply to persons aged 25 or over. The high school column includes people who have had additional education as well. All those in the college column have also been through high school.

EDUCATIONAL ATTAINMENT: 1940–1980

Beginning with 1940, the following proportions of Americans aged 25 or over had completed high school or college:

	PERCENTAGE	
	High School Only	*Four or More Years of College*
1940	24.5%	4.6%
1950	34.3%	6.2%
1960	41.1%	7.7%
1970	55.2%	11.0%
1980	66.3%	16.3%

When persons aged 25 through 29 are considered, the proportion completing high school went from 38.1 percent in 1940 to 85.7 percent in 1980. And in this age group, those who had completed college rose from 5.9 percent to 24.3 percent.

[9, 25, 28]

Among persons aged 25 to 29, a total of 86.3 percent of men had completed high school, as opposed to 84.9 percent of the women.

However, of those slightly younger, between 18 and 24, the proportion of women who had finished high school was 78.8 percent, compared with 76.8 percent of the men.

In the 20-to-24 age range, 77.6 percent of black women finished high school, compared with 71.9 percent of black men. Among whites in that age group, the figures were 85.3 percent for the women and 86.2 percent for the men.

[25]

FROM HIGH SCHOOL TO COLLEGE

In 1960 the proportion of women high school graduates aged 20 to 24 who had completed one or more years of college came to 32.8 percent. By 1970 the proportion was 41.7 percent, and by 1980 it was up to 46.3 percent.

For men of the same age, between 1960 and 1970 the proportion of high school graduates going on to one or more years of college rose from 42.2 percent to 52.4 percent. However, by 1980 that proportion had fallen to 47.7 percent.

[39]

Race and High School Graduation. Among white persons aged 18 to 24 in 1980, a total of 82.5 percent were high school graduates. Among black young people in that age range, only 69.7 percent had completed high school.

Between 1967 and 1980 the proportion of white high school graduates who enrolled in college dropped from 34.5 percent to 32.0 percent. In the same period black high school graduates going on to college rose from 23.3 percent to 27.8 percent.

[39]

YEARS OF SCHOOLING: SEX, AGE, AND RACE

Among persons aged 25 years and older, the median number of school years attended, grouped by sex, age, and ethnicity, are as follows:

	MEN	WOMEN	
White	12.6	12.5	
Black	11.9	11.9	
Hispanic	10.4	10.2	
25–29	13.0	12.8	
35–39	12.8	12.6	
45–49	12.5	12.4	
55–59	12.4	12.3	
65–69	10.7	11.5	
Over 75	8.7	8.9	[25]

OCCUPATIONS AND EDUCATIONAL LEVEL

Among persons employed in professional or technical occupations, 98.0 percent had completed high school, 85.3 percent had had at least a year of college, 67.9 percent were college graduates, and 38.2 percent had done graduate work.

Among those in managerial and administrative positions, the comparable figures are: 89.6 percent, 56.2 percent, 33.8 percent, and 13.4 percent.

Among sales workers, 24.5 percent had finished college, as had 10.1 percent of those in clerical occupations. So had 4.7 percent of craft workers, 3.1 percent of transport drivers, 2.7 percent of laborers, and 8.4 percent of persons employed in farming.

Of white women in professional and technical occupations, 63.5 percent had completed college, compared with 71.6 percent of white men. However, for black women, the figure was 59.2 percent, as opposed to 53.9 percent for black men.

[25]

Graduate Work. Of the 7,041,000 employed men aged 25 to 44 who had at least four years of college, 45.7 percent had also done some graduate work. Of the 3,928,000 women at that age and educational level, 39.4 percent had done graduate work.

Among men aged 25 to 44 who had completed college, 52.2 percent were in professional positions and 23.3 percent were managers or administrators. The comparable figures for women were 65.9 percent and 8.8 percent.

[25]

In 1970 the median income of men who had completed 4 years of college was 42.0 percent higher than that for men who had only finished high school.

By 1980 the median for college men was only 24.9 percent greater than the income of high school graduates.

And between 1970 and 1980, the income advantage of college women fell from 55.8 percent to 31.3 percent as compared with women who had completed high school.

On the other hand, while the 1970 median income of men who had done graduate work was only 6.4 percent above that for men with a bachelor's degree, by 1980 that margin had risen to 13.9 percent.

However, whereas in 1970 women with graduate work were 25.3 percent ahead in salary of women at the bachelor's level, in 1980 their advantage had slipped to 19.5 percent.

[19, 44]

EDUCATIONAL LEVELS

The husband and wife are at the same educational level in 54.7 percent of all marriages. In 26.3 percent he has had more schooling; and in 19.0 percent she has:

	PERCENTAGE OF MARRIAGES
Same levels of education	54.7%
Both not high school graduates	17.8%
Both high school graduates	23.1%
Both some college	4.5%
Both college graduates	9.3%
Different levels: wife less	26.3%
Husband high school graduate, wife less	6.4%
Husband some college, wife less	8.9%
Husband college graduate, wife less	11.0%
Different levels: husband less	19.0%
Wife high school graduate, husband less	9.8%
Wife some college, husband less	5.2%
Wife college graduate, husband less	4.0%

[31]

CHAPTER TWELVE

HOUSING AND TRAVEL

Between 1970 and 1980, the number of occupied housing units in the United States rose from 63,449,747 to 80,378,283, an increase of 26.7 percent, more than double the decade's population growth of 11.5 percent.

The number of rented units—houses plus apartments—went from 23,564,567 to 28,591,179, a rise of 21.3 percent. Housing owned by their occupiers increased from 39,885,180 units to 51,787,104, up 29.8 percent.

In 1970 a total of 37.1 percent of the units were rentals and 62.9 percent were owned. By 1980 rentals had declined to 35.6 percent and owned units had increased to 64.4 percent.

From 1970 to 1980, the proportion of units "lacking complete plumbing for exclusive use" decreased from 6.9 percent to 2.7 percent, which meant facilities were improved or old housing was abandoned. The median number of rooms per unit remained relatively constant, rising from 5.0 to 5.1 rooms over the ten years. However, as the average household declined from 3.11 to 2.75 persons, the Census Bureau concluded that there was "roughly a 15 percent increase in housing space during the decade."

The median monthly rental in the country as a whole went from $89.00 in 1970 to $198.00 in 1980, an increase of 122.5 percent. The median value of owned residences rose from $17,000 to $47,000, a growth of 177.6 percent.

States and Housing Growth. The states with the greatest growth in housing were: Nevada (96.8 percent more units in 1980 compared with 1970), Arizona (89.5 percent), Alaska (78.8 percent), Florida (73.1 percent), and Wyoming (62.2 percent).

The states with the least housing expansion were: New York (9.0 percent over 1970), New Jersey (16.0 percent), Illinois (16.6 percent), Pennsylvania (17.1 percent), and Rhode Island and Iowa (both 17.3 percent).

The following tables rank the states by their percentages of owned residences and by the median value of those homes.

[1.13]

PERCENTAGE OF HOUSING UNITS OCCUPIED BY OWNERS: 1980

		PERCENTAGE			PERCENTAGE
1.	West Virginia	73.6%	26.	North Carolina	68.4%
2.	Michigan	72.6%	27.	Ohio	68.4%
3.	Idaho	72.0%	28.	Florida	68.2%
4.	Iowa	71.8%	29.	Wisconsin	68.2%
5.	Indiana	71.7%	30.	New Mexico	68.0%
6.	Minnesota	71.7%	31.	New Hampshire	67.6%
7.	Mississippi	71.0%	32.	Arizona	66.4%
8.	Maine	70.9%	33.	Virginia	65.6%
9.	Oklahoma	70.7%	34.	Washington	65.6%
10.	Utah	70.7%	35.	Louisiana	65.5%
11.	Arkansas	70.5%	36.	Oregon	65.0%
12.	Alabama	70.2%	37.	Georgia	65.0%
13.	Kansas	70.2%	38.	Colorado	64.5%
14.	South Carolina	70.2%	39.	Texas	64.3%
15.	Kentucky	70.0%	40.	Connecticut	63.9%
16.	Pennsylvania	69.9%	41.	Illinois	62.6%
17.	Missouri	69.6%	42.	Maryland	62.0%
18.	South Dakota	69.3%	43.	New Jersey	62.0%
19.	Wyoming	69.2%	44.	Nevada	59.6%
20.	Delaware	69.1%	45.	Rhode Island	58.8%
21.	Vermont	68.7%	46.	Alaska	58.3%
22.	North Dakota	68.7%	47.	Massachusetts	57.5%
23.	Montana	68.6%	48.	California	55.9%
24.	Tennessee	68.6%	49.	Hawaii	51.7%
25.	Nebraska	68.4%	50.	New York	48.6%

[7]

MEDIAN VALUE OF OWNER-OCCUPIED HOMES: 1980

1.	Hawaii	$118,100	26.	Ohio	44,900
2.	California	84,500	27.	Delaware	44,400
3.	Alaska	76,300	28.	North Dakota	43,900
4.	Nevada	68,700	29.	Louisiana	43,000
5.	Connecticut	65,600	30.	Vermont	42,200
6.	Colorado	64,100	31.	Iowa	40,600
7.	New Jersey	60,200	32.	Pennsylvania	39,100
8.	Washington	59,800	33.	Texas	39,100
9.	Wyoming	58,900	34.	Michigan	39,000
10.	Maryland	58,300	35.	West Virginia	38,500
11.	Utah	57,300	36.	Nebraska	38,000
12.	Oregon	56,900	37.	Maine	37,900
13.	Arizona	54,700	38.	Kansas	37,800
14.	Minnesota	53,100	39.	Indiana	37,200
15.	Illinois	52,800	40.	Georgia	36,900
16.	Wisconsin	48,600	41.	Missouri	36,700
17.	Massachusetts	48,400	42.	South Dakota	36,600
18.	New Hampshire	48,000	43.	North Carolina	36,000
19.	Virginia	48,000	44.	Tennessee	35,600
20.	Rhode Island	46,800	45.	Oklahoma	35,600
21.	Montana	46,500	46.	South Carolina	35,100
22.	New York	45,600	47.	Kentucky	34,200
23.	Idaho	45,600	48.	Alabama	33,900
24.	New Mexico	45,300	49.	Mississippi	31,400
25.	Florida	45,100	50.	Arkansas	31,100

[7]

CHARACTERISTICS OF AMERICA'S HOMES

Of the nation's housing structures, the 1980 Census reported, 62.2 percent were free-standing single-family homes. Another 4.1 percent were also single-family residences which were attached to one or more other buildings. A further 6.1 percent were in two-unit buildings; 5.1 percent were in buildings with three or four units; and 17.5 percent were in structures containing five or more units. The remaining 5.0 percent of America's housing consisted of trailers or mobile homes.

Altogether, 14.8 percent of the housing units had 1 bedroom; 32.4 percent had 2, 37.0 percent had 3, 11.2 percent had 4, and 2.5 percent had 5 or more bedrooms. The remaining 2.1 percent did not contain a separate bedroom.

In addition, 27.2 percent of all housing units had central air conditioning; 27.6 percent had one or more room units; and 45.2 percent had no air conditioning at all.

A total of 92.9 percent of the homes had one or more telephones, while 7.1 percent had none.

These were the years when the nation's housing structures were built, and the years when their current residents moved in:

	PERCENTAGE BUILDINGS BUILT	PERCENTAGE RESIDENTS MOVED IN
1979 or 1980	3.4%	22.8%
1975 to 1978	9.7%	28.3%
1970 to 1974	12.8%	15.9%
1960 to 1969	19.4%	16.5%
1950 to 1959	17.3%	
1940 to 1949	11.3%	16.5%
Before 1940	26.1%	
	100.0%	100.0%

[9]

Rents and Mortgage Payments. A Census survey conducted in 1979 showed that of families which owned their own homes, 29 percent had paid off their mortgages. Among those still making payments, the median amount was $224 per month. For all owners, the value of their house averaged 2.5 times their annual income. For those who had paid off their mortgages, housing costs averaged 12 percent of their income, while for those still paying off a mortgage, the figure came to 19 percent. And among renters, the median monthly rent amounted to $217 that year, with housing costs averaging 26 percent of their income.

Here is how renters and those still paying off a mortgage compared with respect to the percentage of their income consumed by housing costs:

PERCENTAGE OF INCOME CONSUMED BY HOUSING COSTS	PERCENTAGE OF RENTERS	PERCENTAGE OF MORTGAGE PAYERS
Under 14%	16.8%	31.3%
15%–19%	16.4%	21.3%
20%–24%	15.3%	17.1%
25%–34%	19.8%	17.0%
Over 35%	31.7%	13.2%
	100.0%	100.0%

Taxes and Rooms. The median amount owners paid in real estate taxes in 1979 came to $453. Within this group, 82.7 percent had taxes of less than $1,000; 9.2 percent paid between $1,000 and $1,400; 5.0 percent paid from $1,400 to $2,000; and 3.0 percent had tax bills of more than $2,000.

Owned residences had a median of 5.8 rooms, and 30.9 percent had 7 rooms or more. The median for rented residences was 4.0 rooms; and 33.9 percent had 3 rooms or less.

[52]

Race and Residences. The Census provides some information on housing broken down on the basis of race. Of the residences that are owned, 7.2 percent are occupied by black households and 92.8 percent by whites or other races. With rental housing, on the other hand, black households account for 17.1 percent of the total, with white and other races comprising 82.9 percent.

Put another way, 55.6 percent of black families live in rented housing, while this is the case for 32.1 percent of white and other families.

When black families own their homes, the buildings tend to be considerably older:

WHEN BUILT	PERCENTAGE BLACK OWNERS	PERCENTAGE WHITE OR OTHER OWNERS
1970 or later	15.1%	23.1%
1960–1969	18.5%	21.9%
1950–1959	18.2%	19.7%
1950 or before	48.2%	35.2%
	100.0%	100.0%

[52]

HOUSING CONSTRUCTION: 1980

During 1980, construction was authorized to start on 1,181,582 private housing units in states throughout the country. Of these, 704,450 (or 59.6 percent) were to be single-unit homes; 113,754 (or 9.6 percent) were to be in structures with 2 to 4 units; and 363,378 (or 30.8 percent) were to be in buildings having at least 5 apartments.

The states where the highest proportions were to be single-unit homes were: Maryland (83.9 percent), Delaware (81.2 percent), Virginia (78.9 percent), Idaho (77.7 percent), South Dakota (76.1 percent), Georgia (75.7 percent, Nebraska (75.5 percent, and Alaska (72.6 percent).

The states with the highest proportions in buildings with 5 or more apartments were: Hawaii (80.5 percent), Illinois (54.5 percent), Indiana (42.6 percent), Texas (41.0 percent), West Virginia (39.4 percent, Mississippi (38.7 percent), North Dakota (38.0 percent), and Florida (36.9 percent).

[49]

A total of 530,000 newly constructed homes were actually sold in 1980, at an average price of $76,300 including the lot. Of these, 25.1 percent sold for less than $50,000; 33.8 percent were for $50,000 to $70,000; 24.0 percent cost $70,000 to $100,000; and 17.2 percent brought $100,000 or over.

In addition, 92.5 percent were sold with a stove included; 82.3 percent contained a dishwasher, but only 14.0 percent contained a refrigerator.

[51]

THE RISING COST OF RESIDENCE

The following were the average prices for newly constructed one-family homes, including the value of the lot, biennially from 1964 to 1980. The figures have also been adjusted for the purchasing power of the dollar, with 1967 price levels set as 100.0

	ACTUAL PRICE	CONSTANT DOLLARS
1964	$20,500	$22,600
1966	23,300	24,000
1968	26,600	25,500
1970	26,600	22,900
1972	30,500	24,300
1974	38,900	26,300
1976	48,000	28,200
1978	62,500	32,000
1980	76,300	30,900

Between 1964 and 1980, actual sales prices rose by 272.2 percent. However when figures are adjusted for inflation, the increase came to 36.7 percent.

[51]

CHANGES IN RESIDENTIAL CONSTRUCTION

Between 1976 and 1980, the number of homes with air conditioning installed rose from 49.4 percent to 62.5 percent. Those with 2 or more full bathrooms rose from 66.8 percent to 72.5 percent; and those with no attached parking facility rose from 19.7 percent to 24.1 percent.

Also, from 1976 to 1980, the number with 3 or more bedrooms fell from 88.4 percent to 83.0 percent; those with full or partial basements declined from 45.4 percent to 35.5 percent; and those using oil for heating declined from 10.6 percent to 3.0 percent. Those with split-level arrangements also decreased, from 11.9 percent to 8.5 percent.

At the same time, the average size of homes remained relatively constant, going from 1,700 square feet in 1976 to 1,740 in 1980.

[51]

SINGLE- AND MULTIPLE-UNIT CONSTRUCTION

Between 1976 and 1978, the number of new housing units completed (separate homes or apartments) rose from 1,377,000 to 1,868,000, an increase of 35.7 percent. By 1980, however, the number was down to 1,502,000, a decline of 19.6 percent from the 1978 figure.

At the same time, the figures varied considerably for single-family structures and those in multiple-unit dwellings:

	SINGLE FAMILY	MULTIPLE UNITS
1976	1,034,000	343,000
1978	1,369,000	498,000
1980	957,000	545,000
1976–1978	+ 32.4%	+ 45.2%
1978–1980	− 30.1%	+ 9.4%

Moreover, the proportion of construction in multiple-unit structures rose from 24.9 percent in 1976, to 26.7 percent in 1978, and was up to 36.3 percent in 1980.

[51]

CHARACTERISTICS OF SINGLE-FAMILY HOMES

Among the 957,000 single-family homes completed in 1980:

- 17.9 percent had 1 bathroom; 57.5 percent had 1½ or 2; and 24.6 percent had 2½ baths or more.
- 17.0 percent had 2 bedrooms or less, 62.9 percent had 3, and 20.1 percent had 4 or more.
- 35.5 percent had full or partial basements; 19.2 percent had a crawl space; and 45.3 percent were built on slabs.
- 50.4 percent were heated by electricity; 41.2 percent by gas; 3.0 percent by oil; and 5.4 percent by furnaces, space heaters, or other systems.
- 55.6 percent had a 2-car garage, 13.0 percent had a garage for 1 car, 7.2 percent had carports, and 24.1 percent had no attached parking facility.

- 60.4 percent had 1 story, 31.1 percent had 2 or more stories, and 8.5 percent were split-levels.

- 21.0 percent contained less than 1,200 square feet, 50.9 percent had between 1,200 and 2,000 square feet, 13.0 percent had from 2,000 to 2,400 square feet, and 15.1 percent had more than 2,400 square feet. (The average size house had 1,740 square feet.)

- 62.5 percent had air conditioning installed and 56.4 percent had one or more fireplaces.

[51]

MULTI-FAMILY BUILDINGS

In 1980 a total of 545,000 housing units were completed in "multi-family buildings." Of these apartments:

- 44.2 percent were in buildings with less than 10 units; 31.9 percent had 10 to 29 units; 7.9 percent had 30 to 49 units; and 16.0 percent were in buildings with 50 or more units.
- 37.4 percent of the apartments were 1 bedroom or efficiencies; 52.3 percent were 2-bedroom units; and 10.2 percent had 3 or more bedrooms.
- 84.4 percent had installed air conditioning; 87.7 percent were in buildings less than 4 floors in height; and the average apartment contained 979 square feet, compared with 902 square feet in 1978.

[51]

EVALUATIONS OF NEIGHBORHOODS

The Annual Housing Survey for 1978 asked people to evaluate the neighborhoods in which they lived. The responses, which were published in 1981, differ somewhat between homeowners and renters:

	PERCENTAGE OWNERS	PERCENTAGE RENTERS
"Excellent"	41.7%	23.3%
"Good"	44.8%	47.6%
"Fair"	11.3%	22.8%
"Poor"	2.1%	6.3%
	100.0%	100.0%

Mice, Rats, and Leaks. Among homeowners, 11.4 percent said they had mice in their houses; and another 1.2 percent said they had rats or mice or both. In addition, 4.9 percent reported roofs that leaked; and of those homes with basements, 25.6 percent reported water leakage.

[50]

CHIEF COMPLAINTS

The Annual Housing Survey of 1977 asked people what bothered them about their neighborhoods. Their chief complaints (which were released in 1980) were as follows:

Too much street or highway noise (18.0 percent); heavy traffic (14.7 percent); crime in the neighborhood (14.2 percent); streets in need of repair (13.8 percent); odors, smoke, or gas (12.5 percent); presence of trash, junk, or litter (11.0 percent); noise from airplanes (7.8 percent); inadequate street lighting (7.6 percent); other houses in run-down condition (7.1 percent); and boarded-up or abandoned structures (3.8 percent).

Note: These add up to more than 100.0 percent as some people had more than one complaint.

[48]

CHANGES IN RESIDENCE

Within the 5-year period from 1975 to 1980, of the country's 48,180,000 families containing married couples, a total of 21,761,000, or 45.2 percent, changed their residence at least once. The other 26,419,000 families, or 54.8 percent, did not move at all.

The 45.2 percent who moved fell in the following categories:

- 24.2 percent moved but remained within the same county;
- 10.3 percent changed counties but stayed within the state;
- 2.7 percent moved to a contiguous state;
- 6.2 percent moved to a noncontiguous state;
- 1.8 percent came to this country from abroad, either arriving as immigrants or returning from an overseas stay.

Characteristics of Movers. Younger families were considerably more likely to move. Where the husband was under 35, fully 82.0 percent of the households changed their residence during the 5-year period, and 15.6 percent moved to another state. Only 19.7 percent of households with husbands aged 55 or older moved, with only 4.3 percent going to a different state. Also, the higher its income, the less apt a household was to move.

The following table gives the full Census figures. (Information on income is only available for families where the husband is under 55. Also, the Census only classifies families by the husband's age.)

[32]

MOVING AND NONMOVING HOUSEHOLDS: BY HUSBAND'S AGE AND FAMILY INCOME

AGE OF HUSBAND	UNDER 35	35–44	45–54	55 OR OVER
Number of Families	14,089,000	9,881,000	8,930,000	15,280,000
		Percentages		
Nonmovers	18.0%	52.6%	71.8%	80.3%
Moved within county	44.9%	25.1%	15.7%	9.7%
Moved within state	18.4%	10.6%	5.8%	5.3%
To a contiguous state	4.8%	2.9%	2.1%	1.1%
To a noncontiguous state	10.8%	6.6%	3.7%	3.2%
Moved from abroad	3.1%	2.2%	1.0%	0.4%
	100.0%	100.0%	100.0%	100.0%

FAMILY INCOME			
Number of families	7,123,000	11,289,000	14,485,000
		Percentages	
	UNDER $15,000	$15,000–$25,000	OVER $25,000
Nonmovers	32.5%	40.9%	49.8%
Moved within county	34.9%	33.8%	27.0%
Moved within state	13.5%	13.1%	11.8%
To a contiguous state	4.1%	3.2%	3.5%
To a noncontiguous state	10.3%	7.2%	6.5%
Moved from abroad	4.7%	1.8%	1.4%
	100.0%	100.0%	100.0%

[138]

MOVEMENT AMONG REGIONS

The Census computes movements among geographic regions by counting the total number of persons who change their residence, which means all family members including young children. In the 5-year period from 1975 to 1980, a total of 10,141,000 adults and children moved from one region to another. These were the routes they took:

		DESTINATIONS:			
LEAVING FROM:	TOTAL LEAVERS	*Northeast*	*North Central*	*South*	*West*
Northeast	2,591,000	——	412,000	1,452,000	727,000
North Central	3,166,000	268,000	——	1,688,000	1,210,000
South	2,440,000	589,000	950,000	——	901,000
West	1,944,000	249,000	631,000	1,064,000	——
TOTAL ARRIVALS:	10,141,000	1,106,000	1,993,000	4,204,000	2,838,000

The Census's Regions contain the following groups of states:

NORTHEAST: Connecticut, Maine, Massachusetts, New Hampshire, New Jersey, New York, Pennsylvania, Rhode Island, Vermont;

NORTH CENTRAL: Illinois, Indiana, Iowa, Kansas, Michigan, Minnesota, Missouri, Nebraska, North Dakota, Ohio, South Dakota, Wisconsin;

SOUTH: Alabama, Arkansas, Delaware, District of Columbia, Florida, Georgia, Kentucky, Louisiana, Maryland, Mississippi, North Carolina, Oklahoma, South Carolina, Tennessee, Texas, Virginia, West Virginia;

WEST: Alaska, Arizona, California, Colorado, Hawaii, Idaho, Montana, Nevada, New Mexico, Oregon, Utah, Washington, Wyoming.

[138]

REASONS FOR MOVING

The most recent Census study on the reasons people move was conducted over a 3-year period from 1974 through 1976, with the results released in 1979. The report covered people who had moved from one state to another during the twelve months prior to their being interviewed.

Altogether 24 reasons were given for moving. Almost half were associated with employment: transfer by one's employer (23.8 percent); or taking up a new job or looking for work (23.6 percent).

Among the other reasons were: to be closer to relatives (7.5 percent); to attend an out-of-state school (5.4 percent); desire for a change of climate (5.1 percent); entering or leaving the armed forces (4.8 percent); moving to a new locality upon retirement (3.4 percent).

Also: having been widowed, separated, or divorced (2.9 percent); being newly married (1.6 percent); desire to establish one's own household (also 1.6 percent); desire for a better neighborhood (1.5 percent); need for a bigger house or apartment (1.2 percent); to be close to better schools (1.0 percent); easier commuting (also 1.0 percent); looking for less expensive housing (0.8 percent); because of racial or ethnic changes in one's previous neighborhood (0.2 percent).

Why Older People Move. If persons aged 55 and over are examined separately, the most prominent reasons were: to be closer to relatives (22.2 percent); to move to a new community upon retirement (19.8 percent); and desire for a change of climate (12.1 percent).

[34]

In January 1980, the Census Bureau published a study of "housing succession amoung blacks and whites" in the central cities of metropolitan areas. When one family moved out and another family moved in, in 73.4 percent of the cases, one white family replaced another. In 12.6 percent of the cases, one black family replaced another. In 4.4 percent, a black family replaced a white family; and in 4.0 percent a white family replaced a black family. In the remaining 5.6 percent, other races were involved in the succession.

[34]

PERCENTAGE OF PERSONS WHO WERE BORN OUTSIDE THE STATE IN WHICH THEY CURRENTLY RESIDE

	PERCENTAGE		PERCENTAGE
Nevada	78.7%	Illinois	31.1%
Florida	68.7%	New York	31.0%
Alaska	68.4%	Arkansas	30.9%
Arizona	67.5%	Missouri	30.2%
Wyoming	61.6%	South Dakota	29.5%
Colorado	57.3%	Nebraska	29.5%
Oregon	56.3%	Georgia	29.2%
California	54.7%	Michigan	28.7%
Washington	52.2%	Indiana	28.7%
Idaho	50.7%	Massachusetts	28.4%
New Hampshire	50.3%	Ohio	27.9%
New Mexico	48.8%	Tennessee	27.7%
Delaware	48.0%	North Dakota	27.4%
Maryland	46.6%	South Carolina	27.3%
New Jersey	43.9%	Maine	27.1%
Montana	43.1%	Minnesota	25.3%
Connecticut	42.8%	North Carolina	24.2%
Hawaii	42.2%	Iowa	23.2%
Virginia	40.0%	Wisconsin	22.8%
Vermont	38.8%	Louisiansa	21.9%
Kansas	37.7%	Mississippi	21.5%
Oklahoma	37.0%	West Virginia	21.4%
Utah	34.2%	Alabama	21.0%
Rhode Island	33.0%	Kentucky	20.6%
Texas	31.1%	Pennsylvania	19.0%
	U.S.A.	36.2%	

[9]

TRAVEL

The 1980 Census reported the ways in which 96,526,946 Americans travel to work. Altogether, 81,350,994 (or 84.3 percent) went in private motor vehicles, which could mean automobiles, motorcycles, or trucks. In this group, 62,275,065 (or 64.5 percent of all people going to work) drove alone; and 19,075,929 (or 19.8 percent) shared rides with other persons.

Within the remaining 15.7 percent, 6,089,147 (or 6.3 percent) used public transportation; 5,354,846 (or 5.5 percent) walked; and 1,564,032 (or 1.6 percent) used "other means," including bicycles and ferry boats. A final 2,167,927 (or 2.2 percent) consisted of farmers and other individuals who work at home.

Distance and Duration. The Department of Transportation has studied the distance people travel to work and how long it takes them to get there. The average one-way trip is 9.2 miles and takes 20.4 minutes, at an average speed of 28.3 miles per hour.

ONE-WAY DISTANCES	PERCENTAGE	ONE-WAY TIMES	PERCENTAGE
5 miles or less	47.8%	15 minutes or less	54.7%
6 to 10 miles	21.9%	16 to 25 minutes	20.3%
11 to 14 miles	8.0%	26 to 35 minutes	12.5%
15 to 19 miles	8.6%	36 or more minutes	12.5%
20 to 24 miles	5.1%		
25 or more miles	8.6%		
	100.0%		100.0%

The following were the average one-way distances for varying modes of transportation: automobiles, 9.2 miles; trucks, 10.6 miles; buses, 7.2 miles; subways, 9.7 miles; trains, 24.2 miles; taxicabs, 3.3 miles; and streetcars, 7.2 miles. Distances were not published for individuals who walk or use other means of transit.

Shared Rides and Gender. Among those who shared rides with other people, in 77.2 percent of the arrangements 2 people rode together; in 13.5 percent the group consisted of 3; in 3.8 percent there were 4 persons in the vehicle; and in 5.5 percent there were 5 or more.

The typical man who travels to work had a one-way trip of 10.5 miles. The typical woman worker traveled 7.5 miles.

[9, 123]

AUTOMOBILE USE

A study by the Department of Transportation showed that Americans take 108.8 billion automobile trips per year, and that this travel involved 907.6 billion vehicle-miles.

People were asked to estimate how much of their car travel was for particular purposes, and the length of the typical trip in each of these categories. The responses were as follows:

Travel to work and back (30.4 percent of all travel and an average round trip of 18.4 miles); other work-related travel (7.3 percent and an average trip of 11.9 miles); shopping (10.0 percent and 4.9 miles); other personal matters (11.2 percent and 6.7 miles).

Also: civic, educational, and religious activities (4.7 percent and 6.1 miles); visiting friends or relatives (11.3 percent and 11.2 miles); pleasure driving (0.8 percent and 15.7 miles); vacation trips (11.3 percent and 91.0 miles); medical and dental appointments (1.7 percent and 10.8 miles); all other travel (11.3 percent and 9.8 miles).

The amount of travel also varied according to the days of the week: Fridays (16.6 percent of the week's travel), Saturdays (15.6 percent), Wednesdays (14.7 percent), Thursdays (14.6 percent), Tuesdays (14.0 percent), Mondays (12.3 percent), and Sundays (12.2 percent).

[123]

REGISTERED MOTOR VEHICLES

In 1980 there were 161,614,294 motor vehicles registered in the nation. Of these, 159,052,229 were privately owned, and 2,562,065 belonged to public agencies.

Of the 161,614,294 total, 121,723,650 were passenger cars; 33,637,241 were trucks; 5,724,602 were motorcycles; and 528,801 were buses.

Miles Driven and Fuel Consumed. The typical passenger car was driven 9,135 miles during the year and used 603 gallons of fuel, an average ratio of 15.2 miles per gallon.

The average bus went 12,103 miles and consumed 2,034 gallons of fuel, a ratio of 6.0 miles per gallon.

The average single-unit truck (of which there were 32,232,241) drove 10,070 miles and used 907 gallons of fuel, a ratio of 11.1 miles per gallon.

The typical combination truck (there were 1,405,000) went 42,705 miles and used 7,764 gallons of fuel, a ratio of 5.5 miles per gallon.

And the typical motorcycle traveled 3,144 miles during the year on 63 gallons, a ratio of 49.9 miles per gallon.

[124]

Vehicles Per Household. The 1980 Census asked each household how many motor vehicles it had "available" for its use. Of the total number of households, 12.8 percent said they had no vehicle; 35.7 percent said they had 1, which could mean a car, a truck, a camper, or a motorcycle; 33.9 percent replied that they had 2; and 17.7 percent said they had the use of 3 or more.

[9]

LICENSED DRIVERS

In 1980 there were 145,298,996 licensed drivers in the United States. Of these, 77,190,407 (or 53.1 percent) were men, and 68,108,589 (or 46.9 percent) were women.

In 3 of the 50 states, a majority of the licenses were held by women: New Mexico (51.0 percent), Connecticut (50.8 percent), and Utah (50.1 percent).

In the nation as a whole, there were 641 licensed drivers for every 1,000 persons in the population. These states had the highest ratios: Nevada (783 drivers for every 1,000 persons), West Virginia (773 per 1,000), Montana (761), Oregon (756), and Florida (746).

These states had the fewest drivers: New York (526 per 1,000), Louisiana (537), Alaska (551), and Kentucky and Hawaii (both 561).

[124]

SPEEDING AND FATALITY RATES BY STATES: 1980

PERCENTAGE OF VEHICLES CLOCKED AT OVER 55 MILES PER HOUR (U.S.A. = 49.3%)		FATALITIES PER 100 MILLION MILES OF TRAVEL (U.S.A. = 3.36)	
1. New Mexico	67.4%	Nevada	5.67
2. Texas	64.7%	New Mexico	5.42
3. Arizona	63.2%	Arizona	5.03
4. Utah	61.9%	West Virginia	5.03
5. California	61.7%	Montana	4.91
6. North Dakota	58.3%	Wyoming	4.89
7. Kansas	58.1%	Louisiana	4.86
8. Delaware	57.9%	Idaho	4.77
9. Montana	57.8%	Mississippi	4.22
10. Florida	57.6%	Texas	4.01
11. Wyoming	57.5%	South Carolina	3.78
12. Indiana	56.6%	Vermont	3.73
13. Nevada	56.0%	South Dakota	3.68

(continued)

(continued)

	PERCENTAGE OF VEHICLES CLOCKED AT OVER 55 MILES PER HOUR (U.S.A. = 49.3%)		FATALITIES PER 100 MILLION MILES OF TRAVEL (U.S.A. = 3.36)	
14.	Minnesota	55.2%	North Carolina	3.63
15.	Ohio	55.2%	Arkansas	3.62
16.	Vermont	54.9%	Delaware	3.61
17.	Alabama	53.7%	Oklahoma	3.55
18.	Nebraska	53.1%	Nebraska	3.52
19.	Mississippi	52.6%	California	3.52
20.	Rhode Island	52.4%	Maine	3.50
21.	Wisconsin	50.2%	Georgia	3.48
22.	Missouri	50.1%	Missouri	3.45
23.	South Dakota	50.0%	Kansas	3.44
24.	Tennessee	49.7%	Oregon	3.38
25.	Washington	48.9%	New York	3.35
26.	Connecticut	48.8%	Washington	3.34
27.	Iowa	48.6%	Iowa	3.30
28.	West Virginia	48.4%	Alaska	3.30
29.	Massachusetts	48.3%	Tennessee	3.29
30.	Michigan	47.9%	Hawaii	3.29
31.	Oklahoma	47.9%	Alabama	3.28
32.	Maine	46.0%	Kentucky	3.25
33.	Pennsylvania	46.0%	Indiana	3.17
34.	New Jersey	45.9%	Colorado	3.16
35.	Arkansas	45.9%	Wisconsin	3.11
36.	South Carolina	45.5%	Utah	3.09
37.	New York	45.4%	Illinois	3.08
38.	Illinois	45.0%	Minnesota	3.03
39.	North Carolina	44.7%	New Hampshire	3.02
40.	Kentucky	43.1%	Pennsylvania	2.92
41.	Louisiana	41.3%	Connecticut	2.87
42.	Virginia	39.9%	Michigan	2.86
43.	Idaho	39.0%	North Dakota	2.86
44.	Hawaii	38.7%	Ohio	2.82
45.	Oregon	38.1%	Maryland	2.71
46.	Georgia	37.6%	Virginia	2.71
47.	Colorado	35.9%	Massachusetts	2.49
48.	New Hampshire	35.1%	Rhode Island	2.38
49.	Alaska	30.3%	New Jersey	2.23
50.	Maryland	27.0%		

Note: Speeds are based on samples from all roads in the state, ranging from limited access highways to local streets. Fatality information for the state of Florida was not available.

[124]

AIRLINES AND FOREIGN TRAVEL

MAJOR FLIGHT ROUTES

During the month of December 1980, scheduled airlines ran at least a 1,000 flights connecting the following pairs of cities (the figures represent traffic both ways).

Dallas–Houston	3,462	Atlanta–Chicago	1,241
Los Angeles–San Francisco	3,069	Los Angeles–New York	1,240
Chicago–New York	2,534	Dallas–Denver	1,215
New York–Washington, D.C.	2,037	Dallas–New Orleans	1,171
Atlanta–New York	2,029	Los Angeles–San Diego	1,163
Boston–New York	1,842	Detroit–New York	1,138
Miami–New York	1,767	Chicago–St. Louis	1,108
Ft. Lauderdale–New York	1,381	Dallas–Los Angeles	1,058
Boston–Washington, D.C.	1,320	Atlanta–Jacksonville	1,046
Las Vegas–Los Angeles	1,304	Dallas–New York	1,036
Chicago–Washington, D.C.	1,272	Miami–Tampa	1,018
Houston–New Orleans	1,270	Atlanta–Tampa	1,015
Denver–Salt Lake City	1,257	Chicago–Detroit	1,010
Portland–Seattle	1,246		

[126]

AIR TRAVEL COMPLAINTS

During the first six months of 1980, the Civil Aeronautics Board received 9,973 complaints concerning the conduct of domestic airlines.

The following were the major subjects of complaints: late or canceled flights, or unsatisfactory flight conditions (2,265); lost, delayed, or damaged baggage (1,852); rudeness from personnel (1,402); failure to provide expected refunds (978); overbooking of seats (957); complaints about fares (655); problems with reservations or ticketing (601); smoking on the plane (301); misleading advertising (111); and inadequate provisions for special needs of passengers (90).

[127]

FOREIGN TRAVEL: WHY PEOPLE GO ABROAD

During the 5-year period 1976 through 1980, a total of 15,348,743 passports were issued to American citizens. As passports are valid for only five years, this approximates the number of persons holding this document. (Passports may no longer be renewed; you must apply for a new one when the old one has expired.)

Among the 3,020,468 passports issued in 1980, a total of 183,400 went to children under the age of ten, and 171,158 went to individuals aged 70 or over.

Of those who intended to travel abroad, 2,075,810 persons gave "pleasure" or "personal reasons" as their principal "object of travel." Another 161,520 listed "business" and 79,550 put down "education." There were also 112,938 persons associated with the military, and 22,930 on civilian government business. Finally, 10,970 cited "religious" activities for travel; 2,790 put down "scientific"; and 990 said they were traveling for reasons of "health."

[116]

TRAVELERS' OCCUPATIONS

The persons issued passports in 1980 gave the following occupations:

- business or professional employment (686,850), technical or sales work (512,880), clerical occupations (57,350), unskilled labor (1,370).
- teachers (96,360), military personnel (48,000), transportation employees and travel agents (36,540), civilian government personnel (32,660), entertainers (19,360), religious workers (17,270), journalists (10,900), sports figures (1,450).
- and housewives (578,440), students (559,590), retired individuals (172,530).

[116]

FOREIGN DESTINATIONS

In 1980 a total of 8,163,000 Americans traveled overseas. (This figure does not include trips to Canada or Mexico or cruises.) Of these, 3,934,000 (or 48.2 percent) went to Europe and the Mediterranean; 3,218,000 (or 39.4 percent) to Latin America and the Caribbean; and 1,011,000 (or 12.4 percent) to other areas.

Of those going to Western Europe and the Mediterranean, the following numbers visited these countries:

United Kingdom	1,580,000	Israel	289,000
France	888,000	Greece	284,000
Germany	787,000	Belgium	243,000
Italy	749,000	Ireland	239,000
Switzerland	529,000	Portugal	185,000
Austria	420,000	Denmark	181,000
Netherlands	395,000	Sweden	135,000
Spain	368,000	Norway	118,000

Travel: 1965 and 1980. Between 1965 and 1980, the number of Americans traveling to Europe and the Mediterranean rose from 1,405,000 to 3,934,000, or by 180 percent. However, whereas in 1965 the average trip lasted 39 days, in 1980 it was down to 21 days. In 1980 the average traveler to Europe and the Mediterranean spent $867 while abroad.

[172]

VISITORS TO THE UNITED STATES

In 1980 a total of 7,706,000 persons visited the United States from overseas—which means all countries other than Mexico or Canada. Of these, 3,368,000 (or 43.7 percent) came from Europe, 2,003,000 (or 26.0 percent) from Latin America and the Caribbean, and 2,335,000 (or 30.3 percent) from other areas, with about half from Japan.

Of these visitors, 6,312,000 (or 81.9 percent) came for pleasure; 1,040,000 (or 13.5 percent) were on business; 184,000 (or 2.4 percent) were students; and the remaining 170,000 (or 2.2 percent) were in transit to another country.

Between 1973 and 1980, the number of overseas visitors more than doubled, from 3,554,000 to 7,706,000.

[172]

SOURCES

This section lists the publications from which the statistics in *U/S* have been obtained or derived. Most of these documents may be purchased from the U.S. Government Printing Office (Washington, D.C. 20402). They may also be examined in any one of the 1,357 "depository libraries" which receive government documents on a regular basis. These collections are housed in many university libraries and also the reference departments of larger public library systems.

The government publishes its own annual compendium, called *The Statistical Abstract of the United States*. It is an ever-growing volume, now up to 1,000 pages and containing 1,600 finely printed tables. The *Abstract* is an impressive reference work, and can be recommended for its unadorned statistics. It tends to reprint tables much as they have appeared in departmental documents, and no attempt is made to highlight particular figures or suggest their significance. The *Abstract* is a good place to go when you have a fairly clear idea of what it is you want, but it is neither intended nor designed for leisurely reading.

The best and most comprehensive list of public documents is *The American Statistics Index,* which provides detailed descriptions of the figures to be found in government publications. It comes out in monthly installments, which are then combined in an annual edition. The *Index* is published by a private concern (Congressional Information Service, Inc., Washington, D.C. 20014) and most large libraries maintain a subscription.

All figures published by government agencies are in the public domain, which means they are not covered by copyright laws and may be used or reproduced without requests for permission. The user's only obligation is to transcribe these statistics accurately and with an understanding of what they represent.

CENSUS BUREAU PUBLICATIONS

THE 1980 CENSUS

1. *Final Population and Housing Unit Counts.* PHC 80-V-1. (April 1981)
2. *Age, Sex, Race, and Spanish Origin of the Population by Regions, Divisions, and States.* PC 80-Sl-1. (May 1981)
3. *Population and Households by States and Counties.* PC 80-Sl-2. (May 1981)
4. *Race of the Population by States.* PC 80-Sl-3. (July 1981)
5. *General Population Characteristics.* PC 80-1-B. (August 1982)
6. *Standard Metropolitan Statistical Areas and Standard Consolidated Statistical Areas.* PC-Sl-5. (October 1981)
7. *Selected Housing Characteristics by States and Counties.* HC 80-Sl-1. (October 1981)
8. *Urban and Rural Population.* Census Bureau Press Release. (August 1981)
9. *Provisional Estimates of Social, Economic, and Housing Characteristics.* PHC 80-S-1. (March 1982)
10. *Census Bureau Data User News* (January 1981)
11. *Census Bureau Data User News* (April 1981)
12. *Census Bureau Data User News* (October 1981)
13. *Census Bureau Data User News* (February 1982)

THE 1970 CENSUS

14. *Number of Inhabitants.* PC(1)-A1. (December 1971)
15. *Detailed Characteristics.* PC(1)-D1. (February 1973)
16. *Family Composition.* PC(2)-4A. (May 1973)
17. *Marital Status.* PC(2)-4C. (December 1972)
18. *Occupations of Persons with High Earning.* PC(2)-7F. (June 1973)
19. *Earnings by Occupation and Education.* PC(2)-8B. (January 1973)
20. *Race of the Population by Country.* PC(S1)-104. (December 1975)
21. *Historical Statistics of the United States: Colonial Times to 1970.* (1976)

POPULATION AND HOUSING REPORTS

22. *Marriage, Divorce, Widowhood, and Remarriage.* P-20, No. 312. (August 1977)
23. *Relative Progress of Children in School.* P-20, No. 337. (April 1979)
24. *Travel to School.* P-20, No. 342. (September 1979)
25. *Educational Attainment in the United States.* P-20, No. 356. (August 1980)
26. *Households and Families by Type.* P-20, No. 357. (October 1980)
27. *School Enrollment: Social and Economic Characteristics of Students.* P-20, Nos. 360 & 362. (April & May 1981)
28. *Population Profile of the United States.* P-20, No. 363. (June 1981)
29. *Fertility of American Women.* P-20, No. 364. (August 1981)
30. *Marital Status and Living Arrangements.* P-20, No. 365. (October 1981)
31. *Household and Family Characteristics.* P-20, No. 366. (September 1981)
32. *Geographical Mobility: 1975–1980.* P-20, No. 368. (December 1981)

33. *Voting and Registration in the Election of 1980.* P-20, No. 370. (April 1982)
34. *Reasons for Interstate Migration.* P-23, No. 81. (March 1979)
35. *Housing Succession Among Blacks and Whites in Cities and Suburbs.* P-23, No. 101. (January 1980)
36. *Families Maintained by Female Householders.* P-23, No. 107. (October 1980)
37. *Characteristics of Households and Persons Receiving Non-Cash Benefits.* P-23, No. 110. (March 1981)
38. *Child Support and Alimony.* P-23, No. 112. (September 1981)
39. *Characteristics of American Children and Youth.* P-23, No. 114. (January 1982)
40. *Coverage of the National Population in the 1980 Census.* P-23, No. 115. (February 1982)
41. *Ancestry and Language in the United States.* P-23, No. 116. (March 1982)
42. *Trends in Child Care Arrangements of Working Mothers.* P-23, No. 117. (June, 1982)
43. *Money Income of Families and Persons in the United States: 1978.* P-60, No. 123. (June 1980)
44. *Money Income and Poverty Status of Families and Persons in the United States: 1980 and 1981.* P-60, Nos. 127 and 134. (August 1981 and July 1982)
45. *Characteristics of Households Receiving Non-Cash Benefits.* P-60, No. 128 (October 1981)
46. *Money Income of Families and Persons in the United States: 1979.* P-60, No. 129.
47. *Farm Population of the United States.* P-27, No. 54. (September 1981)
48. *Indicators of Housing and Neighborhood Quality.* H-150-77. (May 1979)
49. *Housing Units Authorized by Building Permits.* C-40-80-12. (February 1981)
50. *Indicators of Housing and Neighborhood Quality.* H-150-78. (June 1981)
51. *Characteristics of New Housing.* C-25-80-13. (July 1981)
52. *General Housing Characteristics.* H-150-79. (August 1981)

CENSUS OF GOVERNMENTS

53. *Popularly Elected Officials.* 9C77(1)-2. (October 1979)
54. *State Government Tax Collections.* GF-80, No. 1. (January 1981)
55. *Public Employment.* GE-80, No. 1. (June 1981)
56. *County Employment.* GE-80, No. 4. (June 1981)
57. *City Employment.* GE-80, No. 2. (July 1981)
58. *City Government Finances.* GF-80, No. 4. (September 1981)

NON-CENSUS SOURCES

NATIONAL CENTER FOR HEALTH STATISTICS

59. *Natality: 1977.* Vital Statistics of the United States: Vol. I. (1981)
60. *Mortality: 1977.* Vital Statistics of the United States: Vol. II, Parts A & B. (1980 & 1981)

61. *Mortality: 1961.* Vital Statistics of the United States: Vol. II, Part A. (1964)
62. *Marriage and Divorce: 1977.* Vital Statistics of the United States: Vol. III. (1981)
63. *Utilization of Short Stay Hospitals.* Health and Vital Statistics: Series 13, No. 46. (March 1980)
64. *Characteristics of Visits to Female and Male Physicians.* Health and Vital Statistics: Series 13, No. 49. (June 1980)
65. *National Estimates of Marriage Dissolution and Survivorship.* Health and Vital Statistics: Series 3, No. 19. (November 1980)
66. *Inpatient Health Facilities.* Health and Vital Statistics: Series 14, No. 24. (March 1981)
67. *Contraceptive Utilization.* Health and Vital Statistics: Series 23, No. 7. (March 1981)
68. *Current Estimates from the National Health Interview Survey.* Health and Vital Statistics: Series 10, No. 136. (April 1981)
69. *State Life Tables.* (1975)
70. *Health: U.S.* (December 1981)

BUREAU OF LABOR STATISTICS

71. *Perspectives on Working Women.* Bulletin 2080. (June 1980)
72. *Directory of National Unions and Employee Associations.* Bulletin 2079. (September 1980)
73. *Handbook of Labor Statistics.* Bulletin 2020. (December 1980)
74. *Consumer Prices: Energy and Food.* (December 1980)
75. *Geographic Profile of Employment and Unemployment.* Report 619. (December 1980)
76. *Current Wage Developments.* (January 1981)
77. *Marital and Family Characteristics of the Labor Force.* Report 237. (January 1981)
78. *Employment and Earnings.* (January & March, 1981)
79. *Employment and Unemployment in 1980.* Report 244. (April 1981)
80. *Earnings and Other Characteristics of Organized Workers.* Bulletin 2105. (September 1981)
81. *Urban Family Budgets and Comparative Indexes for Selected Urban Areas.* Press Release. (April 1982)

NATIONAL CENTER FOR EDUCATION STATISTICS

82. *Digest of Educational Statistics.* (1981)
83. *Degrees Awarded to Women.* (January 1981)
84. *Residence and Migration of College Students.* (February 1981)
85. *Education in the United States.* (April 1981)
86. *Faculty Salaries, Tenure, and Benefits* (May 1981)
87. *Earned Degrees Conferred* (September 1981)
88. *Fall Enrollment in Colleges and Universities: 1981.* (November 1981)

89. *Education Directory*. (December 1981)

90. *Condition of Education*. (1982)

BUREAU OF JUSTICE STATISTICS

91. *Prisoners in State and Federal Institutions*. (May 1980)

92. *Profile of Jail Inmates*. (October 1980)

93. *Expenditure and Employment for the Criminal Justice System*. (March 1981)

94. *Criminal Victimization in the United States*. (September 1981)

95. *Prisoners at Mid-Year 1981*. (September 1981)

96. *Capital Punishment* and *Death Row Prisoners*. (December 1981 and July 1982)

DOCUMENTS FROM OTHER DEPARTMENTS

97. *Abortion Surveillance*. Centers for Disease Control. (November 1980)

98. *Fluoridation Census*. Centers for Disease Control. (April 1977)

99. *Public Assistance Statistics*. Department of Health and Human Services. (August 1980)

100. *Recipient Characteristics Study*. Department of Health and Human Services. (September 1980)

101. *Report of the Graduate Medical Education National Advisory Committee*. Department of Health and Human Services. (1981)

102. *Survey of Earned Doctorates*. National Research Council. (October 1981)

103. *Uniform Crime Reports: 1980*. Federal Bureau of Investigation. (September 1981)

104. *Uniform Crime Reports: 1979*. Federal Bureau of Investigation. (September 1980)

105. *Uniform Crime Reports: 1970*. Federal Bureau of Investigation. (August 1971)

106. *Sole Proprietorship and Partnership Returns*. Internal Revenue Service. (March & April, 1981)

107. *Individual Income Tax Returns: 1978*. Internal Revenue Service. (1981)

108. *Agricultural Statistics*. Department of Agriculture. (1981)

109. *Federal Meat and Poultry Inspection*. Department of Agriculture. (March 1981)

110. *Estimates of the Cost of Raising a Child*. Department of Agriculture. (November 1981)

111. *Economic Indicators*. Council of Economic Advisers. (November 1981)

112. *National Income and Product Accounts*. Department of Commerce. (June 1981)

113. *Statistics of Presidential and Congressional Elections*. Clerk of the House of Representatives. (Various Dates)

114. *Selected Manpower Statistics*. Department of Defense. (1981)

115. *Special Analyses of the Budget of the United States*. Office of Management and Budget. (1981)

116. *Summary of Passport Statistics*. Department of State. (January 1981)

117. *Federal Work Force Statistics.* Office of Personnel Management. (January 1981)
118. *Occupations of Federal White Collar Workers.* Office of Personnel Management. (1981)
119. *Sexual Harrassment in the Federal Workplace.* Merit System Protection Board. (March 1981)
120. *Cost of Owning and Operating Automobiles and Vans.* Federal Highway Administration. (1980)
121. *Characteristics of 1977 Licensed Drivers.* Department of Transportation. (December 1980)
122. *Home-to-Work Trips and Travel.* Department of Transportation. (December 1980)
123. *Purposes of Vehicle Trips and Travel.* Department of Transportation. (December 1980)
124. *Highway Statistics.* Department of Transportation. (1981)
125. *Rail-Highway Crossing Accident-Incident Inventory.* Federal Railroad Administration. (June 1981)
126. *Scheduled Arrival Performance.* Civil Aeronautics Board. (December 1980)
127. *Consumer Complaint Report.* Civil Aeronautics Board. (1980)
128. Proxy Statements of Business Corporations. These statements are submitted to the Securities and Exchange Commission. The figures in the text were collated by *Business Week,* May 10, 1982.

ANNUAL REPORTS

129. Postmaster General. Report for 1980. (1981)
130. Veterans Administration. Report for 1980. (1981)
131. Consumer Product Safety Commission. Report for 1981. (1982)
132. Federal Prison System. Report for 1980. (1981)
133. Commissioner of Internal Revenue. Report for 1980. (1981)
134. Attorney General. Report for 1980. (1981)
135. Immigration and Naturalization Service. Report for 1980. (1981)
136. National Transportation Safety Board. Report for 1980. (1981)
137. National Labor Relations Board. Report for Year ending September 30, 1980. (1981)
138. Office of Personnel Management. Report for Year Ending September 30, 1980. (1981)

SERIES AND PERIODICALS

MONTHLY VITAL STATISTICS REPORT (National Center for Health Statistics)

139. May 29, 1981
140. June 11, 1981
141. July 31, 1981
142. September 17, 1981
143. September 28, 1981

144. September 29, 1981
145. March 18, 1982
146. April 16, 1982
147. May 27, 1982

MORBIDITY AND MORTALITY WEEKLY REPORT *(Centers for Disease Control)*

148. January 9, 1981
149. September 11, 1981
150. January 8, 1982
151. February 5, 1982
152. *Annual Supplement: 1980*

SOCIAL SECURITY BULLETIN *(Social Security Administration)*

153. June 1981
154. July 1981
155. November 1981
156. December 1981
157. January 1982
158. February 1982
159. March 1982
160. *Annual Supplement: 1980*

MONTHLY LABOR REVIEW *(Bureau of Labor Statistics)*

161. August 1980
162. November 1980
163. January 1981
164. February 1981
165. April 1981
166. June 1981
167. October 1981
168. February 1982
169. April 1982
170. September 1982

SURVEY OF CURRENT BUSINESS *(Department of Commerce)*

171. April 1981
172. May 1981
173. August 1981

STATISTICS OF INCOME BULLETIN *(Internal Revenue Service)*

174. Summer 1981
175. Winter 1981–1982

HEALTH CARE FINANCING REVIEW (Health Care Financing Administration)

176. Fall 1981
177. Winter 1981

HEALTH CARE FINANCING TRENDS (Health Care Financing Administration)

178. Spring 1981
179. Summer 1981

INDEX

ANDREW HACKER is the author of *The End of the American Era*, and his articles have appeared in *The Atlantic, Harper's, Time, Newsweek,* and *The New York Review of Books.* He lives in New York and teaches in the Division of the Social Sciences at Queens College.